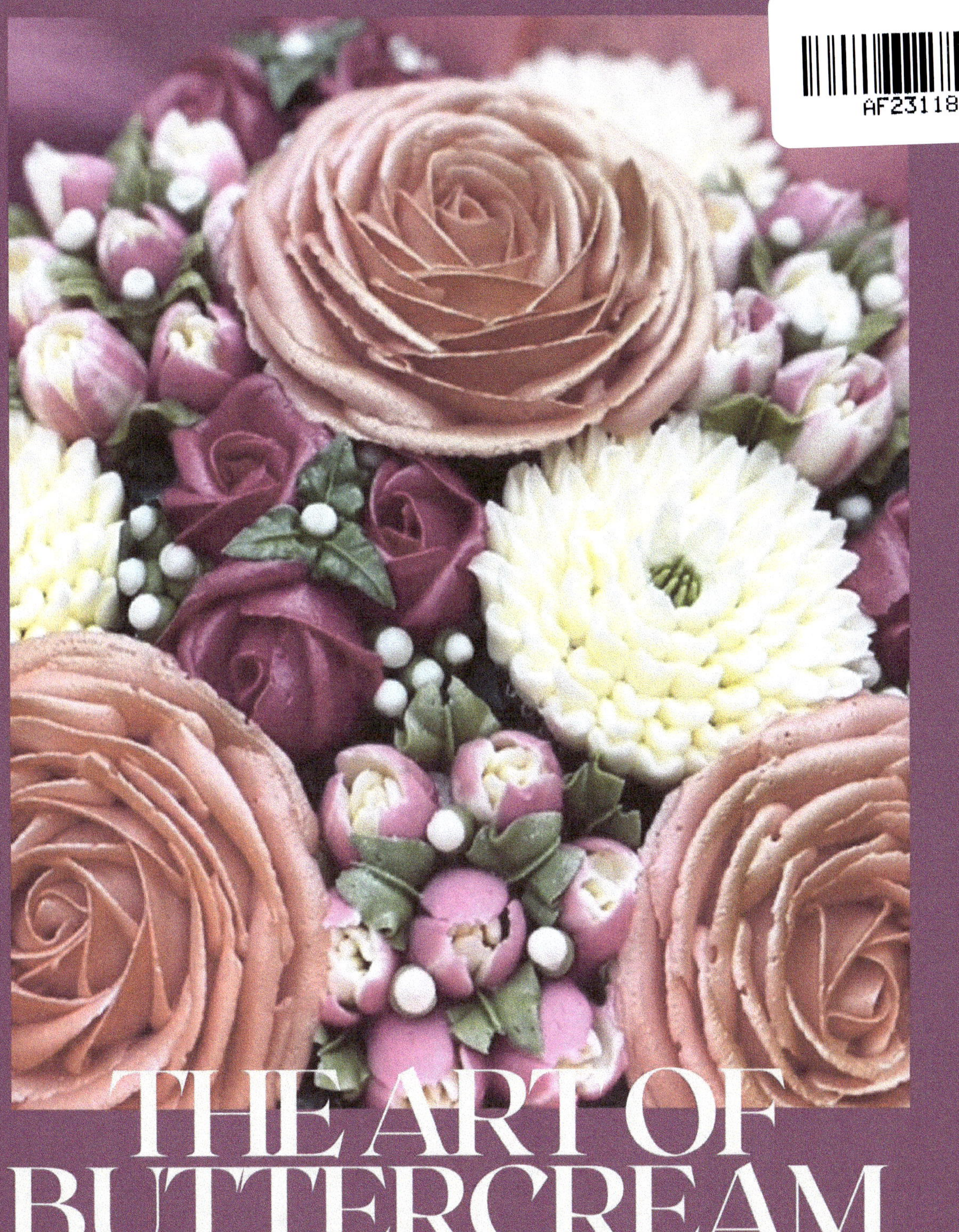

THE ART OF BUTTERCREAM BLOOMS

A Guide to Hand-Piped Floral Cupcakes

FARHANA UDDIN

First published in Great Britain in 2025 by TEP publishing

The Empire Publishers Publishing
131 Finsbury Pavement, London EC2A 1NT

https://www.theempirepublishers.co.uk/

Our books may be purchased in bulk for promotional, educational or business use. Please contact Book writing founders at +44 20 4579 8116, or by email at support@theempirepublishers.co.uk

First Edition February 2025

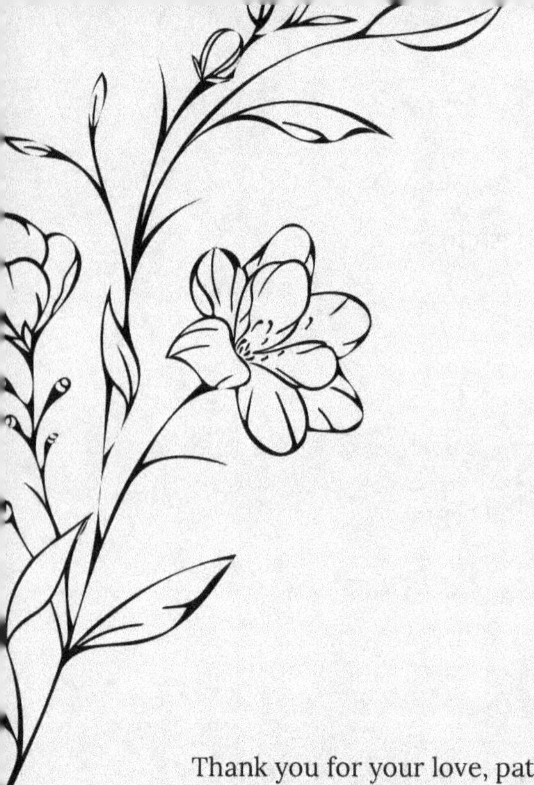

Dedication

To my incredible family.

Thank you for your love, patience, and wholehearted support—especially when the house smelled like frosting for days and every flat surface was covered in cupcakes "for practice."

To my husband—thank you for always nodding at my buttercream rants like you knew exactly what I was talking about, and for calling every flower "beautiful," even the wobbly ones.

To my daughter—your talent behind the camera turned my piped petals into art. Thank you for capturing the magic, even when I said "just one more angle" twenty times.

To my son—thank you for being the most enthusiastic taste-tester and for reminding me (loudly) when there were no cupcakes left to "sample." You've got a sweet tooth and a sweeter heart.

To my mum—your quiet strength, loving encouragement, and lifelong support have been the foundation for everything I do. Also, thank you for not judging the number of piping nozzles I own.

You've all filled my life (and this book) with joy, humour, and sugar-fuelled memories. I couldn't have done it without you—and probably wouldn't have wanted to.

I love you more than buttercream. And that's saying something.

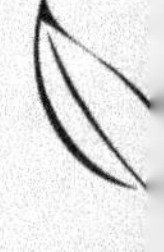

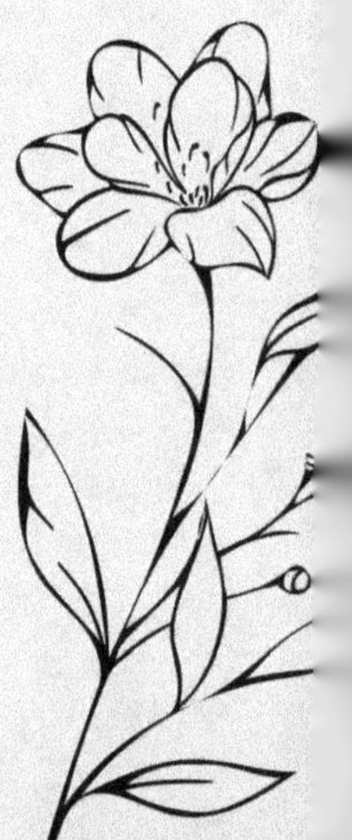

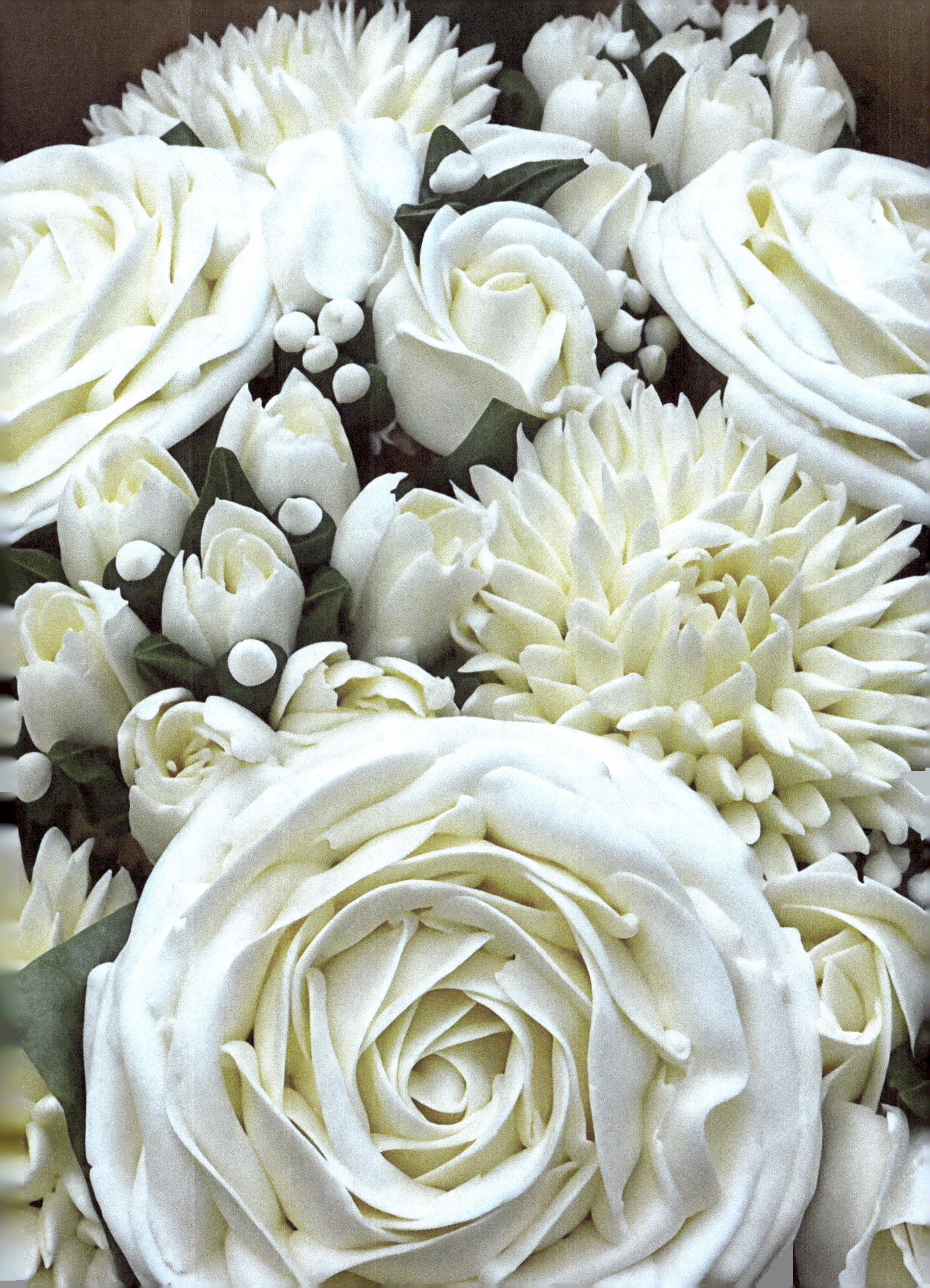

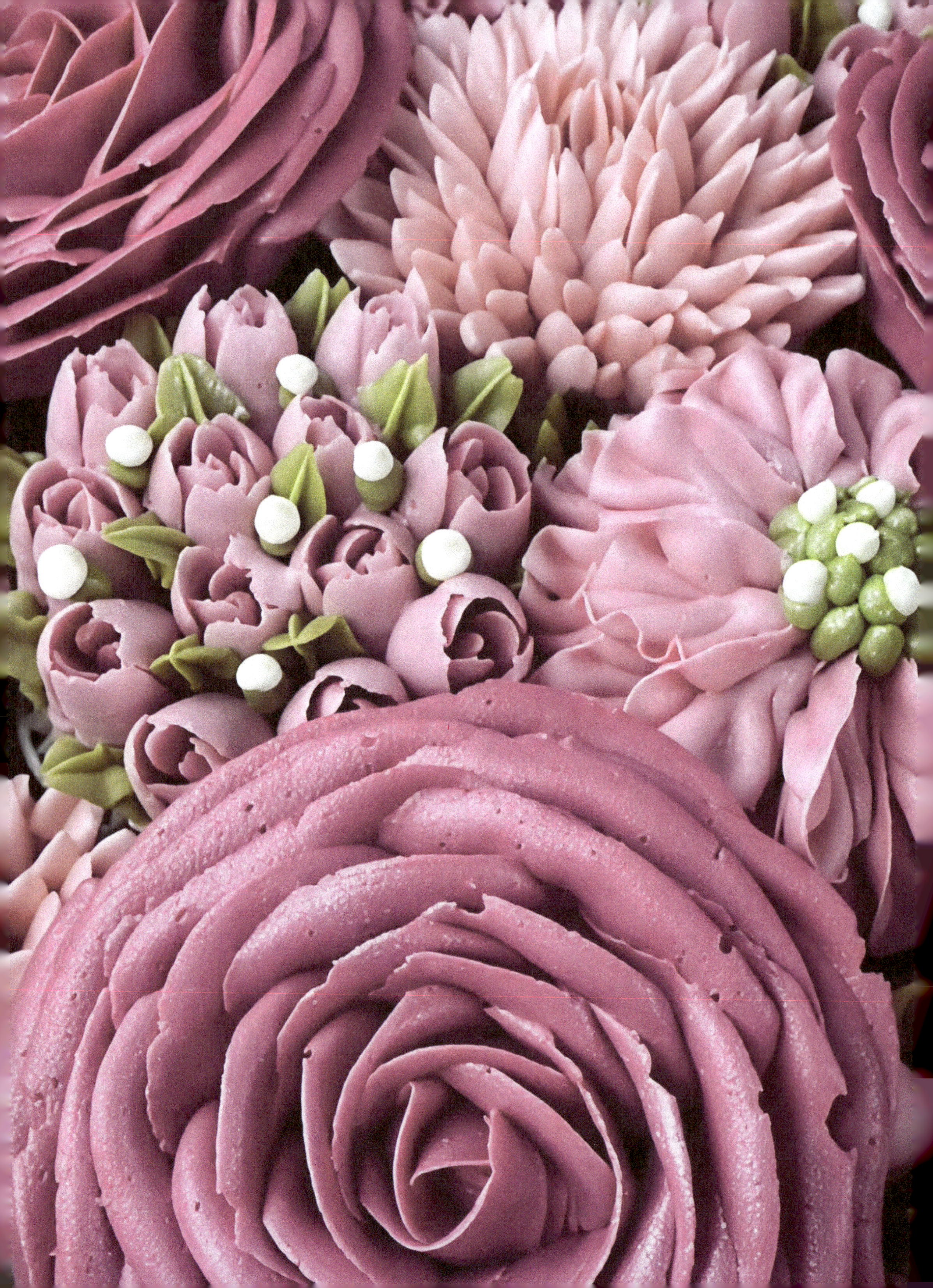

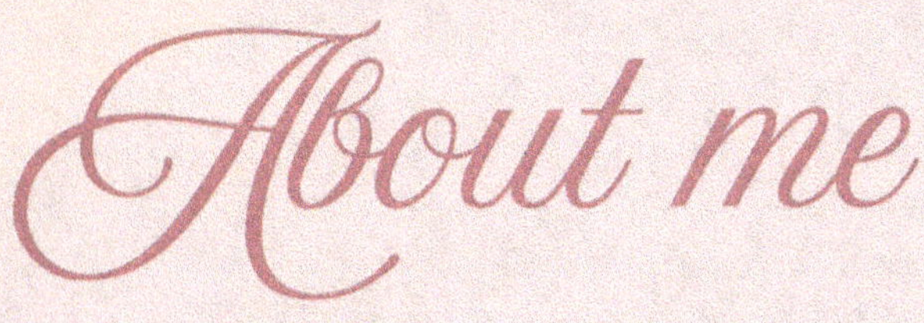

About me

Five years ago, I embarked on a journey of learning how to pipe buttercream flowers through online tutorials; dedicating countless hours to practice and perfecting my craft. The process of piping delicate blooms with buttercream has brought me immense joy and a sense of comfort like no other. Witnessing the transformation of simple ingredients into intricate floral designs filled my heart with happiness, and the reactions from both myself and those who admired the finished products have been priceless. With determination and passion, I have transitioned from crafting buttercream flower cupcakes for personal enjoyment to selling them in elegantly packaged boxes.

The overwhelmingly positive response from my customers has fueled my ambition further, leading me to explore the creation of buttercream flower bouquets. Seeing the awe and delight on customers' faces when they receive these edible arrangements has been truly gratifying, with comments like, "We didn't want to eat the flowers as they looked so real," serving as a testament to the lifelike quality of my creations.

After years of being asked when I would share my expertise, I have now decided to take the leap and write a beginner's book on piping buttercream flowers from the comfort of one's home. This book aims to provide step-by-step guidance; from mastering the most basic flower designs to embellishing cakes and cupcakes with exquisite floral adornments. It is my hope that this book will inspire and empower others to embark on their own journey of buttercream flower piping, spreading beauty and happiness through their sweet creations.

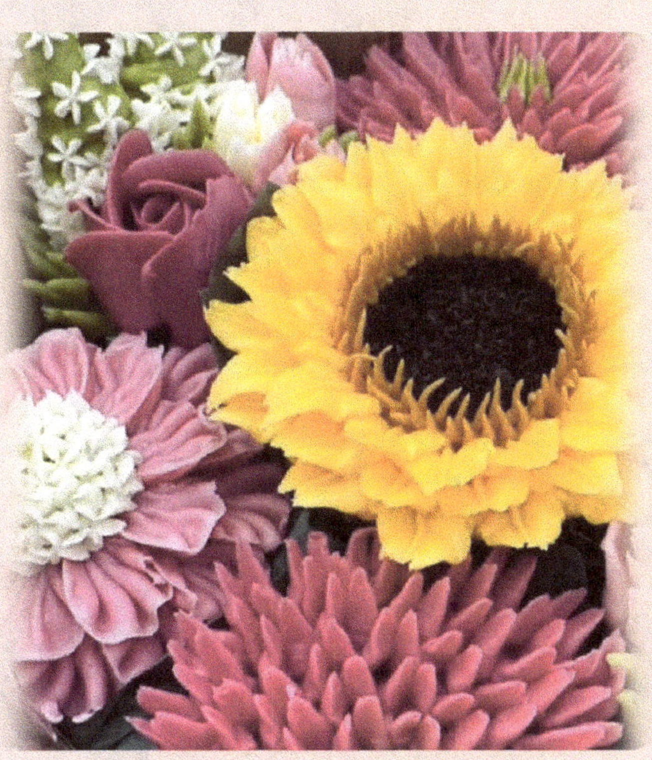

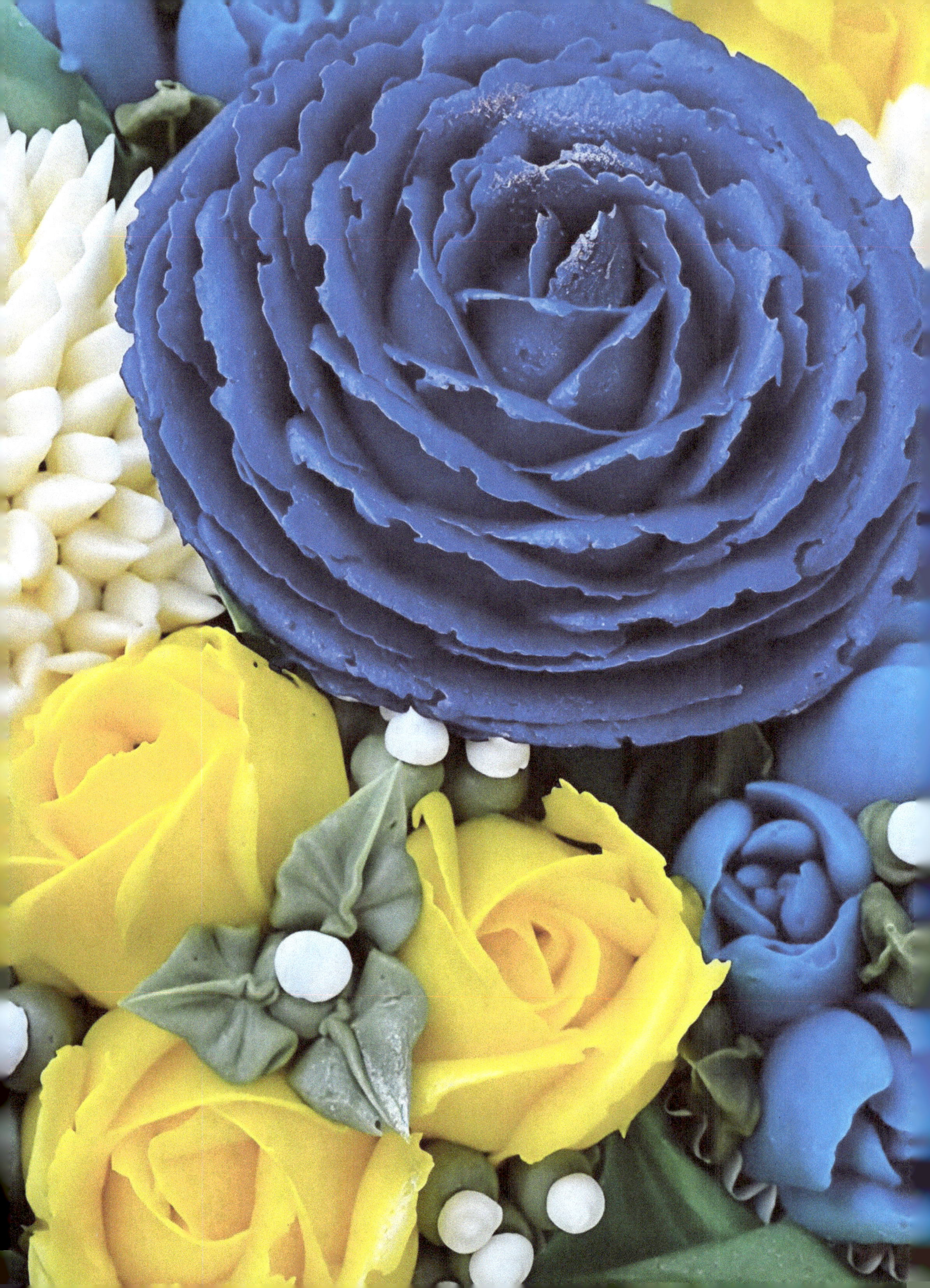

COLOURING

Colouring buttercream is an art inspired by the vibrant palette of the world around us. Drawing from the rich hues of blooming flowers, the serene shades of a sunset, or the lively tones of a bustling market, we can create buttercream that mirrors these natural wonders. The infusion of colours transforms simple buttercream into a canvas of creativity, where each shade adds depth and dimension to the design. Whether it is the soft pastels of spring blossoms or the bold, dramatic tones of an autumn landscape, the effect of colouring buttercream is transformative. It elevates cakes and pastries from mere desserts to visual masterpieces, captivating the eyes and evoking emotions even before the first bite. The result is a stunning, edible work of art that not only tastes divine but also tells a story through its beautiful and intricate hues.

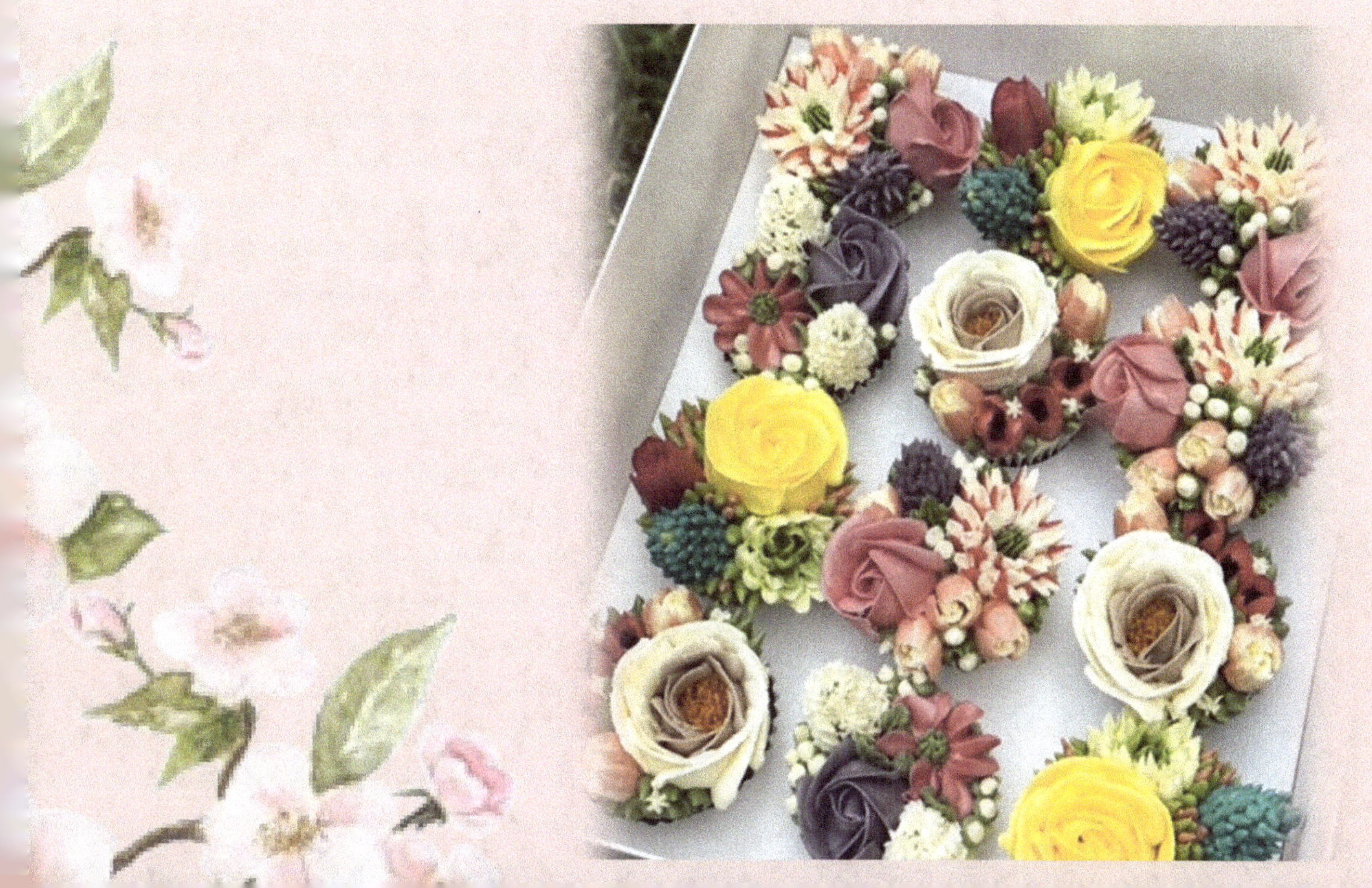

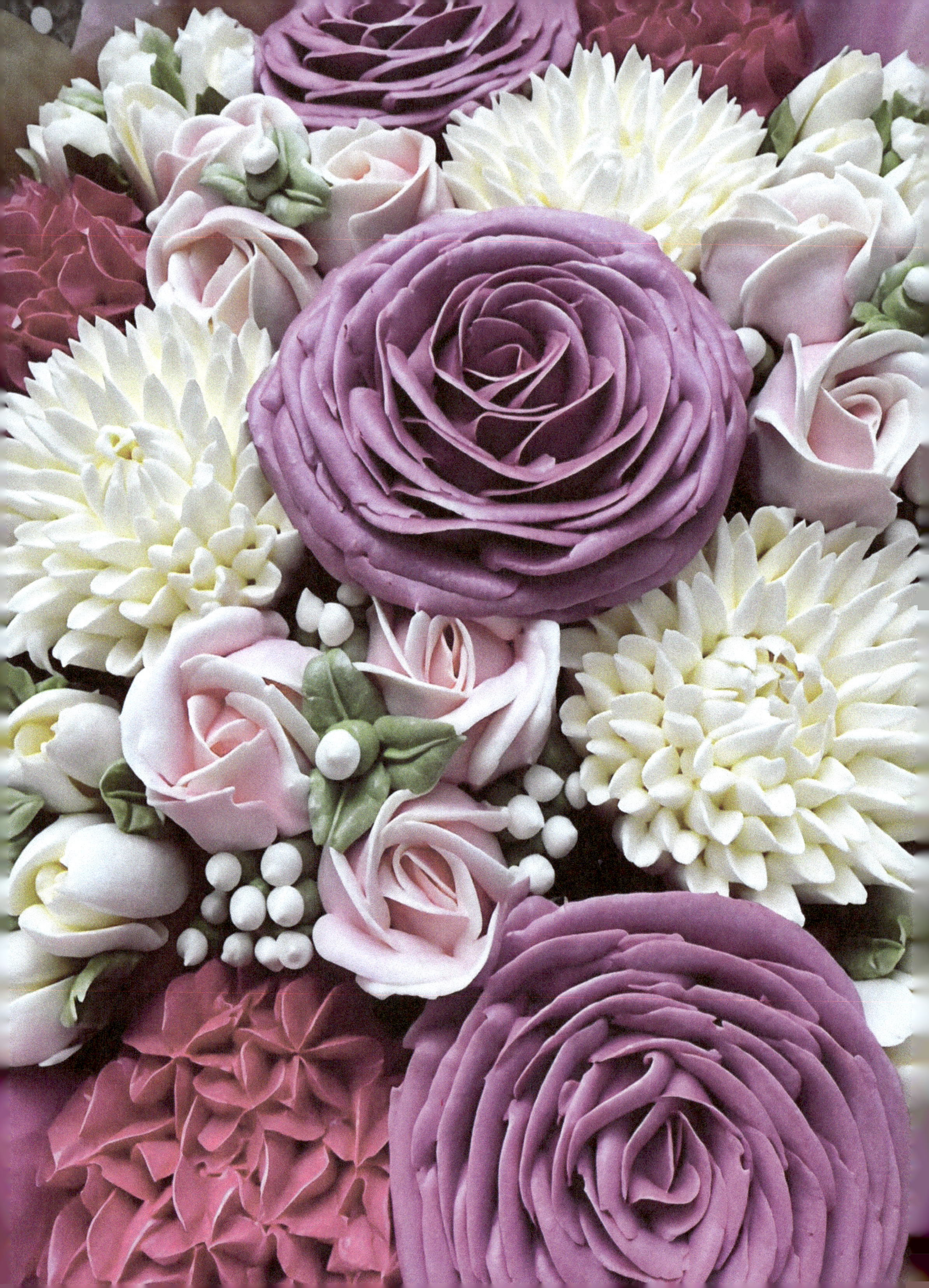

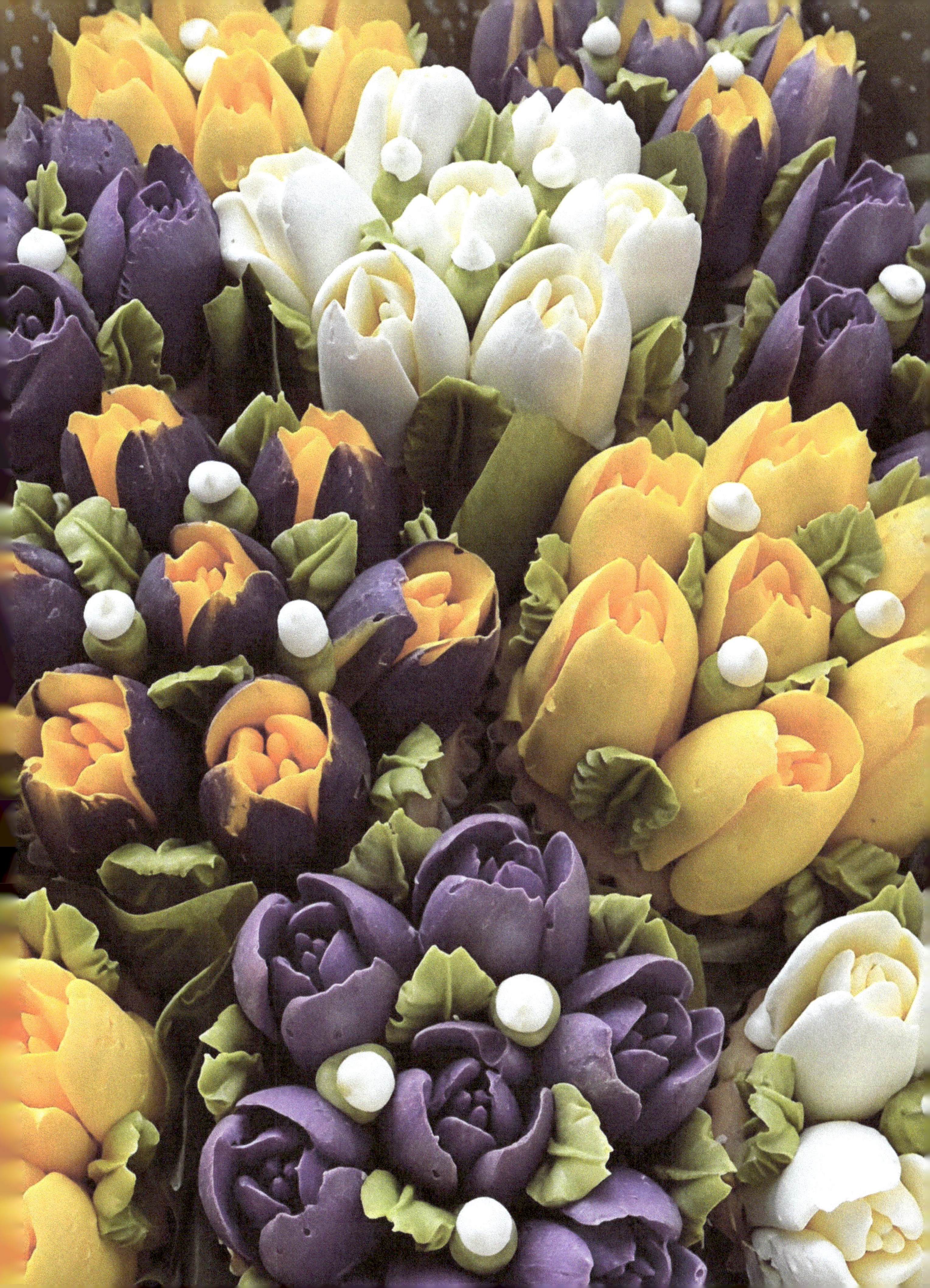

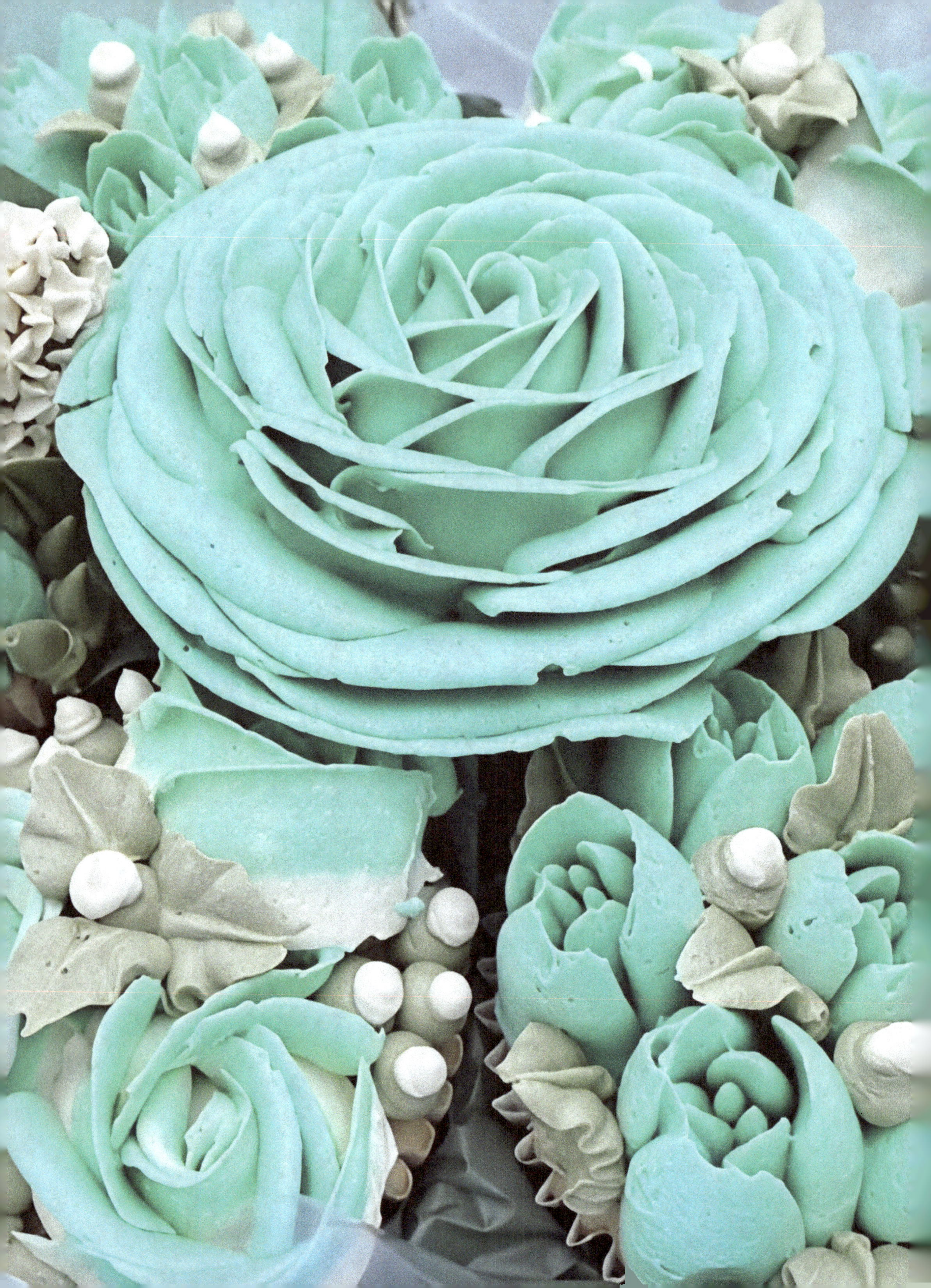

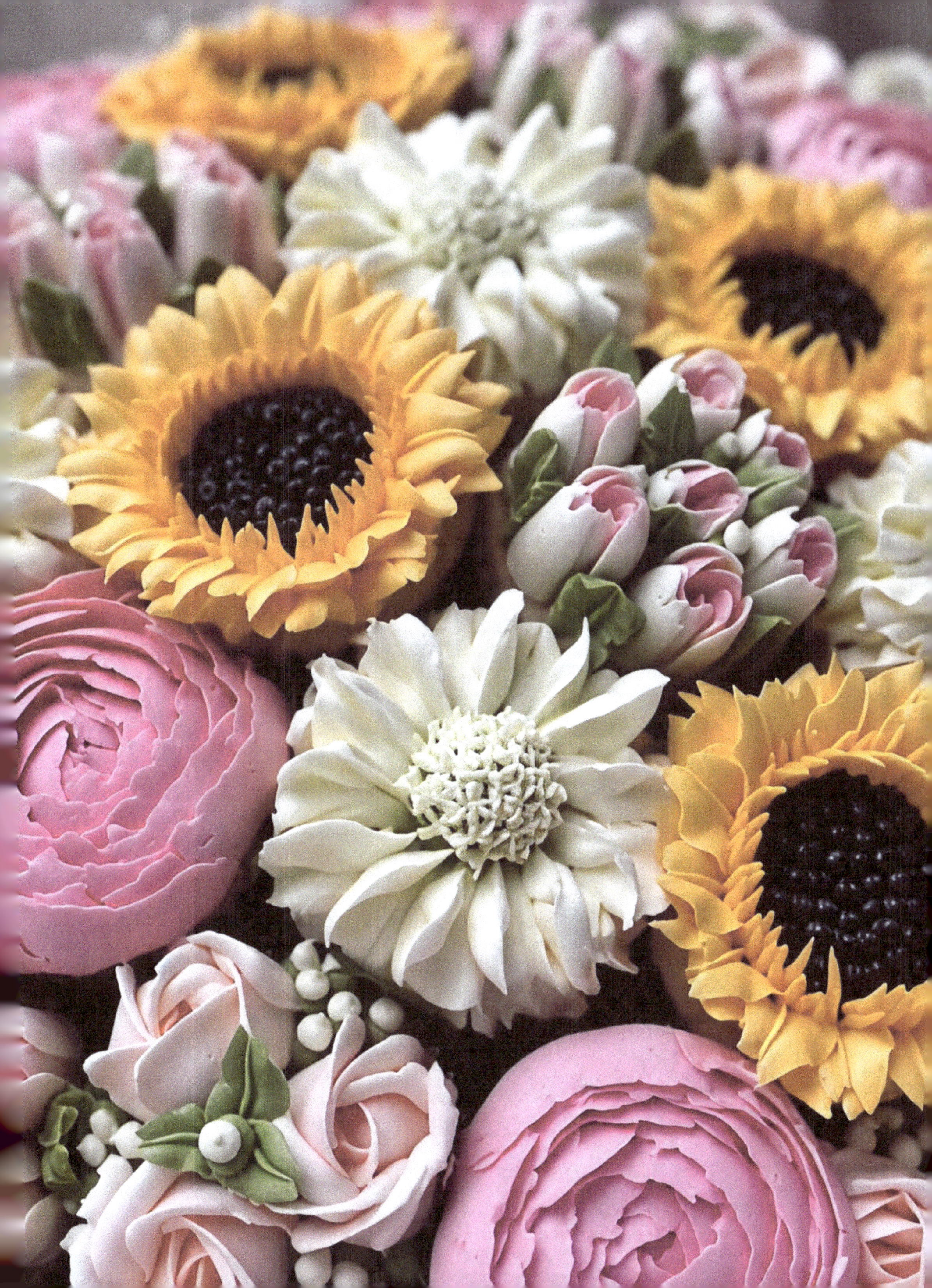

Floral Designs Featured in This Guide

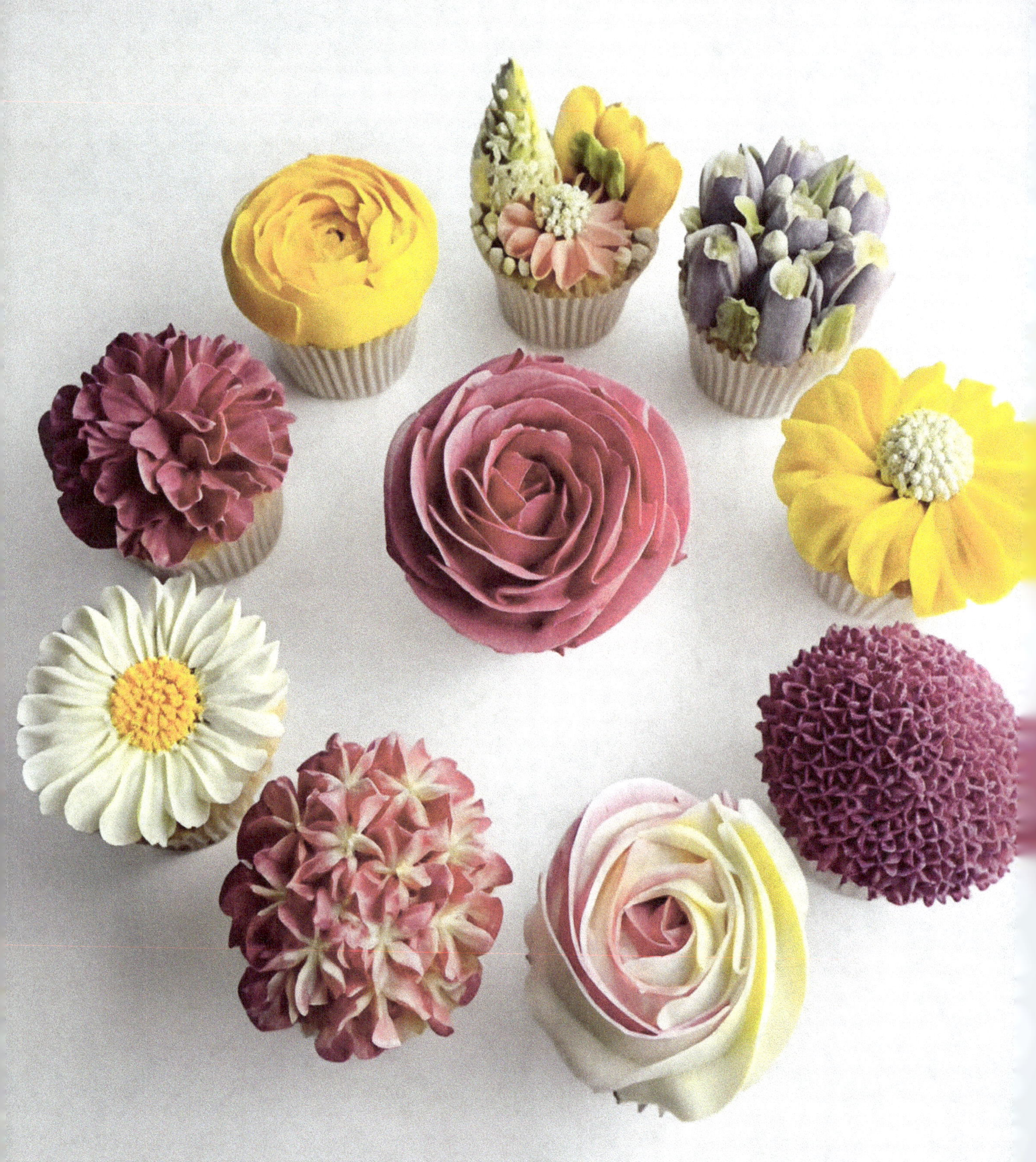

This book will introduce you to 10 basic buttercream flowers, guiding beginners through the process of hand-piping with clear, real-life instructions. Mastering the Scabiosa, with its delicate, clustered petals that form a dainty bloom. Next, you will learn the classic Rose, focusing on achieving smooth, overlapping petals and a natural spiralled centre. The Allium Flower teaches techniques for creating tall, spiky bursts that radiate from a round centre, offering contrast to the softer flowers. The Peony showcases how to layer voluminous, ruffled petals for a lush, full-bodied bloom, while the Carnation Flower introduces intricate rippling effects that mimic its signature frilly look.

You will also discover the Hydrangea Flower, which is created by piping small clusters of petals to form a full, rounded ball, perfect for adding texture to any floral arrangement. The Simple Rosette Flower focuses on mastering the swirl technique, ideal for quick and elegant designs.

For the Tulip Flower, you will learn how to pipe tall, pointed petals that come together to form the signature cup shape, while the Daisy Flower helps you practice creating long, slender petals that radiate from a golden centre.

To push your skills further, the book introduces a challenge flower towards the end: a floral arrangement that includes the Tall Veronica Flower, with its long, delicate spikes, as well as Mini Scabiosa and Mini Tulips, perfect for practicing fine detailing. Each step is broken down with easy-to-follow guidelines, helping beginners understand the importance of buttercream consistency, piping tips, and hand control. By the end, you will not only be able to pipe beautiful, realistic flowers but also develop confidence in experimenting with your own unique designs.

Decorating Tips and Floral Designs

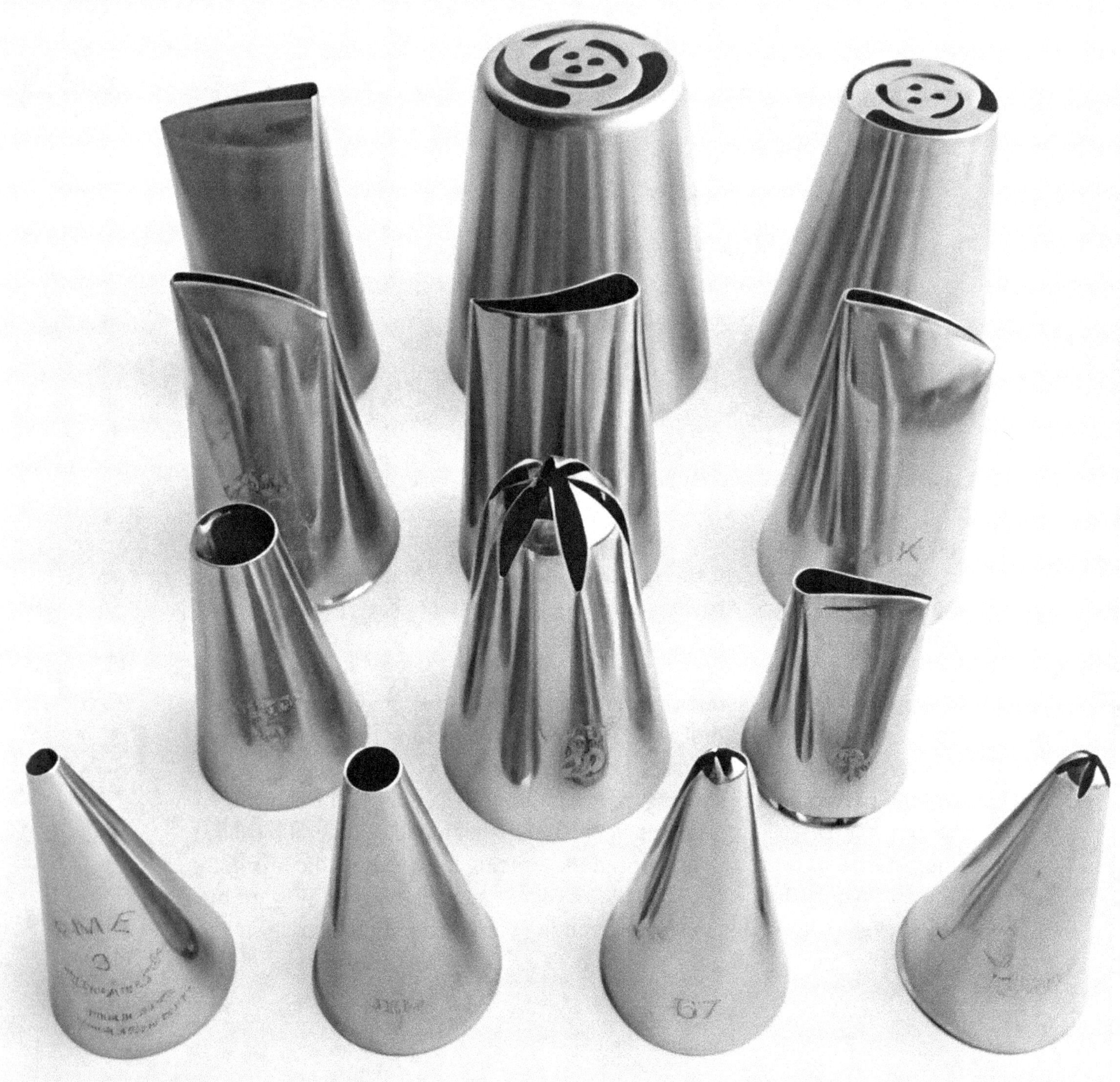

Scabiosa flower

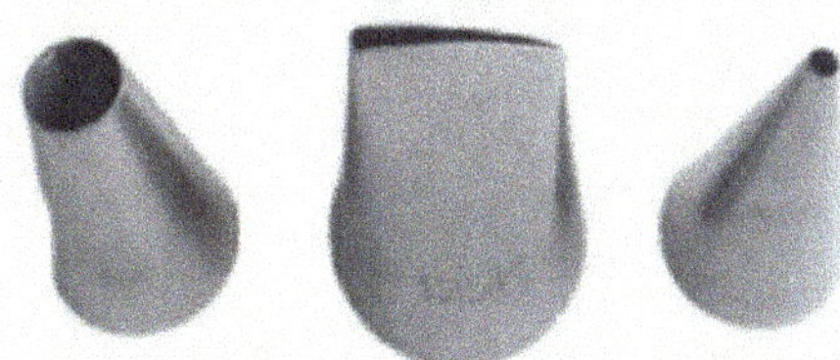

**Nozzle 125K, PME 3 &
Wilton 12**

Carnation flower

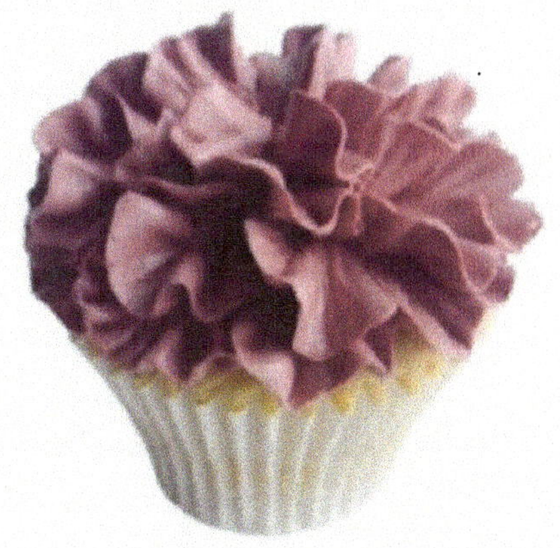

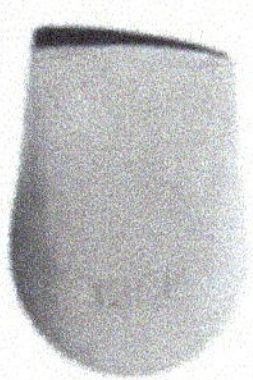

Nozzle 125K

Daisy flower

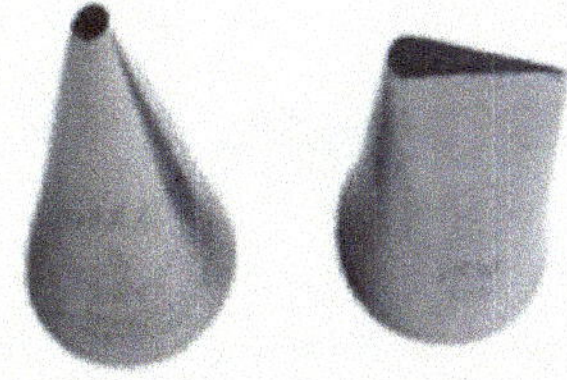

JEM 104 and PME 3

Peony flower

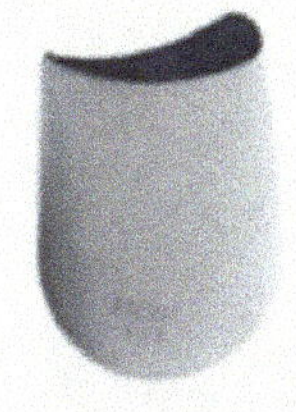

Nozzle JEM 123

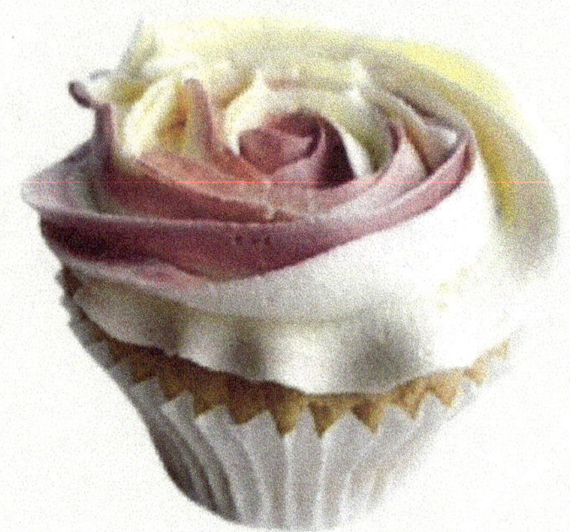

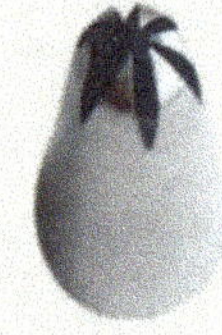

Nozzle Wilton 2D

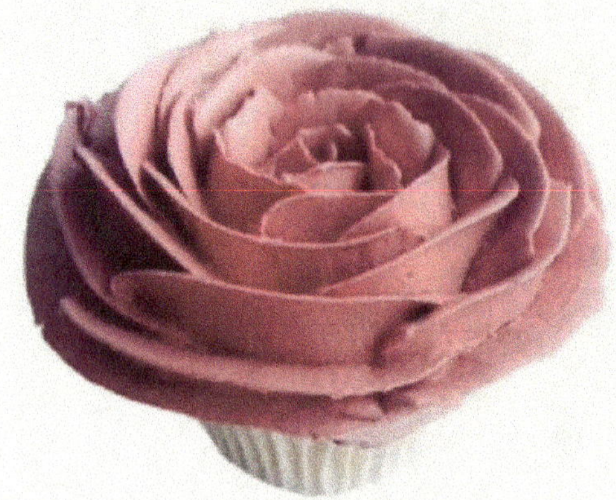

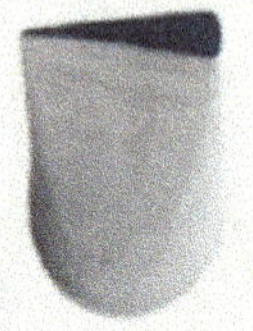

Nozzle 127

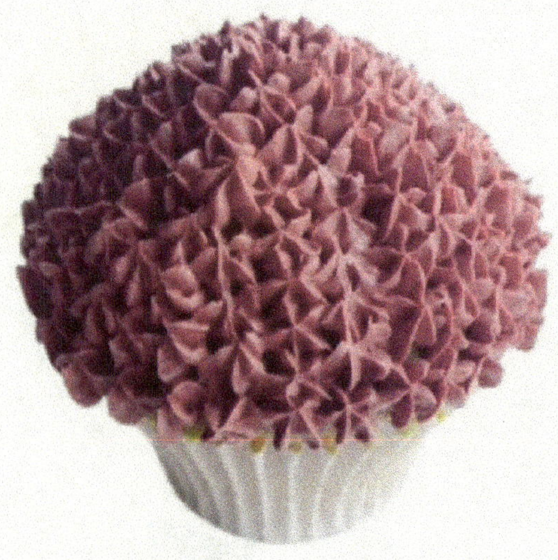

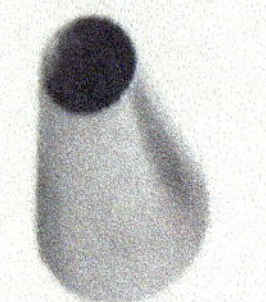

**Any star Nozzle or
No 24 And Wilton 12.**

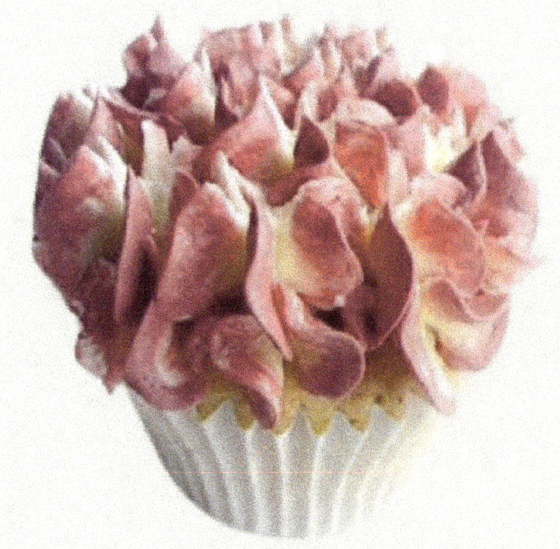

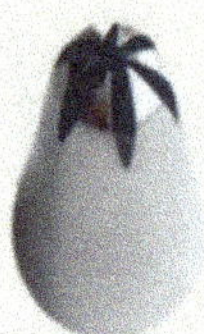

Nozzle Wilton 2D

Flower Garden

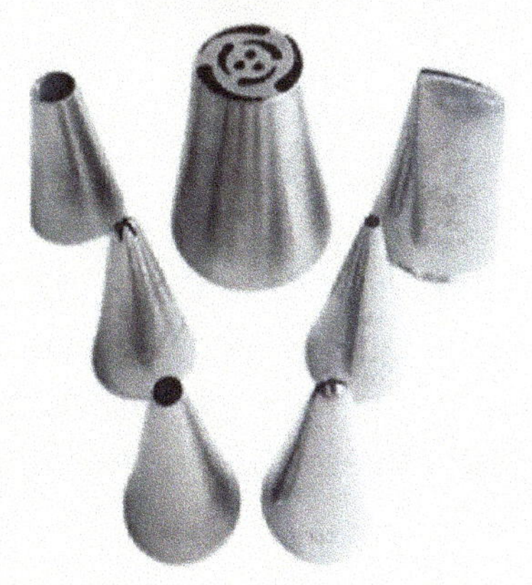

**Mini Russian nozzle,
Wilton 12, ATECO124K, PME 3,
No 24 star nozzle, JEM 7 nozzle
67 leaf nozzle or any small leaf nozzle**

Tulip Flower

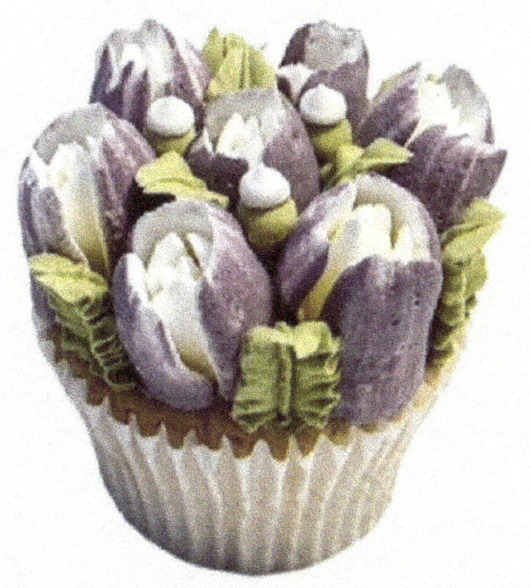

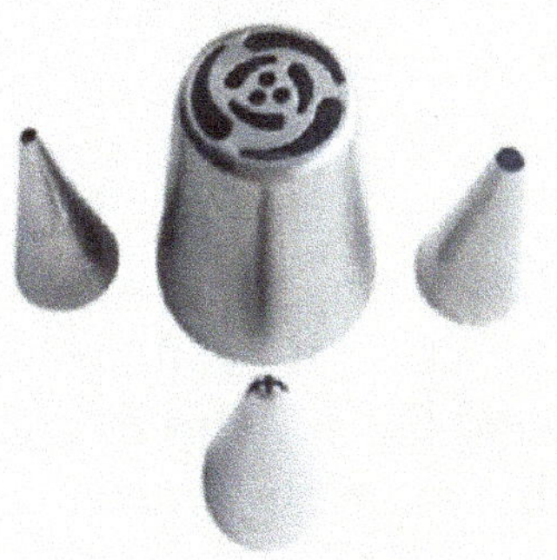

Large Russian Nozzle, PME 3,
No 67 & JEM 7

Using a coupler.

Using a coupler with piping nozzles is a game-changer when decorating buttercream roses, allowing for easy nozzle changes without switching piping bags.

1. To use a coupler, first insert the base of the coupler into the piping bag, ensuring the wider end fits snugly inside. Trim the bag tip if needed for a precise fit.

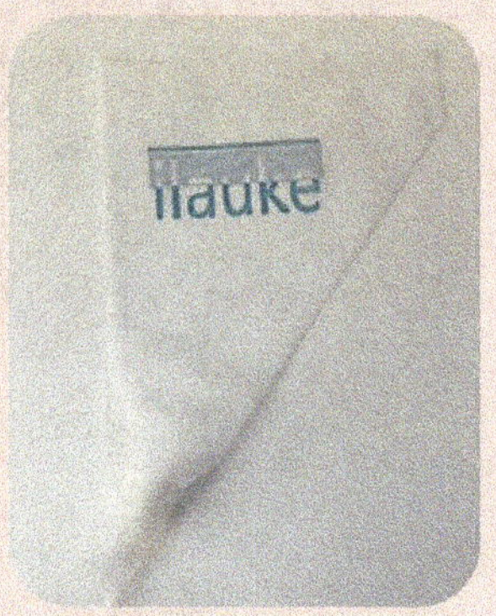

2.Then, place your chosen nozzle over the exposed coupler base and secure it with the coupler ring by twisting it tightly. This setup allows you to switch between different petal tips or if you are piping different shapes using the same coloured icing. It helps to create varying petal sizes and effects without needing multiple bags of buttercream.

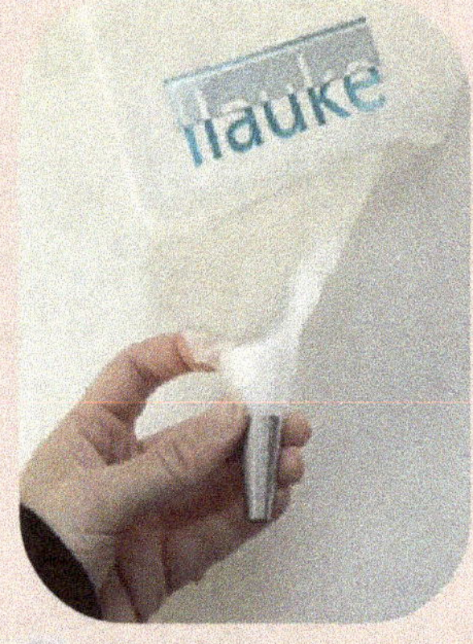
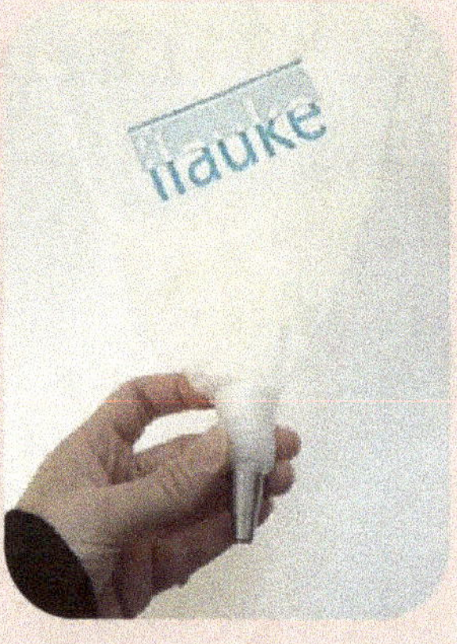
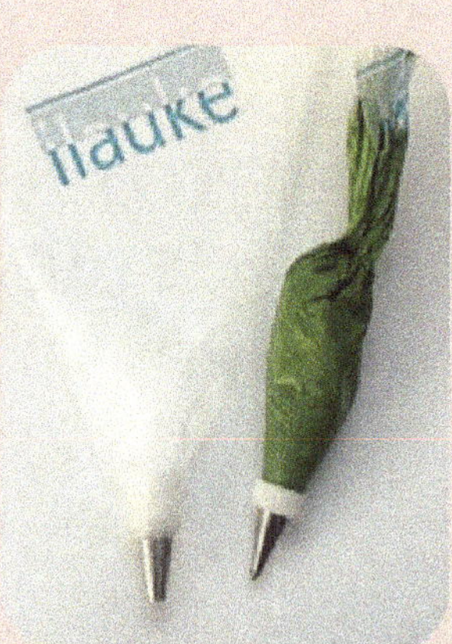

Piping Tips

Available widely in supermarkets, homeware stores and online, a vast array of nozzles are designed for various decorating tasks, each serving a unique purpose. Among the most common types are round nozzles, ideal for writing and creating dots; star nozzles, perfect for piping stars, shells, and swirls; and petal nozzles, essential for crafting detailed flower petals. Leaf nozzles create realistic foliage, while multi-opening nozzles are used for producing grass or hair-like textures. Additionally, there are speciality nozzles like basketweave and ruffle nozzles, which add intricate patterns and textures to cakes. This book will cover the essential nozzles needed for creating simple yet beautiful flowers, providing a solid foundation for anyone looking to enhance their cake decorating skills.

Piping tips are metal, cone-shaped nozzles with an opening at the narrow end. To use a piping tip with a piping bag, insert the tip into the narrow end of the bag, then fill the bag with buttercream. Cut the tip off the piping bag with scissors to expose the piping hole. The shape of the piping tip is where the endless possibilities begin. These tips can be used to create a wide variety of flower petals, flower centres, leaves, borders, and much more. The choice can be overwhelming, with hundreds of shapes available, but this beginner's guide will cover the basic tips to teach you the fundamentals of floral piping.

Basic Piping Tips for Beginners

1. Round Tips: Best for writing, outlining, and creating dots and lines.
2. Star Tips: Ideal for piping stars, swirls, and rosettes.
3. Petal Tips: Essential for creating delicate flower petals and ruffles.
4. Leaf Tips: Designed to create realistic leaves, adding a finishing touch to floral designs.
5. Multi-Opening Tips: Perfect for creating grass, hair, or other fine textures.

Do's and Don'ts for Piping Buttercream Flowers

Do's

Do Practice with Each Tip

Before decorating your cupcakes or cakes, take the time to practice with each piping tip on parchment paper. This will allow you to understand how much pressure you need to apply and the technique required to create specific shapes and designs. Each tip produces a different effect, so practicing beforehand helps you master the intricacies of each one, ensuring cleaner, more precise results on your final product.

Do Use the Right Consistency of Buttercream

The consistency of your buttercream is crucial for successful piping. If the buttercream is too soft, the flowers will lose their shape and appear droopy. On the other hand, if the buttercream is too stiff, it will be difficult to pipe, and your hands will tire quickly. Adjust your buttercream consistency depending on the tip you are using—stiffer for detailed flowers, softer for smooth, flowing petals —and always test it before starting your project.

Do Keep Tips Clean

As you pipe, especially when switching between colours or designs, buttercream can clog or smudge in the piping tips, affecting the shape and precision of your work. Clean your tips regularly by wiping them with a damp cloth or rinsing them in warm water between uses. This will ensure that you maintain clean, sharp lines and prevent colour contamination, giving your flowers a professional, polished look.

Don'ts

Don't Overfill the Piping Bag

Overfilling your piping bag can make it difficult to control the flow of buttercream, leading to uneven or inconsistent designs. It also puts extra strain on your hands, making the piping process harder. Fill the piping bag only about halfway to allow space for gripping and controlling the pressure. If you need more buttercream, it is better to refill the bag than to overfill from the start.

Don't Use Cold Buttercream

Cold buttercream is too stiff to pipe smoothly and will resist flowing through the piping tip, leading to jagged, uneven edges. Always work with buttercream at room temperature for the best results. If your buttercream has been refrigerated, let it sit at room temperature for a while, and give it a quick mix to restore its creamy, pipeable consistency.

Don't Apply Pressure Unevenly

Consistency is key when piping buttercream flowers. Applying uneven pressure will result in distorted shapes and uneven sizes. Practice applying a steady, even pressure to create uniform petals and designs. It is especially important when making detailed flowers, where any variation in pressure can disrupt the symmetry and flow of the petals.

By following these do's and don'ts, you will ensure smoother, cleaner piping and more professional-looking buttercream flowers!

Troubleshooting Common Issues with Piping Buttercream Flowers

Buttercream Not Holding Its Shape

Issue: If your buttercream is too soft, it will not hold its shape properly, causing the petals and designs to appear droopy or less defined.

Solution: Start by chilling the buttercream briefly for about 10-15 minutes. This will firm it up, making it easier to pipe. Alternatively, you can add more powdered sugar to stiffen the buttercream, adjusting the consistency until it is firm yet pipeable. Another tip is to let freshly made buttercream rest for a day. Using buttercream that has been allowed to set overnight (covered with cling film) can make a significant difference when piping intricate flowers. After resting, the buttercream becomes more stable, meaning your decorations will hold their shape better. This also allows time for the flavours to meld, improving the overall taste.

Uneven Lines or Shapes

Issue: Uneven or inconsistent lines are usually caused by applying uneven pressure while piping or using buttercream that is not the right consistency.

Solution: To resolve this, practice applying steady, even pressure with your hands while piping. If the buttercream is too stiff, it may result in jagged or broken lines, so adjust the consistency by adding a small amount of milk or cream. If the buttercream is too soft, stiffen it by adding more powdered sugar. Consistent practice will help you master controlling the pressure and achieve uniform shapes and clean lines.

Clogged Tips

Issue: Clogged piping tips can interrupt the flow of buttercream, resulting in incomplete or uneven designs.

Solution: To clear a clogged tip, gently use a toothpick or pin to remove the blockage. To prevent clogs, ensure your buttercream is smooth and free of lumps before filling the piping bag. A common cause of clogs is lumpy icing sugar, so I recommend sieving the powdered sugar before adding it to your whipped buttercream. This extra step guarantees a silky texture, making it easier to pipe clean and consistent lines. If the buttercream becomes too firm while working, place the tip in warm water for a few seconds - but make sure to wipe it dry before continuing.

By troubleshooting these common issues, you will find it easier to pipe precise, professional-looking buttercream flowers, ensuring a smoother decorating process and better results.

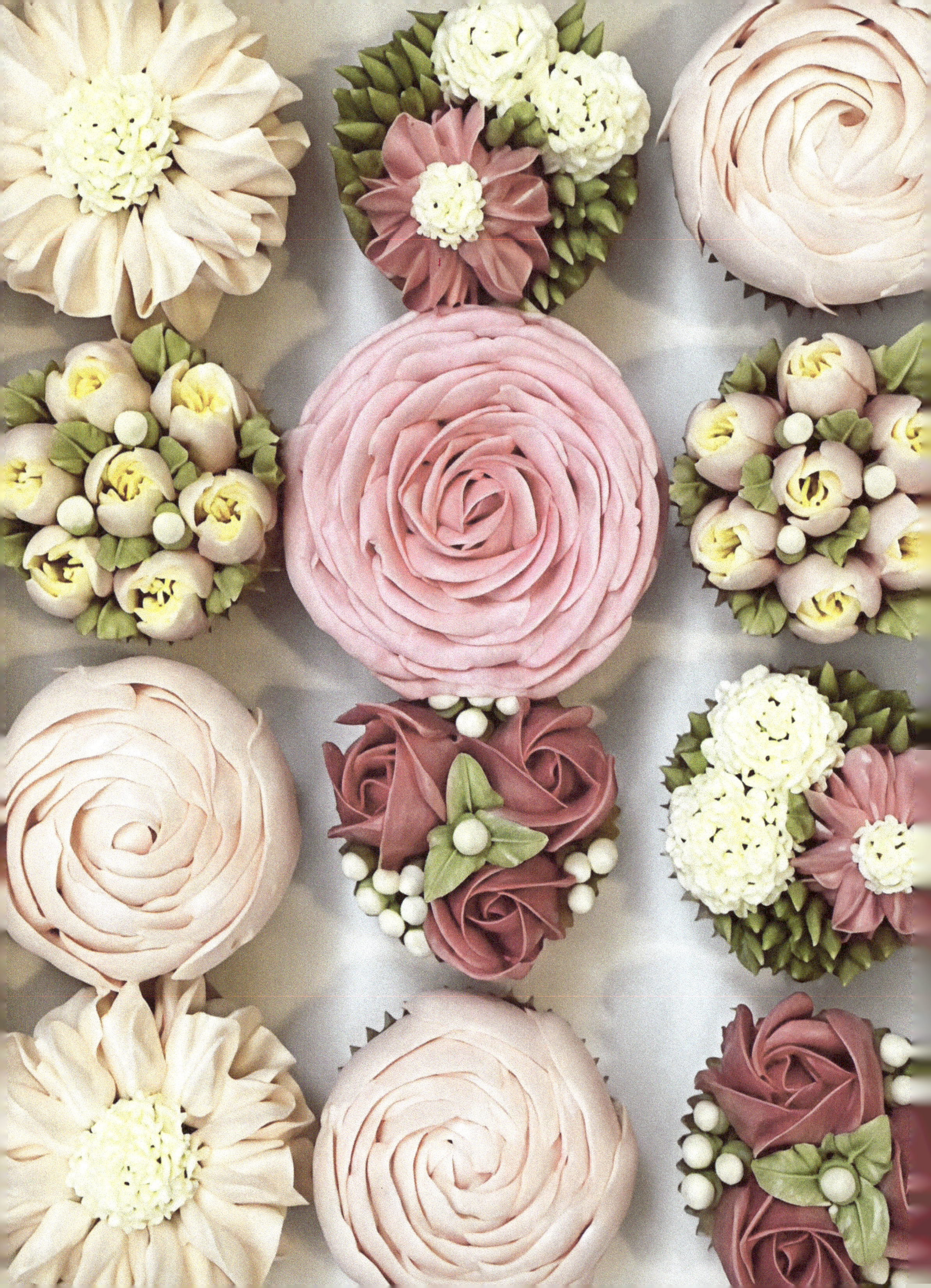

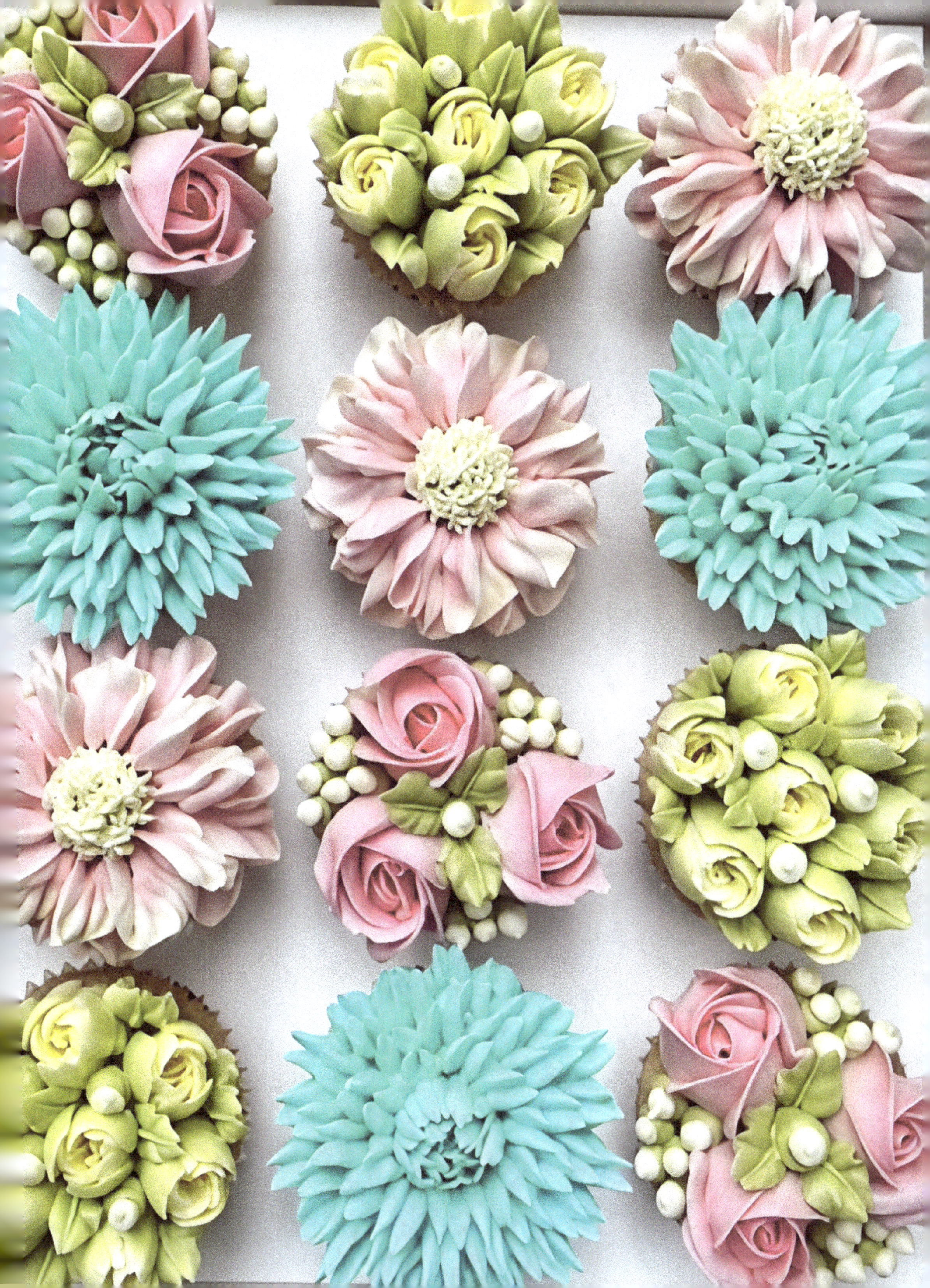

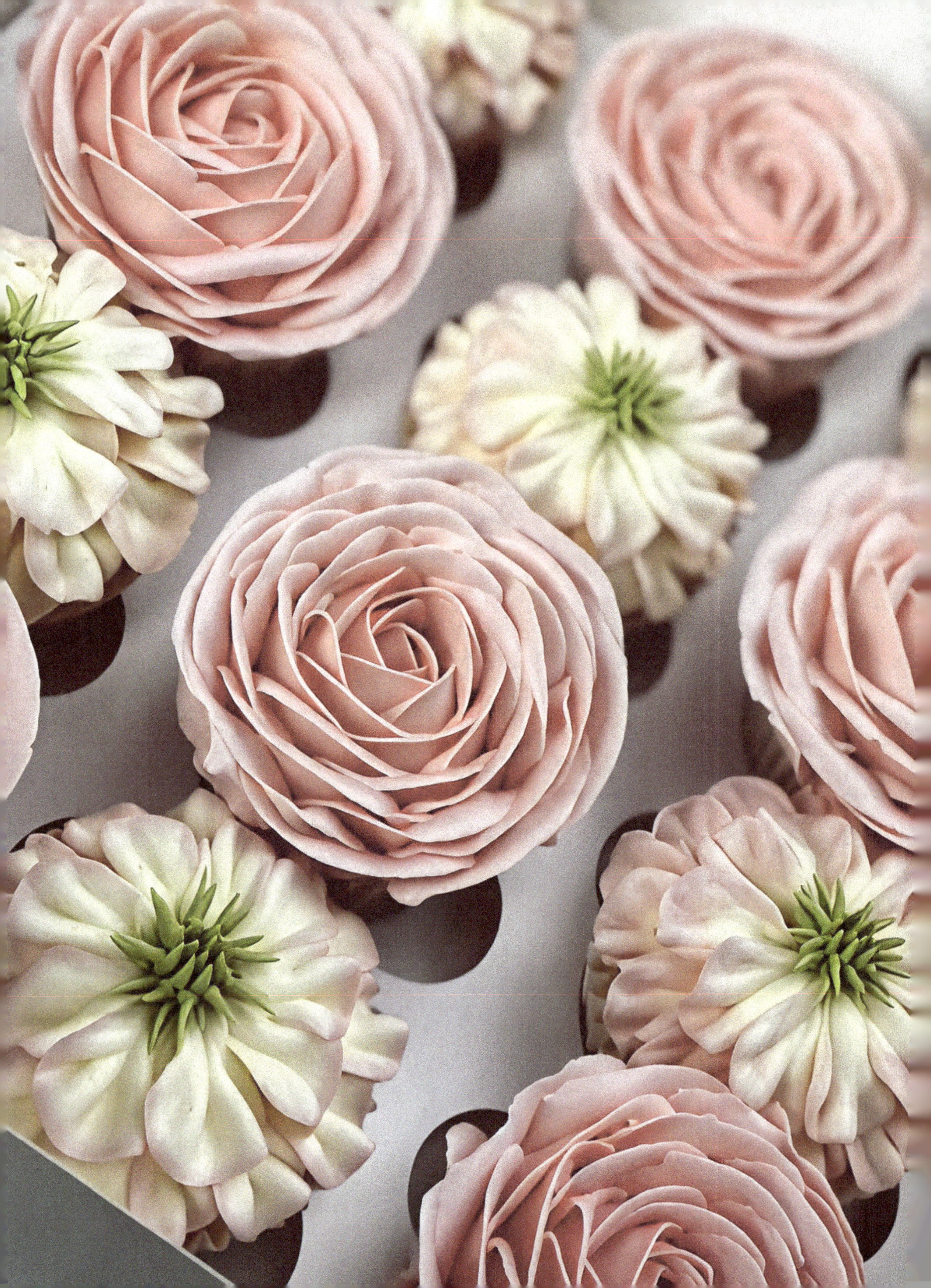

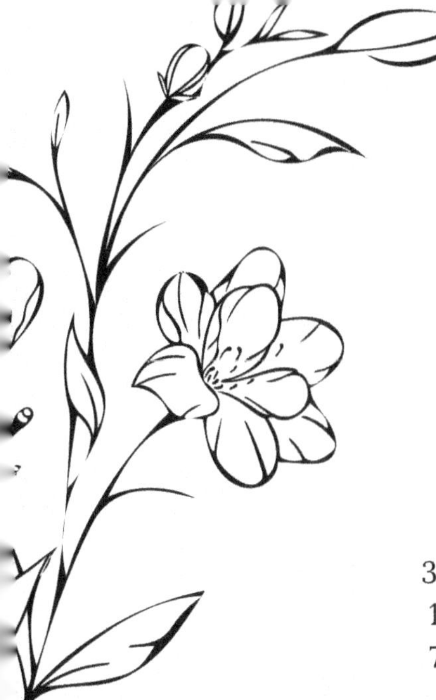

Smooth Buttercream Recipe

Ingredients:
3 blocks of 250 grams unsalted butter, softened
1 tablespoon vanilla essence
700 grams icing sugar

Instructions:
- Ensure your unsalted butter is soft to the touch. This will make it easier to mix into a smooth buttercream. Take out three blocks of unsalted butter and let them sit at room temperature until they are soft.
- Measure out the vanilla essence and the icing sugar.
- Have these ingredients ready before you start mixing to streamline the process.
- Place the three blocks of softened unsalted butter into the bowl of a stand-alone mixer.
- Begin mixing the butter at medium speed. This initial mixing step is crucial as it incorporates air into the butter, resulting in a light and fluffy buttercream.
- Continue mixing until the butter transforms into a pale, almost white colour. This indicates that enough air has been incorporated and the butter is ready for the next step.
- Once the butter has reached the desired consistency and colour, add one tablespoon of vanilla essence. This will infuse the buttercream with a delightful vanilla flavour.
- Mix the butter and vanilla essence together until the essence is fully incorporated and evenly distributed throughout the butter.
- Gradually add the icing sugar to the butter mixture. To avoid a cloud of icing sugar dust, start the mixer on a low speed when adding each portion of icing sugar.

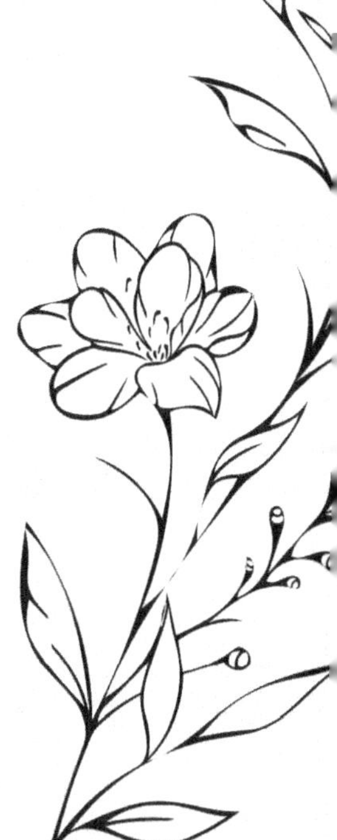

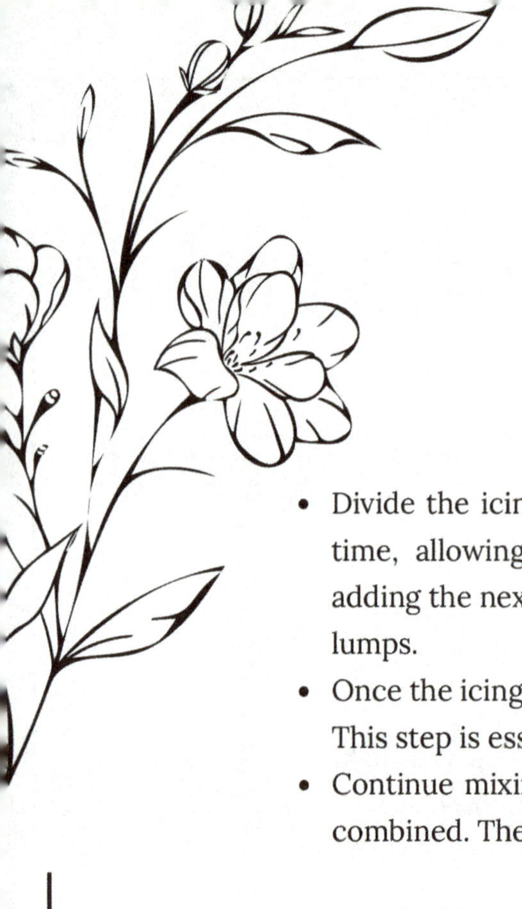

- Divide the icing sugar into three equal parts. Add each part one at a time, allowing the mixer to fully incorporate each portion before adding the next. This ensures that the sugar mixes evenly and prevents lumps.
- Once the icing sugar has been added, increase the mixer speed to high. This step is essential for achieving the desired smooth, airy texture.
- Continue mixing until the buttercream becomes light, fluffy, and well combined. The texture should be creamy and spreadable.

- The final buttercream should be smooth, creamy, and white in colour. If the buttercream is too stiff, you can adjust the consistency by adding a small amount of milk. If it is too soft, add more icing sugar until the desired stiffness is achieved.
- Your smooth buttercream is now ready to be used for icing cakes, cupcakes, or any other baked goods.
- If you have any leftover buttercream, store it in an airtight container in the refrigerator. It can be kept for several days and should be re-whipped before use to regain its fluffy texture.

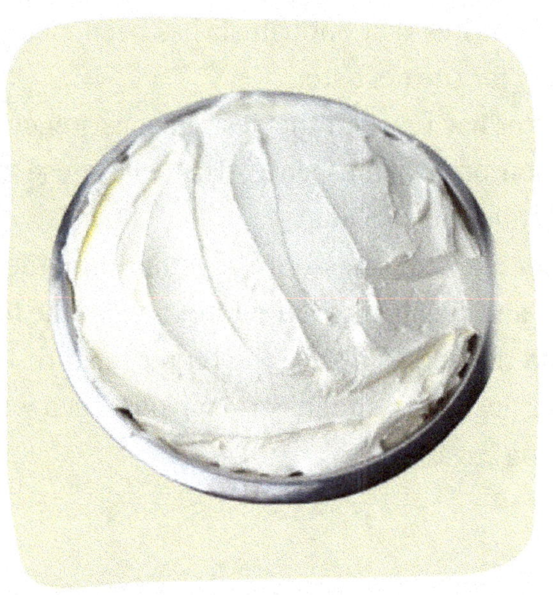

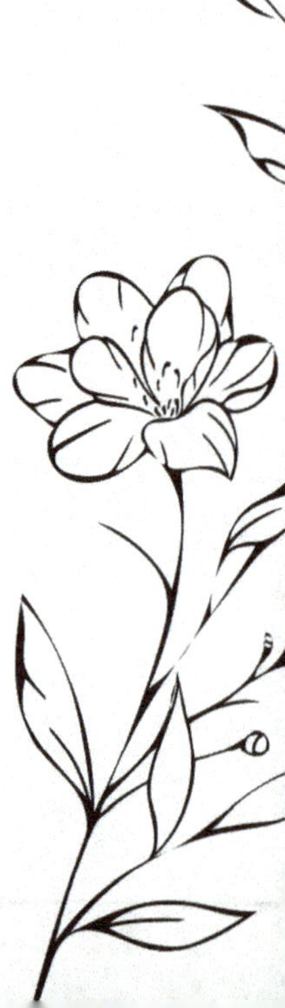

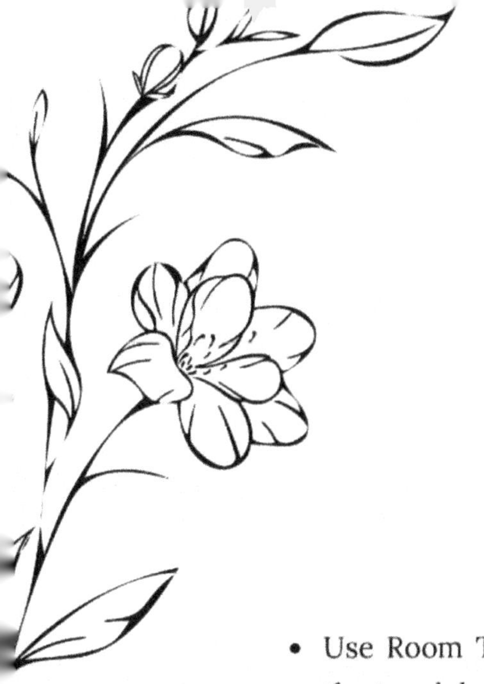

Do's

- Use Room Temperature Butter: Make sure your butter is soft to the touch before starting to ensure a smooth, creamy consistency.
- Sift Your Icing Sugar: This helps to avoid lumps in the buttercream, resulting in a smoother texture.
- Taste as You Go: Adjust the sweetness by adding more icing sugar or a pinch of salt if needed.
- Mix on High Speed at the End: This helps incorporate air, making the buttercream light and fluffy.

Don'ts

- Use Cold Butter: Cold butter won't mix properly and will result in a lumpy buttercream.
- Add All the Sugar at Once: Gradually adding the icing sugar prevents a powdery cloud and ensures better incorporation.
- Overmix: Overmixing can cause the buttercream to become too airy or even separate.
- Skip the Consistency Check: Always check the consistency before using the buttercream; it should be easy to spread but firm enough to hold its shape.

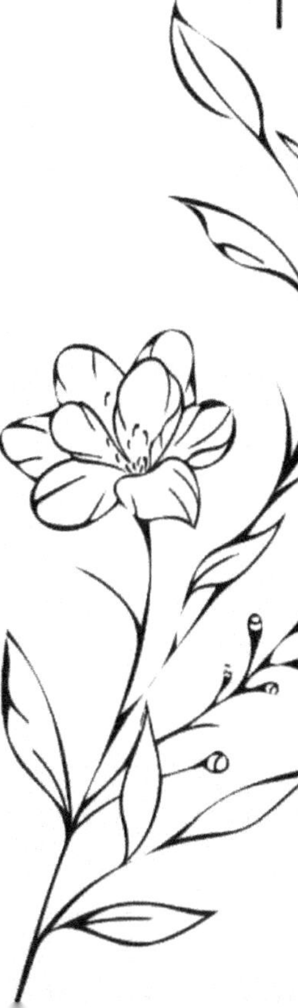

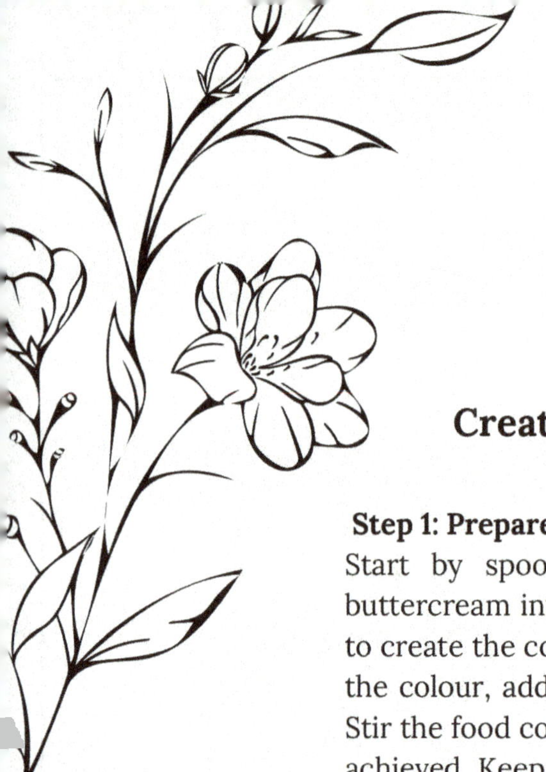

Creating Two-Tone Buttercream

Step 1: Prepare Coloured Buttercream

Start by spooning approximately one-third of your prepared buttercream into a separate mixing bowl. This portion will be used to create the coloured swirls. Depending on the desired intensity of the colour, add a few drops of food colouring to the buttercream. Stir the food colouring into the buttercream until the desired hue is achieved. Keep in mind that the intensity of the colour will deepen slightly as the buttercream sits.

Step 2: Prepare Piping Bag

With the piping bag fitted with the desired tip, use a butter knife or spatula to spread the coloured buttercream around the edges of the inside of the piping bag. Ensure an even coating of coloured buttercream on the inner surface of the bag. Once the coloured buttercream is spread evenly, spoon the remaining uncoloured vanilla buttercream into the centre of the piping bag.

Step 3: Load the Piping Bag

Twist the open end of the piping bag to close it which prevents the buttercream from leaking out. With the buttercream loaded into the piping bag, gently squeeze the bag to push the buttercream down toward the tip. Squeeze a small amount of the buttercream out onto a plate until both the coloured and white buttercream streams are coming out together. This ensures that the piping bag is properly filled with both colours and ready for piping.

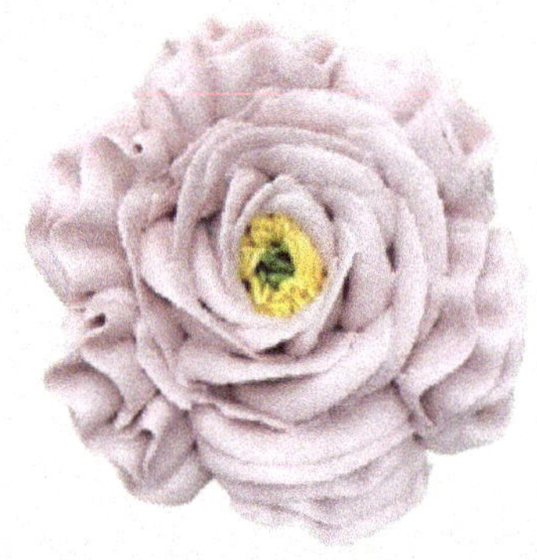

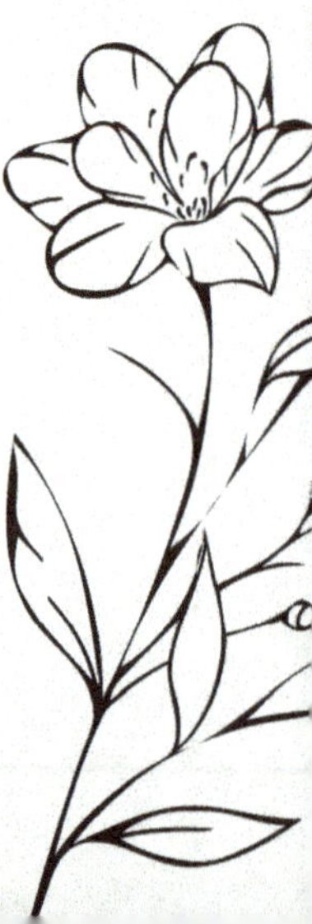

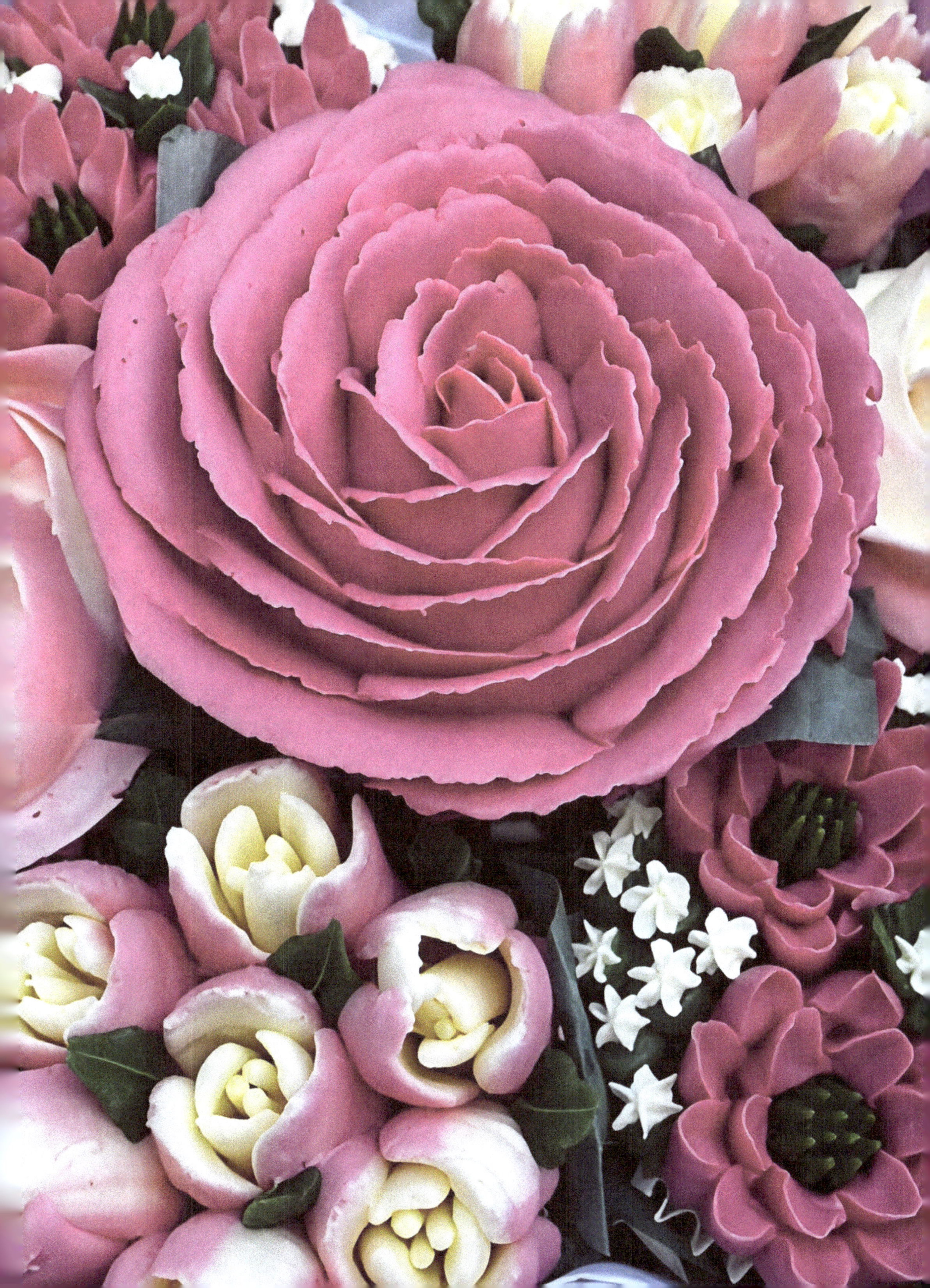

Rose Flower

The Rose is a tribute to my dad's garden—where every bloom told a story, and the roses, in all their colours and forms, were always the most enchanting. Each petal I pipe brings me back to those quiet, fragrant moments spent with him among the flowers.

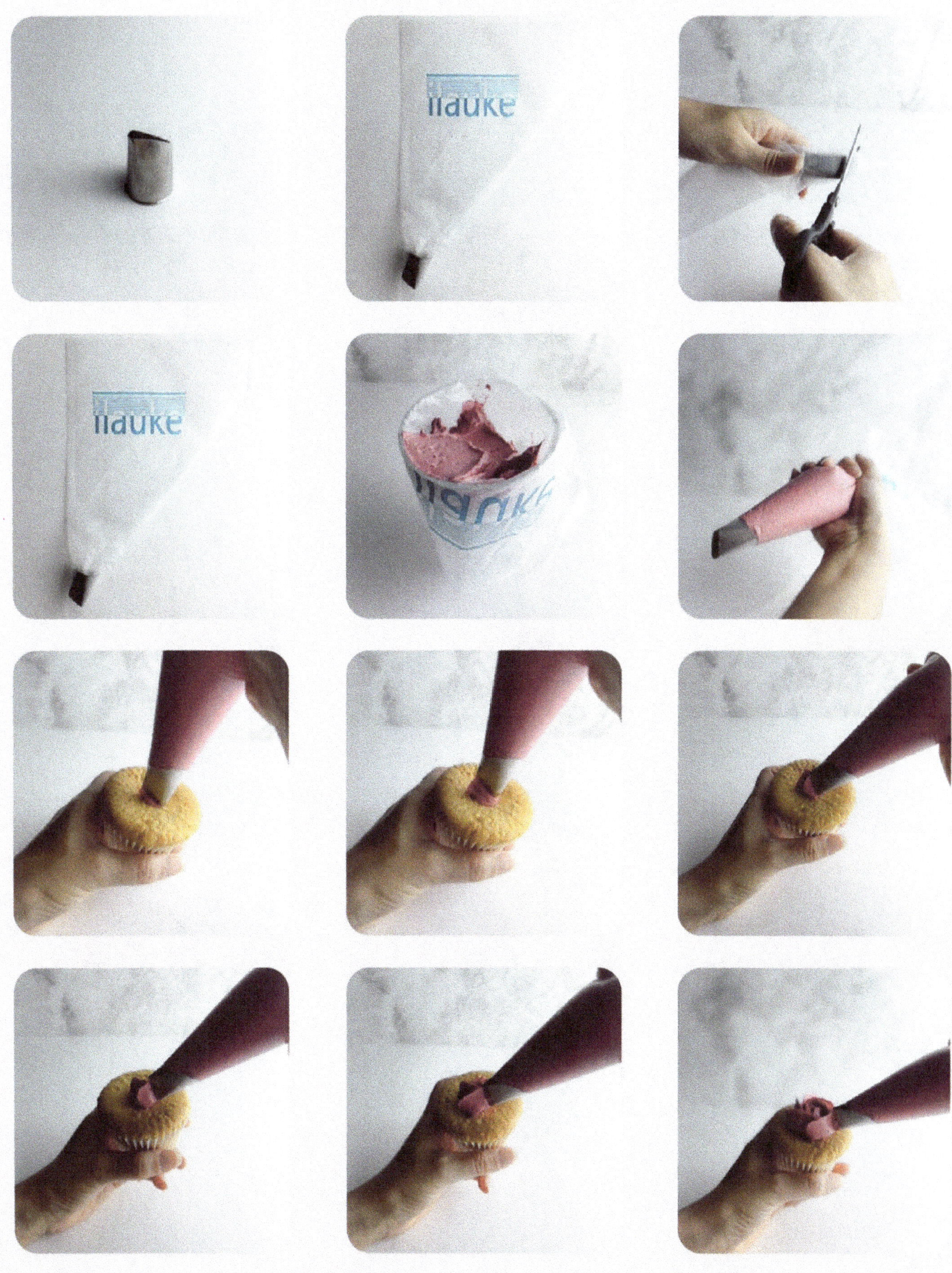

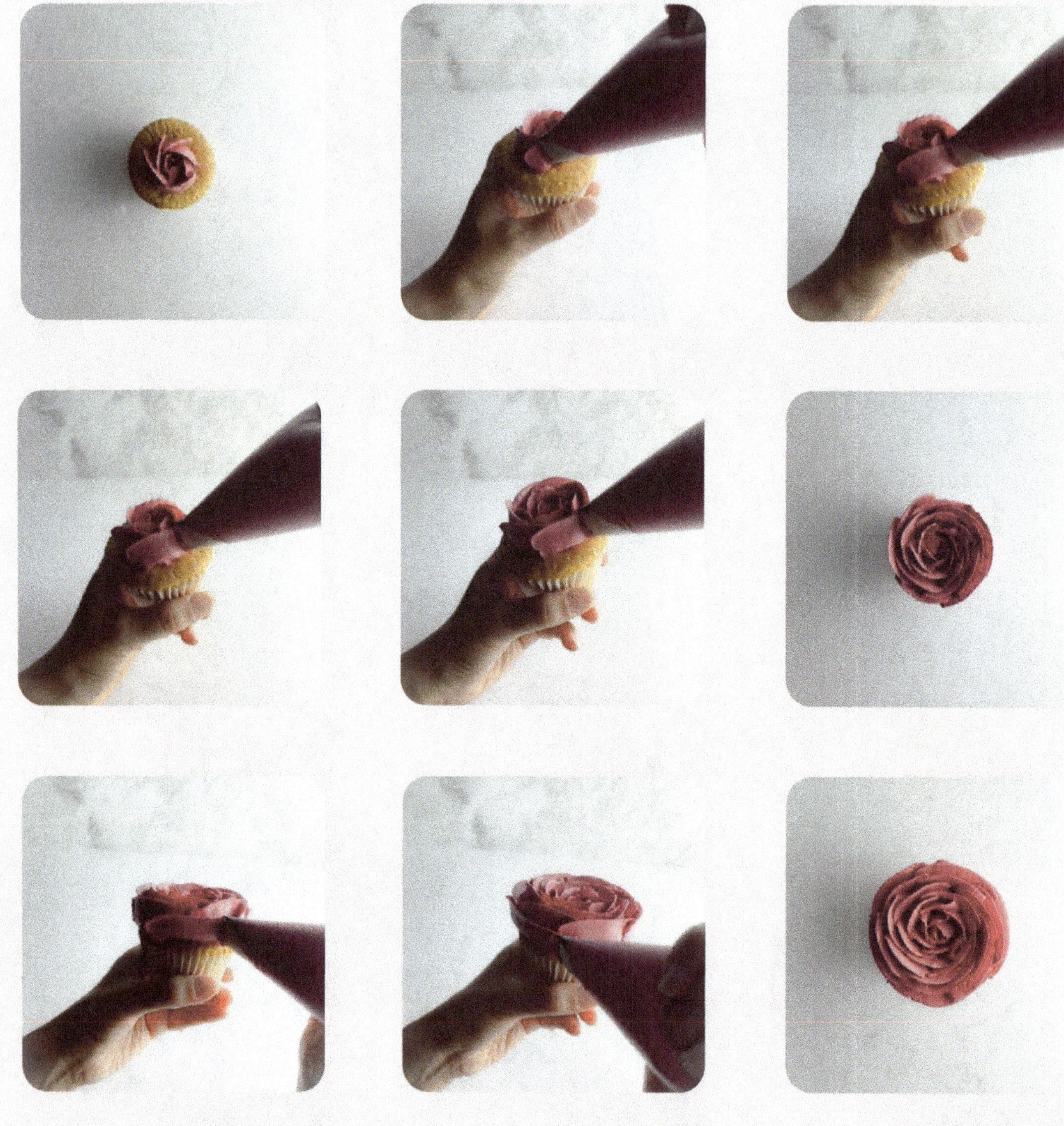

Instructions

Before starting, ensure that your piping bag is fitted with a petal tip (such as No 127). Hold the cupcake in your non-dominant hand and the piping bag in your dominant hand for better control. The icing should be smooth and of a medium consistency—not too soft or firm - so that it holds its shape but is still easy to pipe.

Hold the piping bag at a 90-degree angle against the cupcake, with the wider end of the piping tip facing down. Begin applying firm but even pressure to squeeze out the icing while simultaneously pulling the bag upwards to create a cone shape. The cone should be narrow at the top and approximately ½ inch tall. If the base is too tall, this can make your rose top-heavy and unstable. The base is essential for providing structure, so ensure that the cone stands firm and stable on the flower cupcake.

Now that the base is ready, position the piping tip near the top of the cone. Hold the piping bag at a slight angle (about 45 degrees) to the cupcake, with the wider end of the petal tip touching the cone and the narrow end pointing slightly outward.

Begin piping by applying steady pressure to the bag as you simultaneously rotate the cupcake slowly with your other hand. This movement creates a spiral of icing that wraps around the top of the cone; forming the centre of the rose. Keep your movements smooth and consistent, as the spiral will serve as the foundation for the petals.

If the spiral looks too small or undefined, you can add another layer by repeating the process until you achieve a rounded, well-defined centre. This step is crucial for creating a realistic looking rose.

Once the spiral centre is complete, hold the piping bag so that the wider part of the tip touches the base of the spiral, with the narrow end angled slightly outward. Begin piping the first petal by applying pressure to the bag, while rotating the cupcake slowly in the opposite direction.

This petal should create a slight arc around the spiral. Make sure that the petal covers about one-third of the space around the spiral centre. You do not want to cover too much as this will affect the balance of your petals later on.

Pipe the second petal next to the first, leaving a small gap between the two. Again, hold the piping bag at a slight angle, with the narrow end of the petal tip pointing outward. Rotate the cupcake as you pipe the petal.

When viewed from above, the first three petals should form a triangular shape around the spiral centre. Ensure that each petal overlaps the previous one slightly at the edges. This helps to form a natural flow and adds to the realism of the rose.

For the second layer of petals, begin slightly lower than the first layer and hold the piping bag at a slightly more outward angle. The goal is to make the petals appear to be opening up, so angle the piping tip so the petals curve outward and away from the centre.

The second layer of petals should overlap the first layer without actually covering them. The tips of the petals in the second layer should gently touch the top edges of the first layer, giving a sense of fullness and depth.

For the third layer of petals, you will need to increase the outward angle of the piping tip, making it almost parallel to the surface of the cupcake. Hold the piping bag with the wider end of the petal tip touching the base of the previous petal layer, and the narrow end positioned almost horizontally.

Pipe five petals around the base of the rose. These petals should slightly overlap each other and the previous layer, blending them together for a seamless aesthetic. This step adds volume and begins to make the rose look fuller and more realistic.

If at any point the petals appear too thin or fragile, they may start to collapse or look flat. If this happens, carefully scrape off the affected petals using a small offset spatula or a toothpick; taking care not to disturb the underlying layers.

To correct this, apply more pressure when piping your next set of petals. The extra icing will give the petals more structure and stability, ensuring that they hold their shape. Additionally, ensure that each new petal connects securely to the previous ones, helping to reinforce the overall structure of the rose.

As you continue, gradually tilt the piping tip further outward with each successive petal. By the end of this final layer, the piping tip should be nearly horizontal to the surface of the cupcake.

Add a final set of five petals around the outermost layer. If you want a fuller bloom, you can add a third set of five petals. Make sure each petal overlaps the previous one slightly for a cohesive look. The petals should fan outwards, giving the appearance of a fully opened rose in bloom.

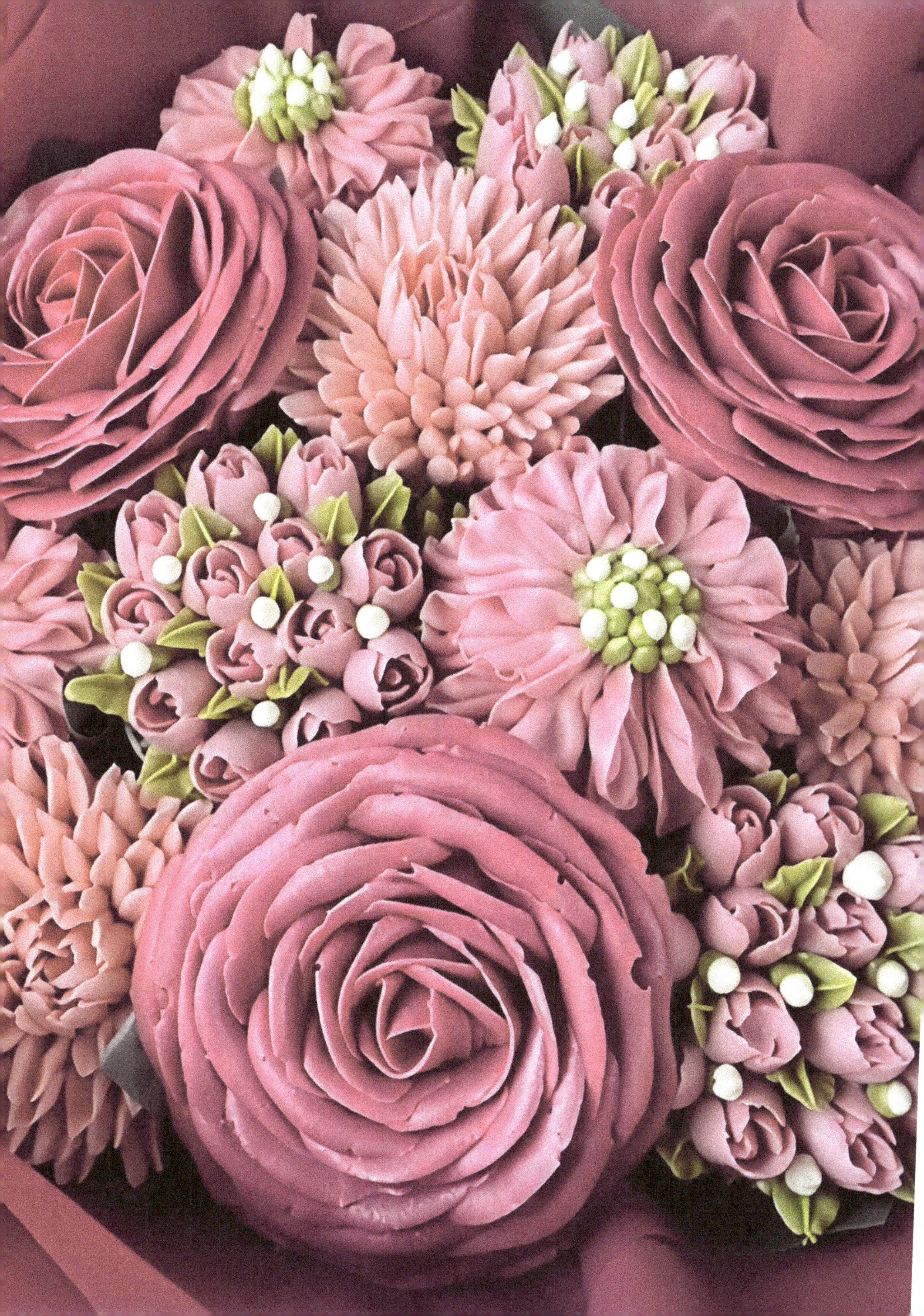

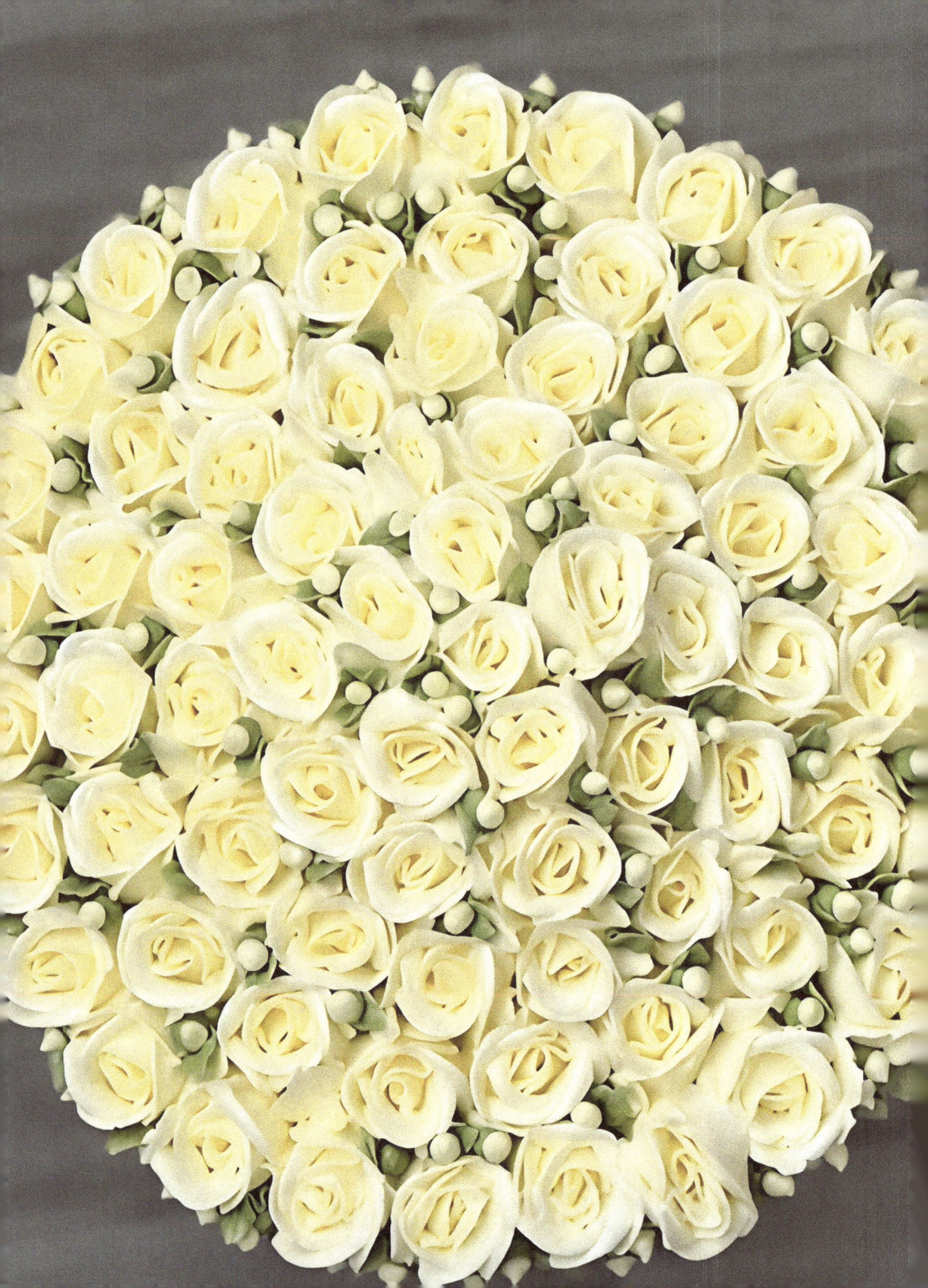

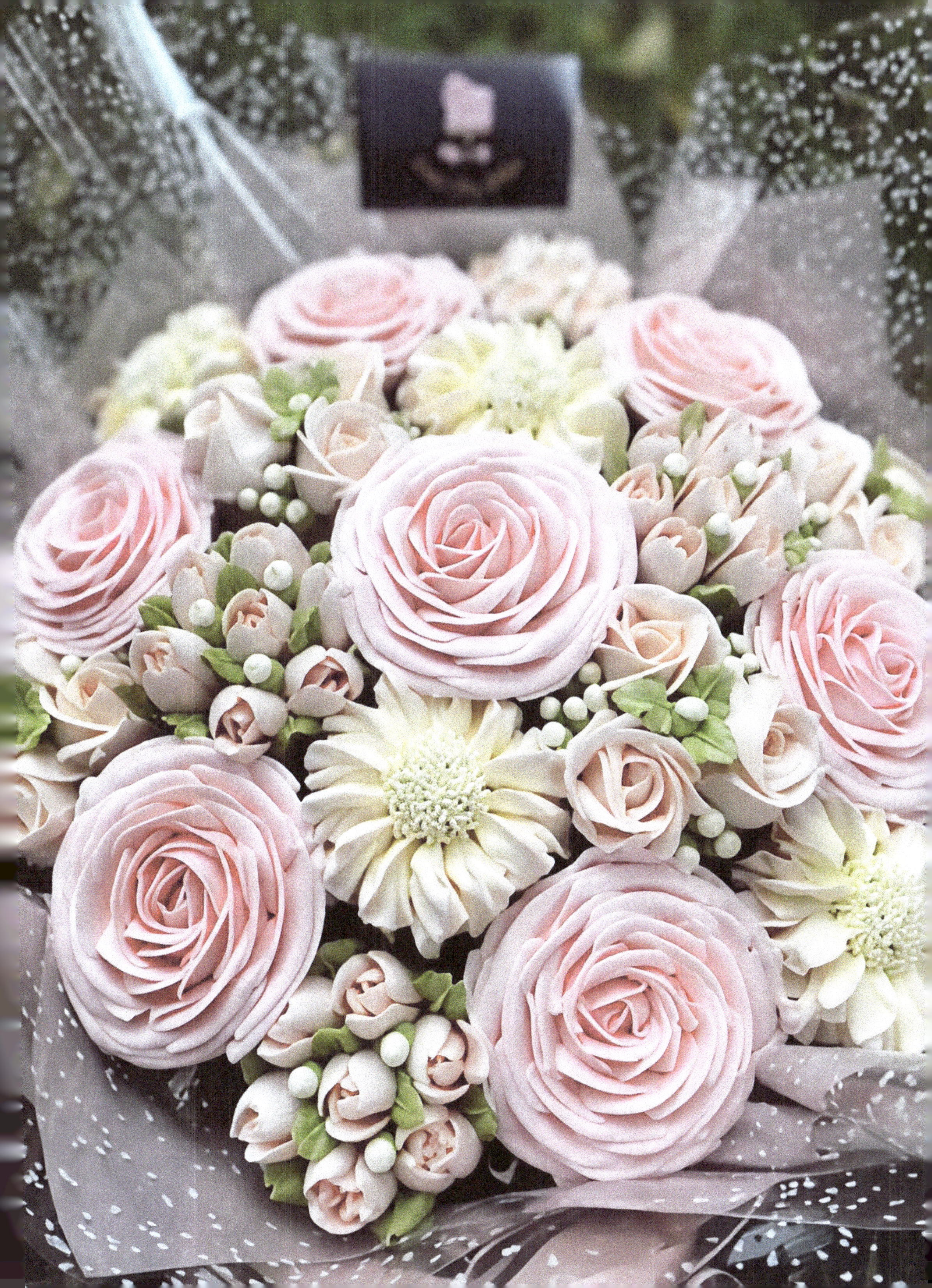

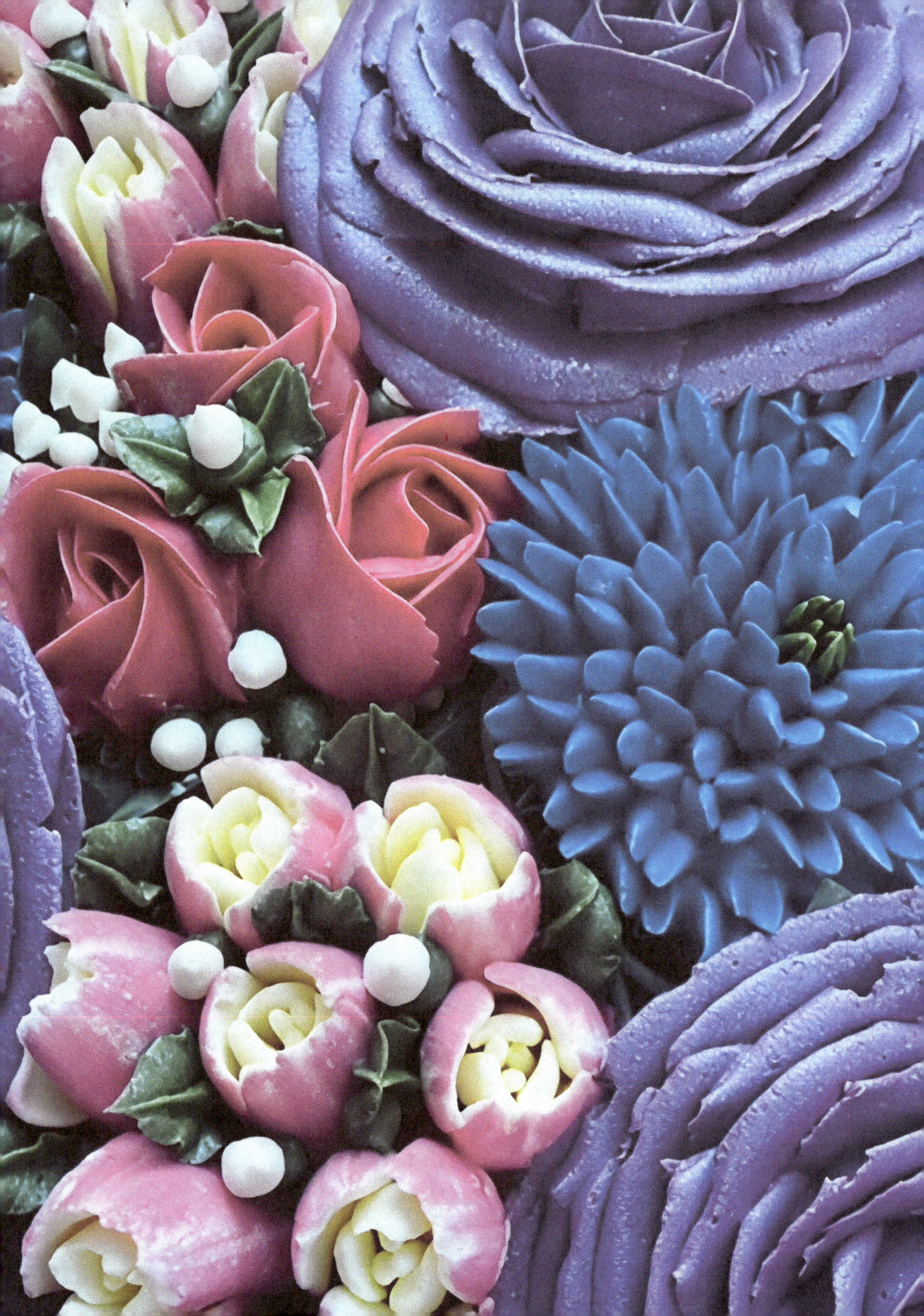

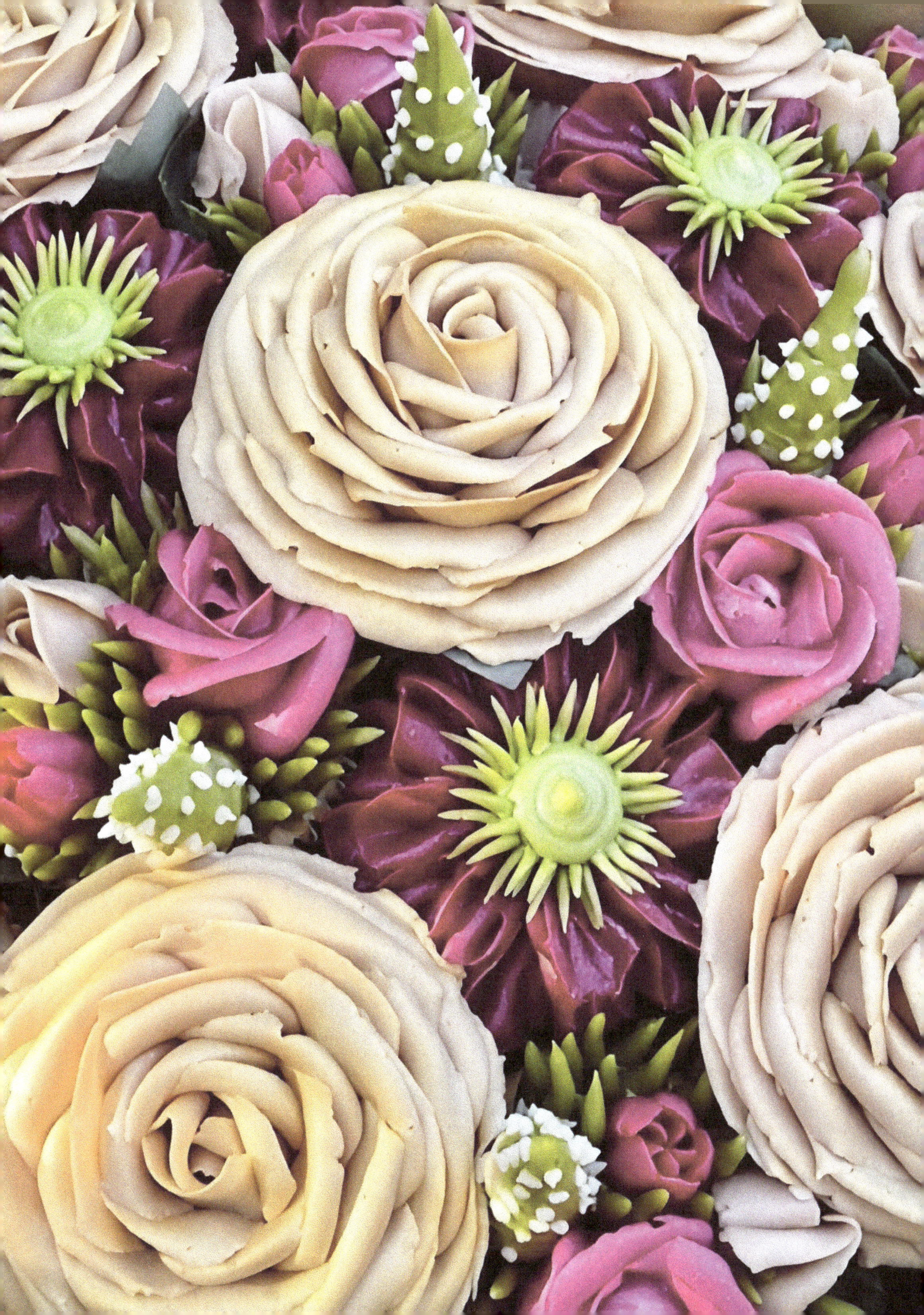

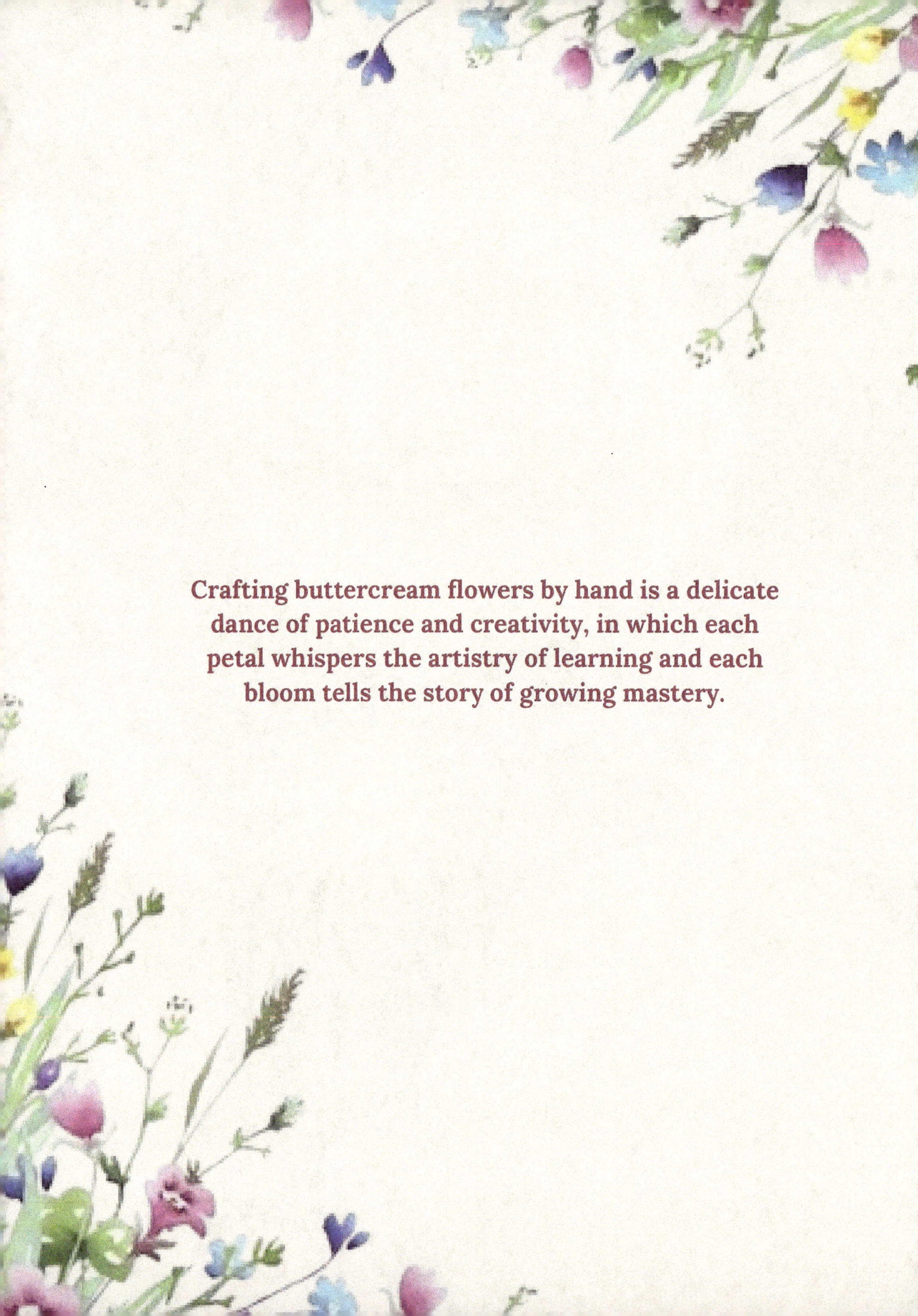

Crafting buttercream flowers by hand is a delicate
dance of patience and creativity, in which each
petal whispers the artistry of learning and each
bloom tells the story of growing mastery.

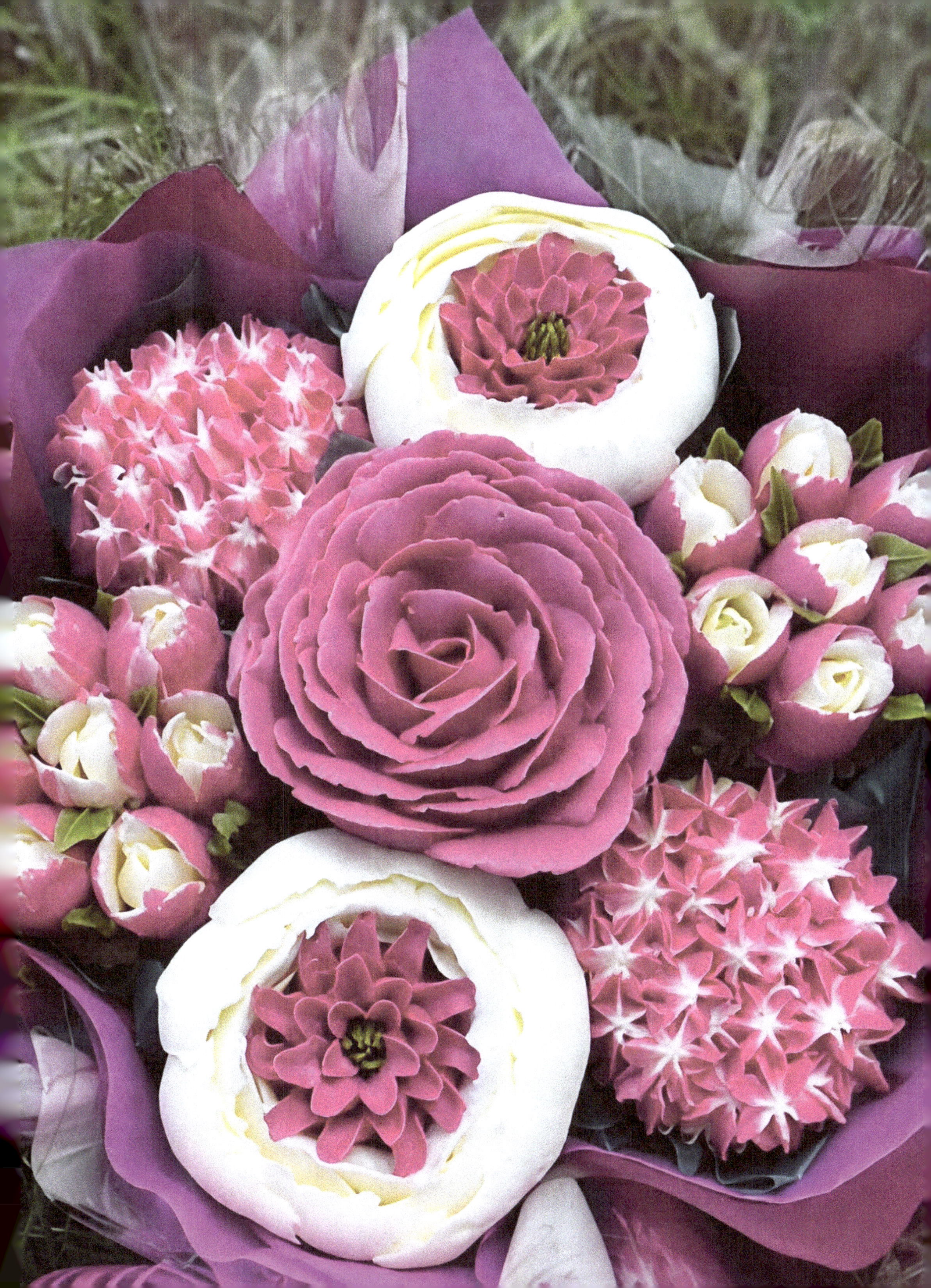

Hydrangea Flower.

I included the Hydrangea because it reminds me of the cheerful mornings; dropping my children at nursery, passing by gardens overflowing with big, colourful blooms. Those hydrangeas always made the simplest routines feel a little more magical.

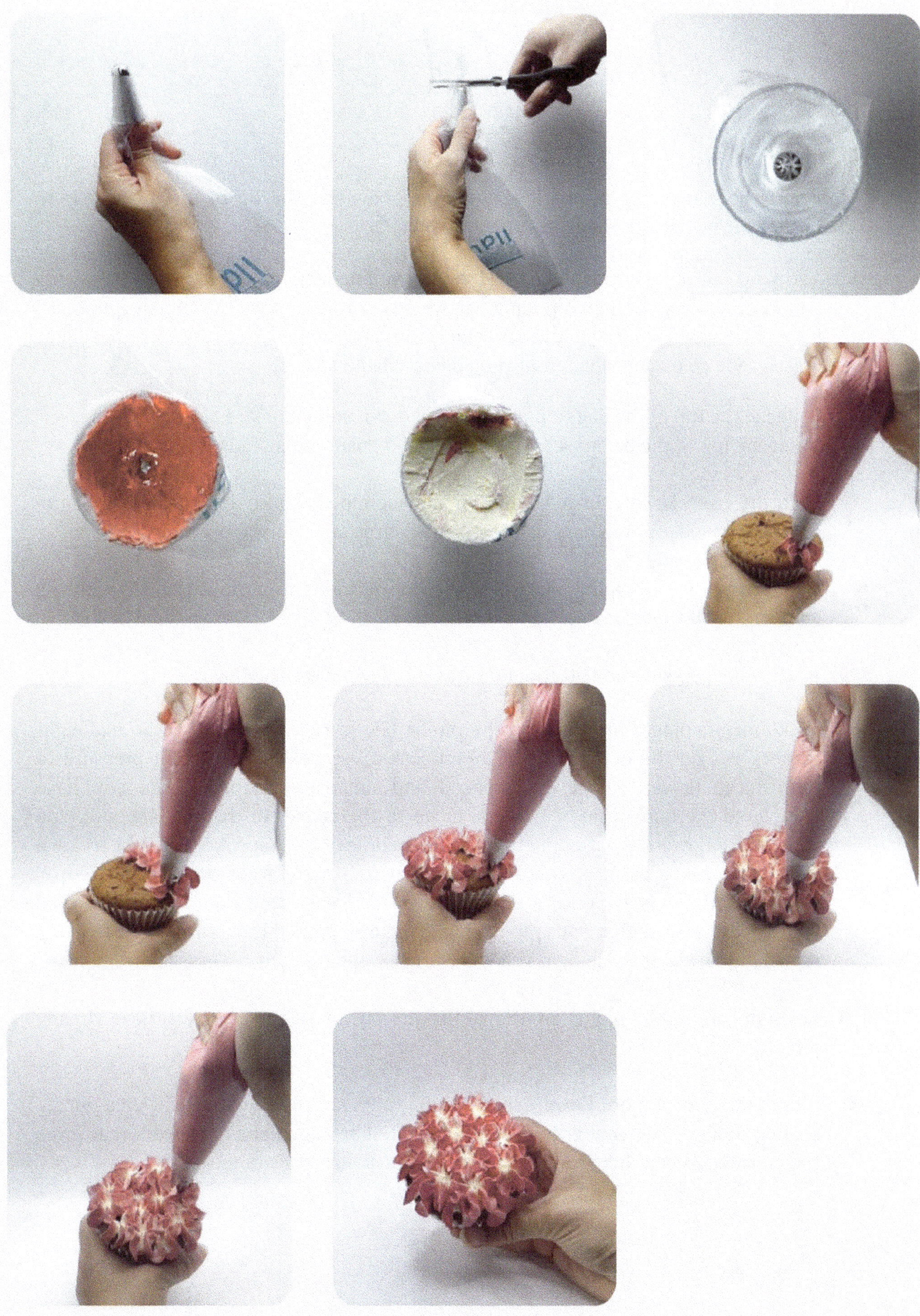

Instructions

Insert the star piping nozzle into the piping bag. Cut the tip of the piping bag to ensure the nozzle fits snugly through the hole.

Add your chosen icing to the bag. Here, I have lined the piping bag with pink icing and filled the bag with cream icing to give a two-toned effect. The icing gels that I have used are from Progel and are widely available online. You can also use Colour Splash food colouring which is also readily available online.

Squeeze the top of the bag to push the icing down and eliminate any air pockets. Twist the top of the bag to secure the icing and ensure it is ready for use.

Hold the cupcake in your left hand (or non-dominant hand) and the piping bag in your right hand (or dominant hand) at a 90-degree angle above the cupcake.

Gently squeeze the piping bag. Allow the nozzle to create a flower shape with the icing on top of the cupcake.

Release the pressure and lift the nozzle away to complete the flower.

While maintaining a firm grip on the piping bag, carefully pipe an additional eight flowers around the outer edge of the cupcake. Use gentle, consistent pressure to ensure the flowers are evenly spaced and uniformly shaped. Once you have completed the outer ring of flowers, move to the centre of the cupcake and pipe three more flowers, positioning them in the middle of the cupcake. This will create a visually appealing pattern with a decorative border and a focal point in the centre. Gently set the cupcake onto a flat, stable surface, such as a countertop or a cake board. Next, ensure that your piping bag is securely closed by tightening or twisting it, making sure that the icing is ready for precise application.

Begin decorating by piping additional flowers on top of the ones you have already piped.

Aim to add 3 or 4 more flowers, positioning them strategically to build up a dome-shaped mound. The goal is to create a lush, full arrangement of flowers that gives the cupcake a beautifully rounded, three-dimensional appearance.

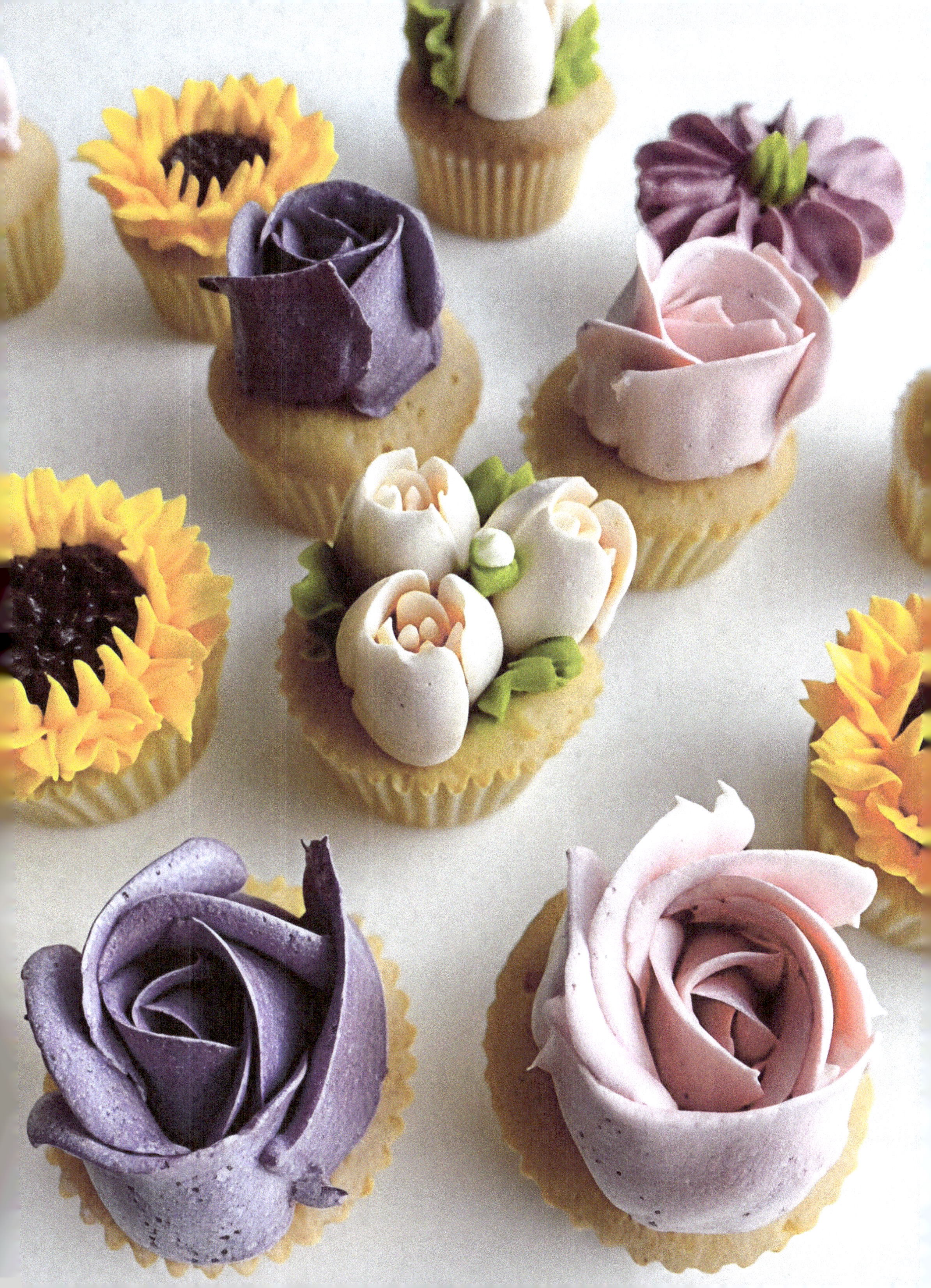

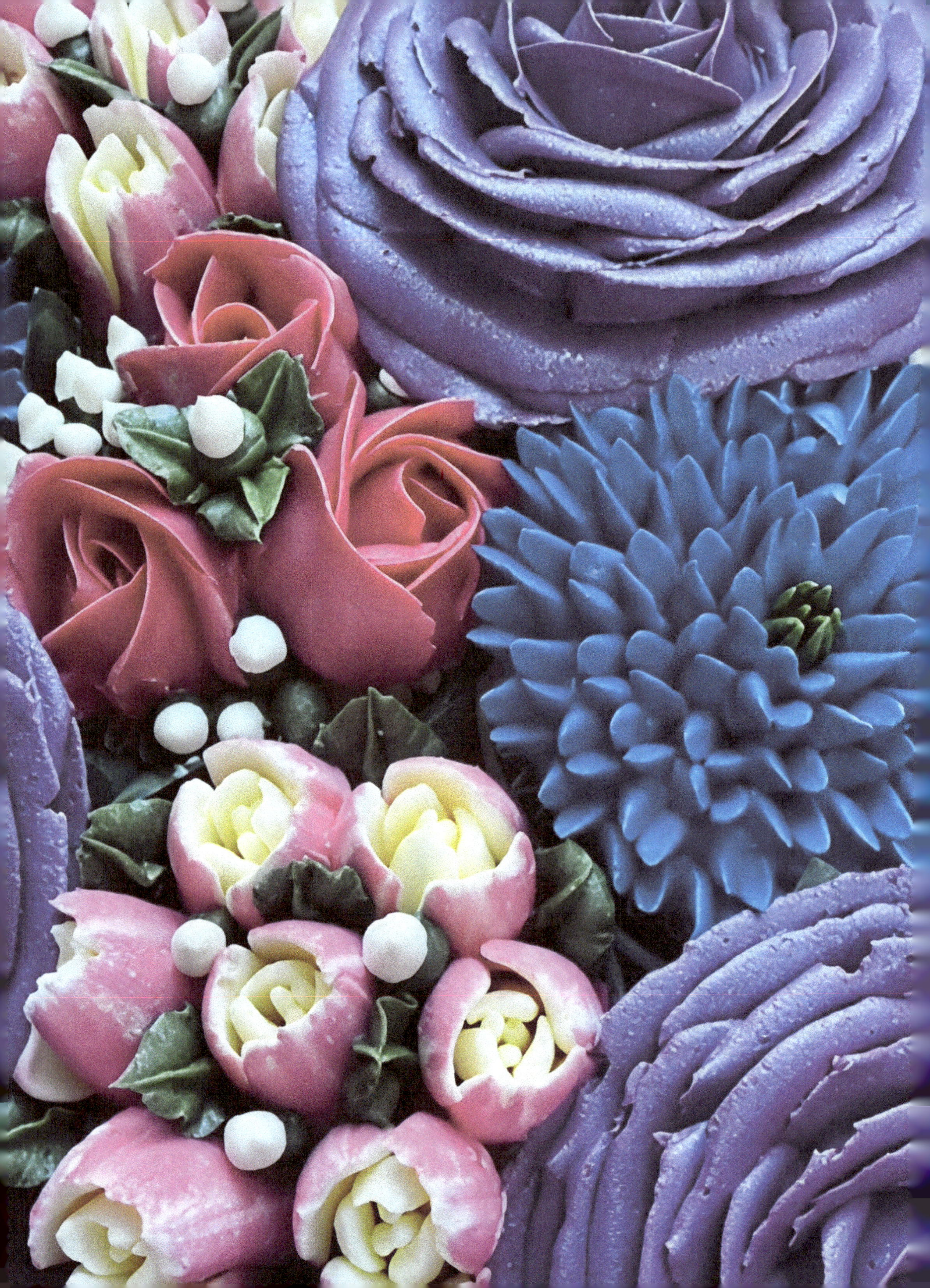

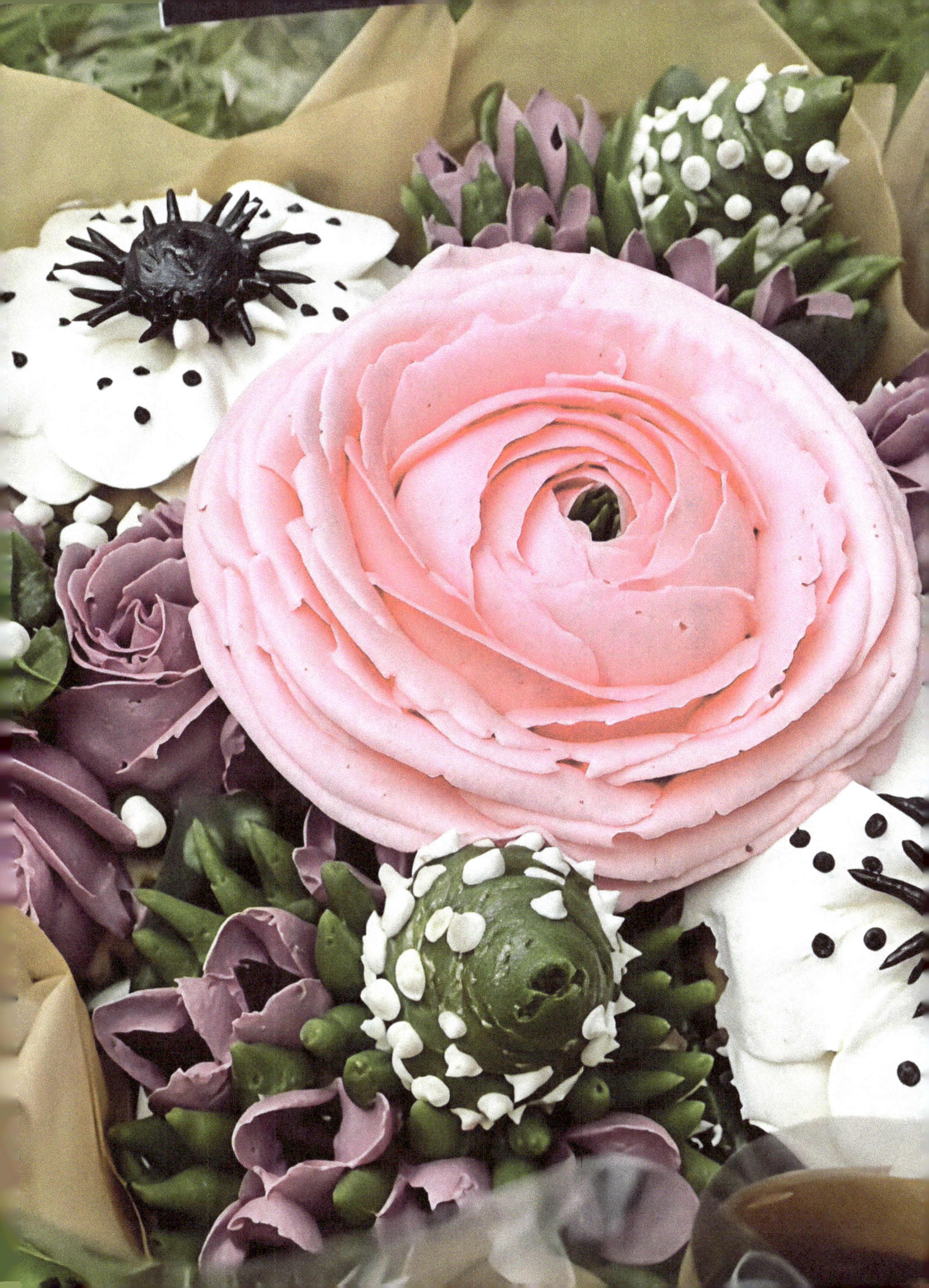

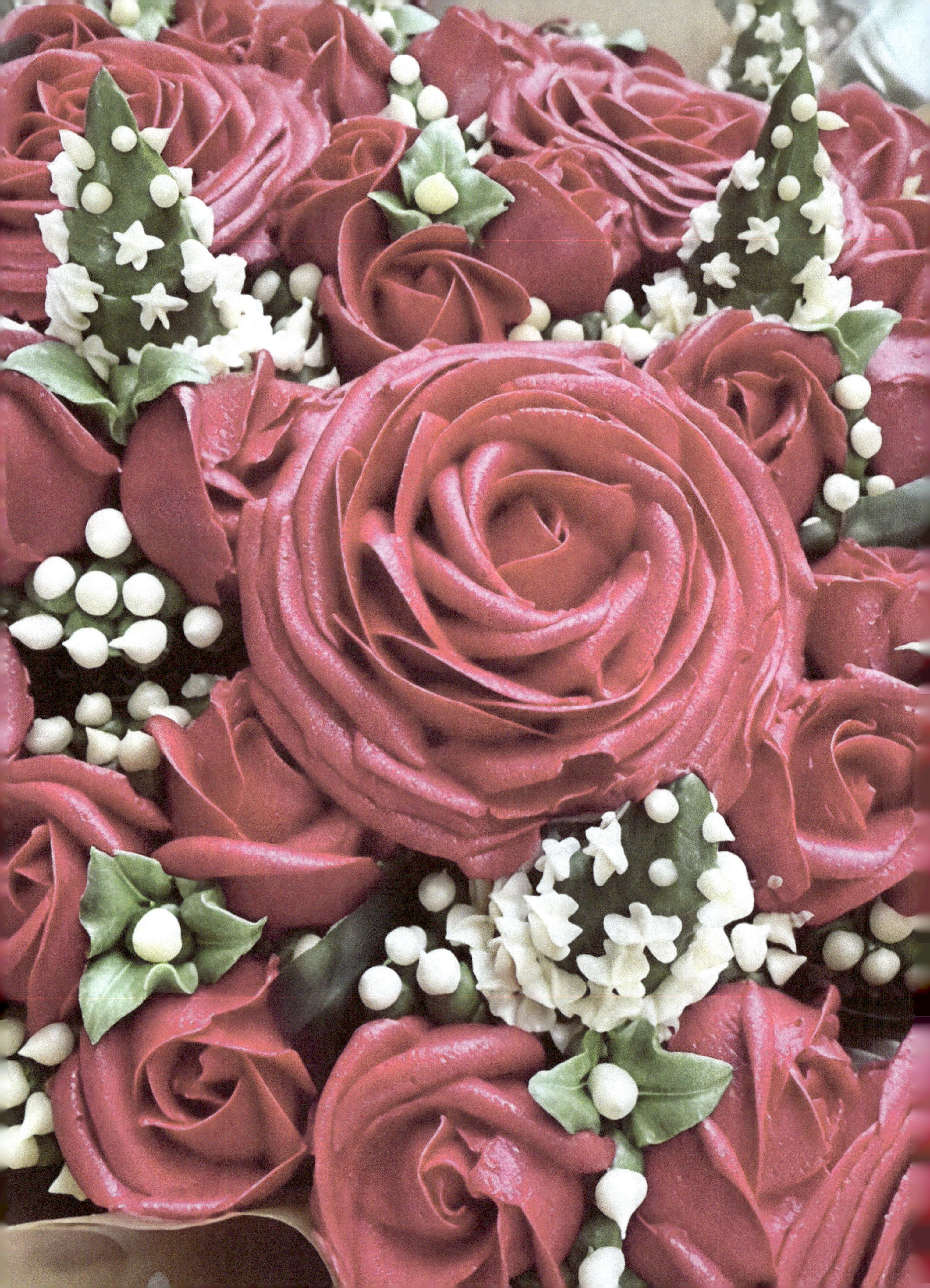

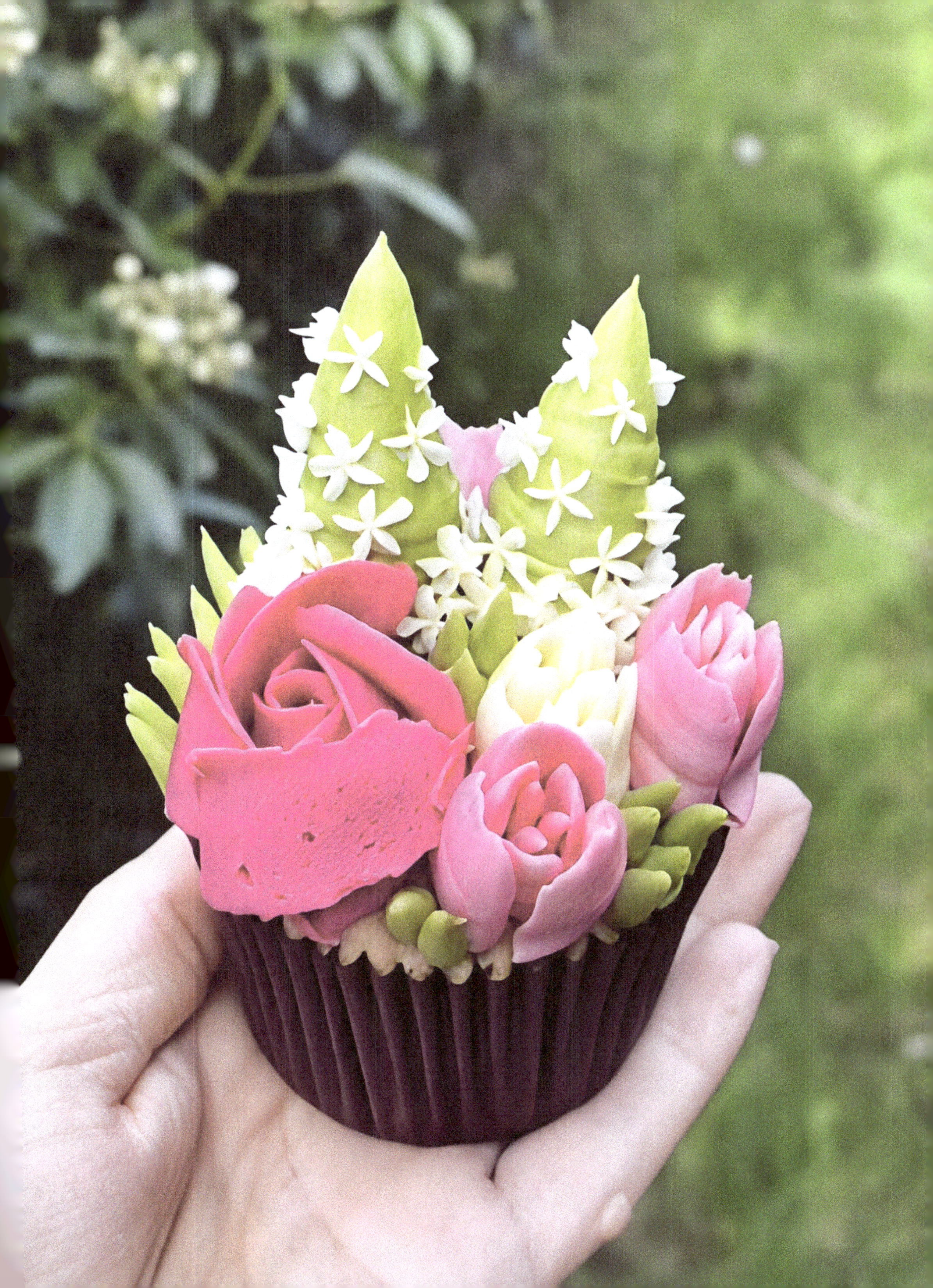

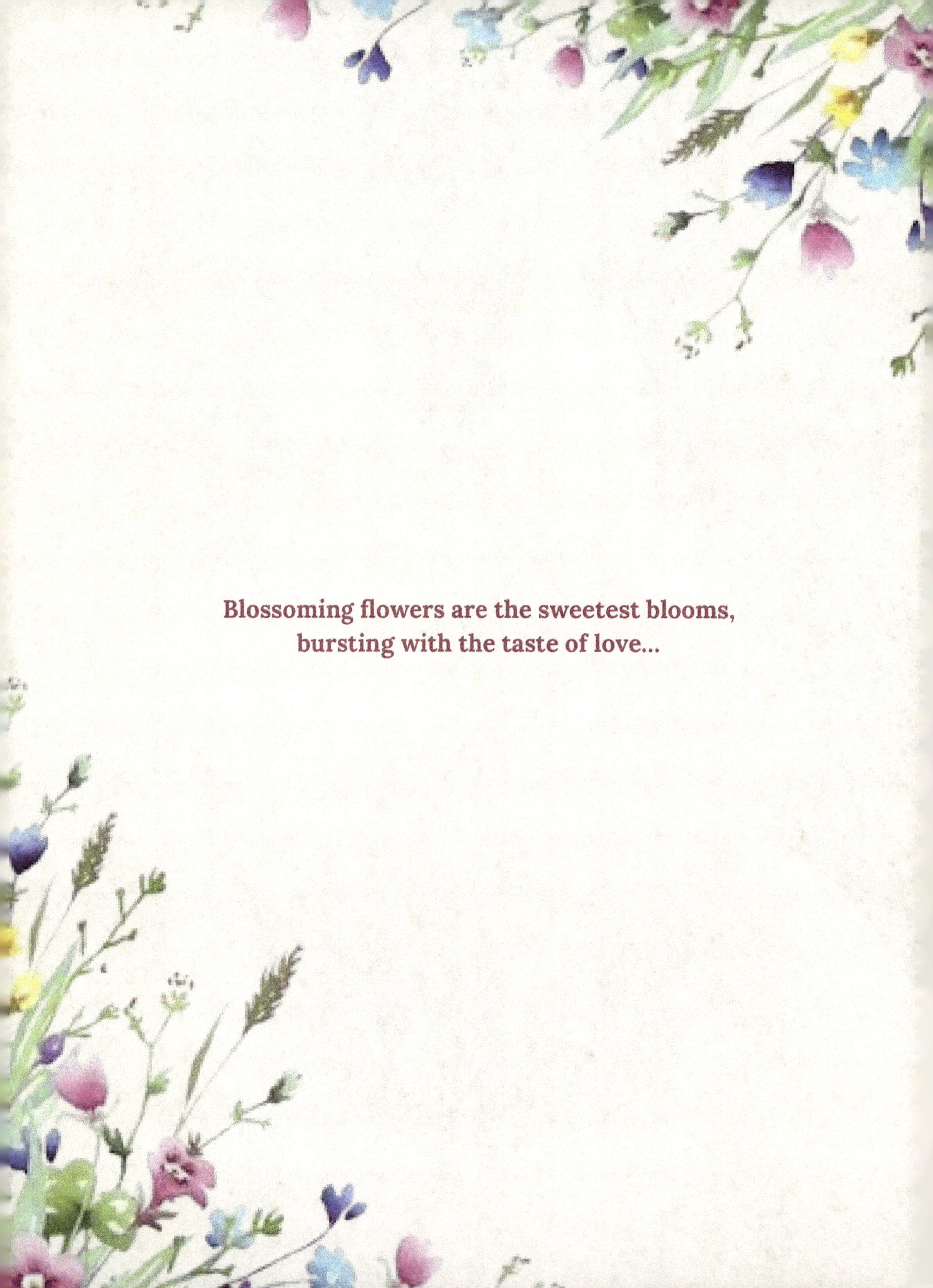

Blossoming flowers are the sweetest blooms,
bursting with the taste of love...

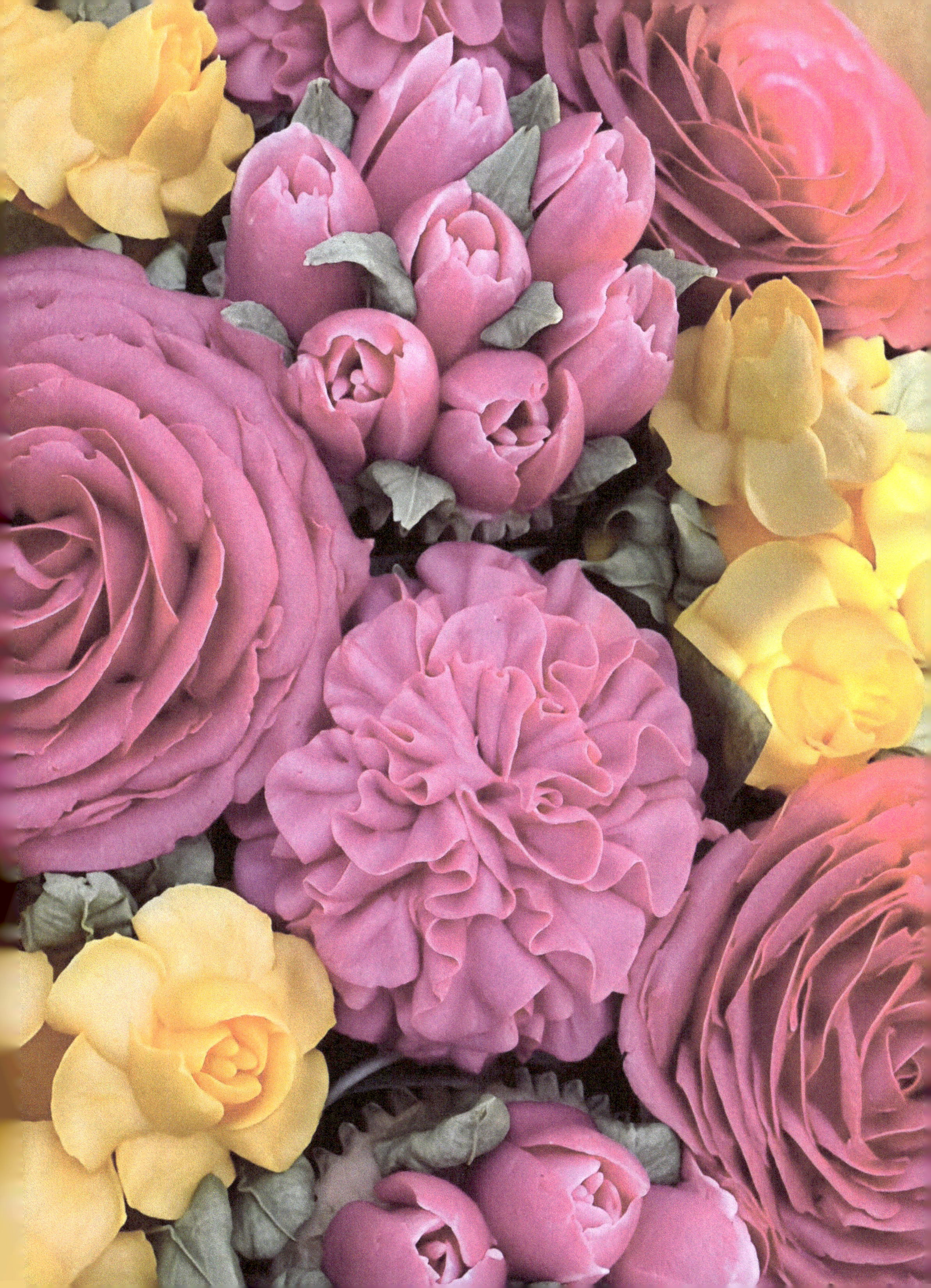

Carnation Flower

I chose to include the Carnation because it reminds me of the quiet strength and love of the women in my life, especially my mother —delicate in appearance, yet full of resilience and grace, just like this timeless flower.

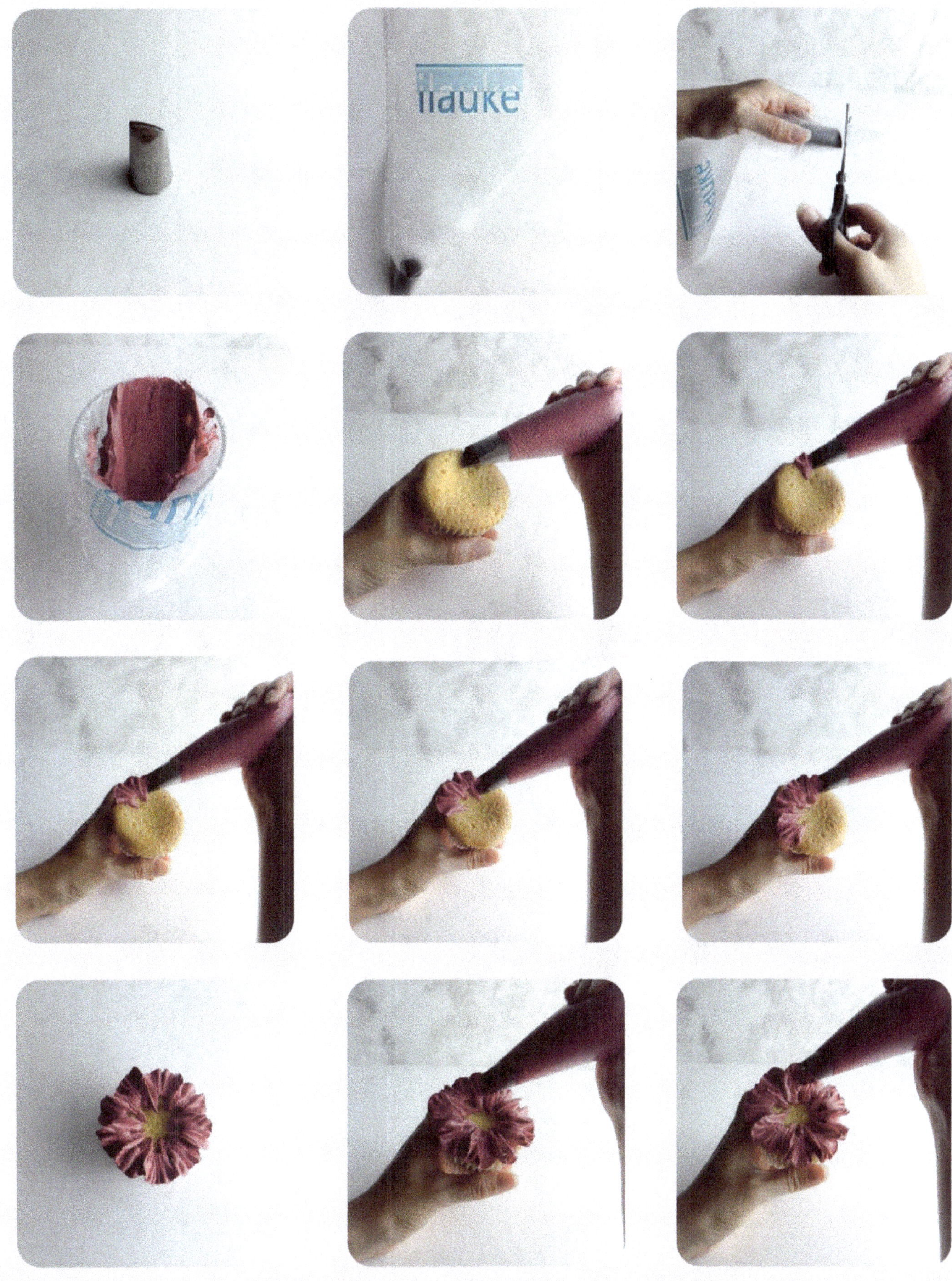

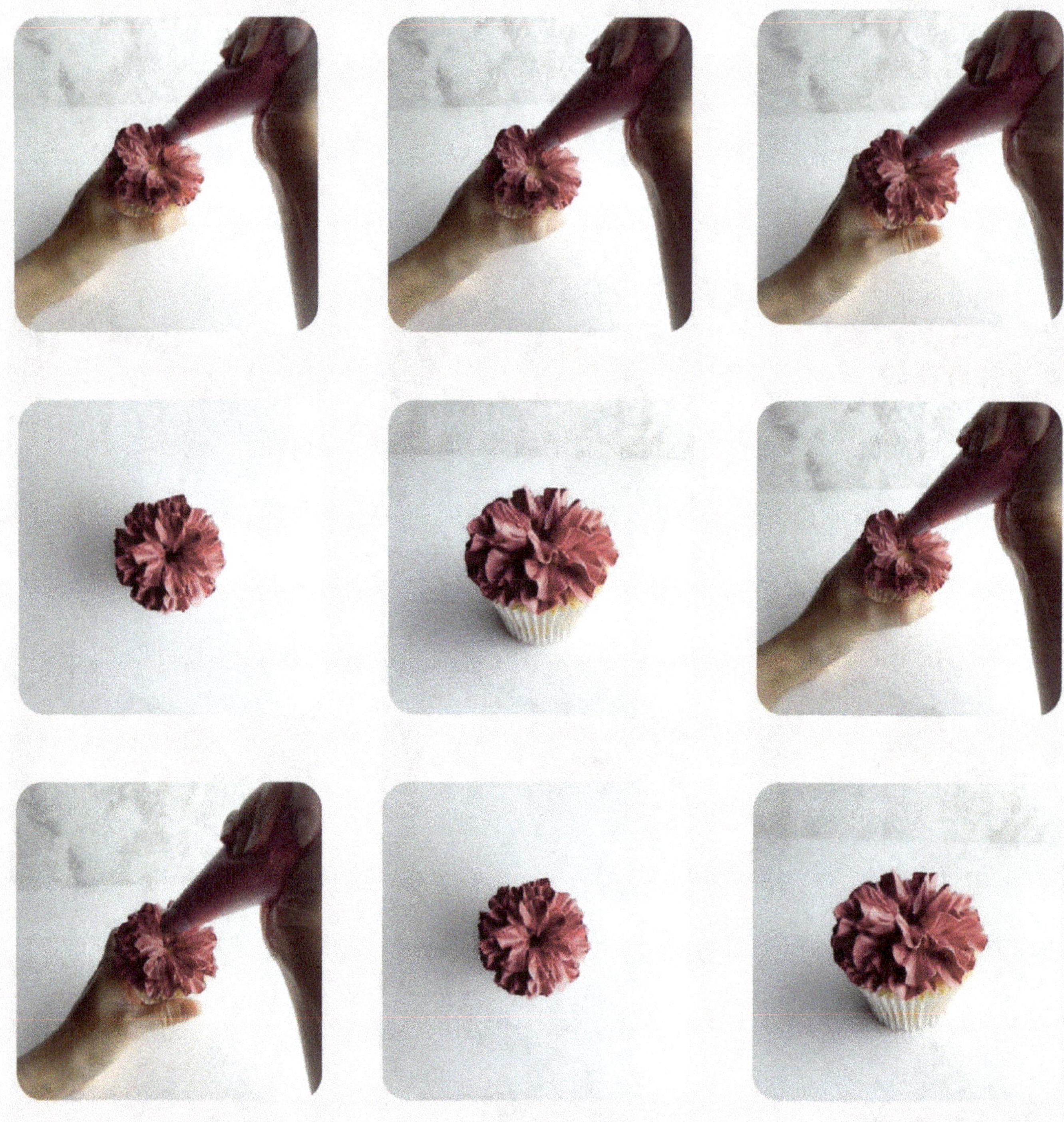

Instructions

Fit the piping bag with your 125K nozzle, then measure and cut the bag as needed. Place the piping bag in a tall glass and fill with your favourite coloured icing to pipe the carnation flower. Here, I have used Progel pink icing.

Hold the piping bag in one hand at a 45-degree angle and the cupcake in your other hand. This angle allows for better control and helps to create natural petal shapes. The wider end of the tip should always face outward, away from the centre of the cupcake. Begin at the outer edge of the cupcake. Position the tip so it is just above the surface. Use just enough steady pressure for the icing to come out.

Squeeze the piping bag gently to release the icing whilst simultaneously pulling the tip toward the centre in an upside down rounded 'W' shape. Aim to create a petal that tapers off as you pull away.

As you finish the petal, gradually release pressure on the bag while lifting the tip away from the cupcake. This action helps create a ruffled edge of the petal.

Pipe ruffled edges in an upside 'W' but in a gentle, rounded shape.

Move slightly to the right (or left) to start your next petal, ensuring that it overlaps with the edge of the first petal. This overlap creates a fuller look and mimics the natural layering of a real carnation.

Repeat the squeezing and pulling technique for each petal, maintaining the 45-degree angle and the petal tip orientation.

Aim for between 5-7 petals in total for a lush appearance. Take your time to ensure each petal is distinct yet harmoniously blends with the others.

Once the outer layer is complete, it is time to create the inside layer. This time, start piping petals closer to the centre of the flower. The second layer will be created on top of the first layer but will be piped smaller in size.

Use the same squeezing and pulling technique but make these new petals slightly smaller than the outer ones. This difference in size helps to create depth and dimension in your flower.

Position the inner petals so they overlap with the outer layer, filling in any gaps and enhancing the overall look.

The carnation flower should resemble with the picture below with lots of ruffles and definition plus a hole in the middle.

After piping the second layer of petals, it is time to add the final layer, which will consist of a small circle of ruffled petals. To do this, hold the piping bag at a 60-degree angle, ensuring that the wider end of the nozzle is facing inward toward the centre of the flower.

This technique will neatly close the hole in the middle, creating a fully bloomed and polished look. Take your time to ensure even, overlapping petals for a beautiful, seamless finish.

As you continue to practice piping carnations, you will find that each attempt brings you closer to mastering the technique. It's completely normal for the ruffles to vary in shape and size when you are first starting out so do not be discouraged. With each new flower, your piping skills will improve, and you will develop a feel for the pressure and movement needed to create even, delicate petals. Patience and persistence are key—before you know it, you will be able to pipe beautiful, consistent carnations with ease, adding a stunning touch to any cake or dessert that you decorate. Keep practicing and enjoy the creative process!

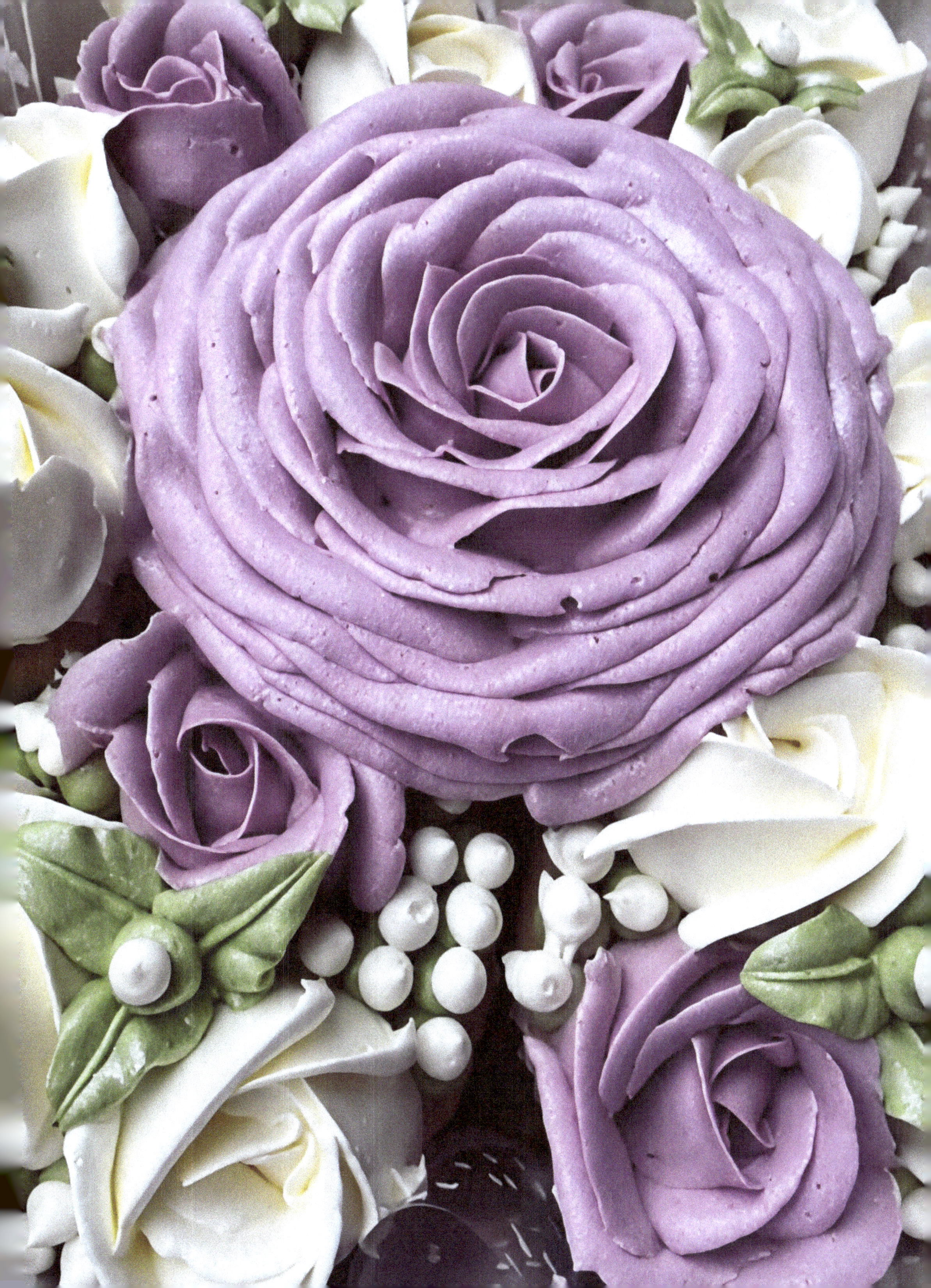

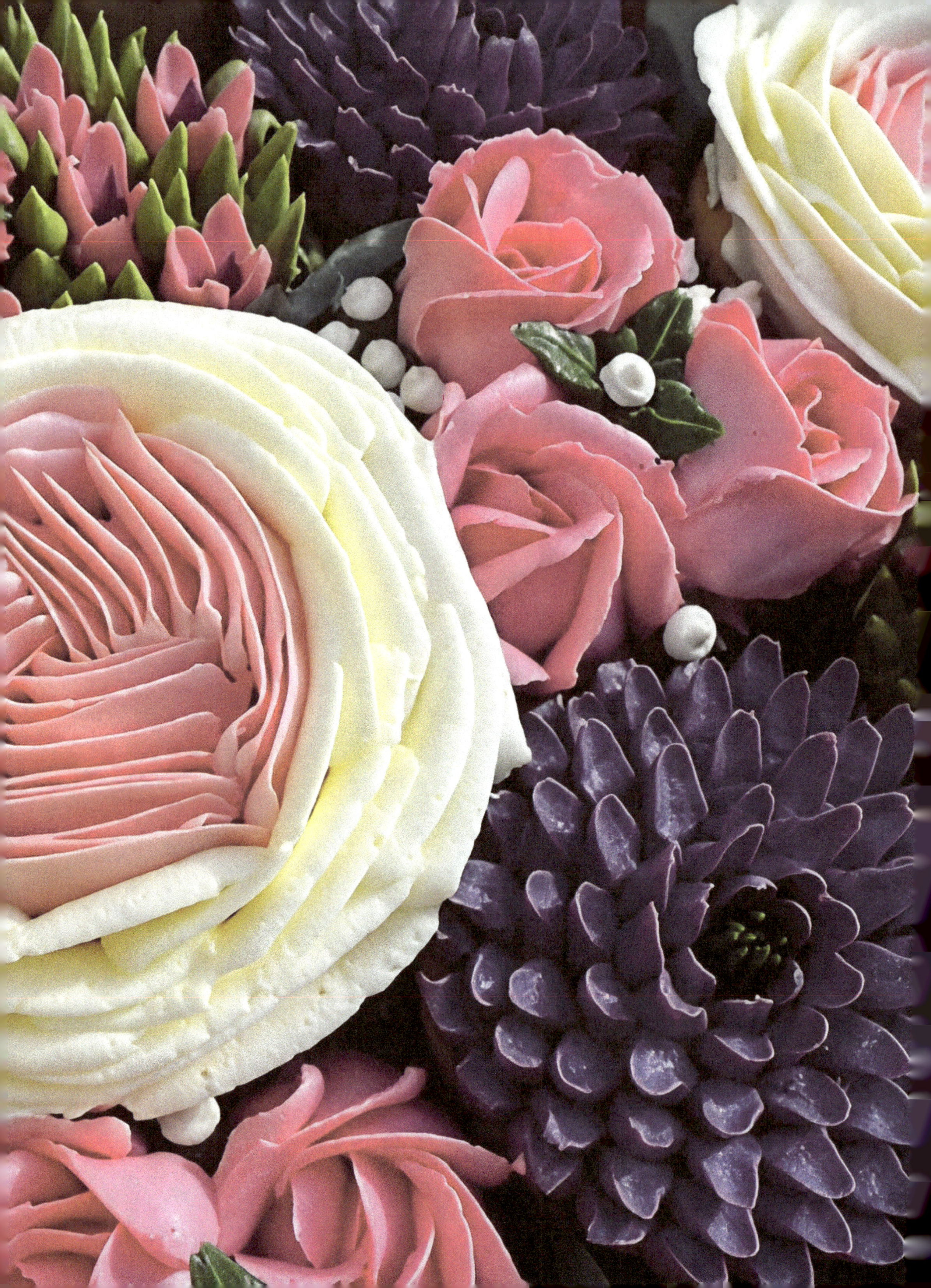

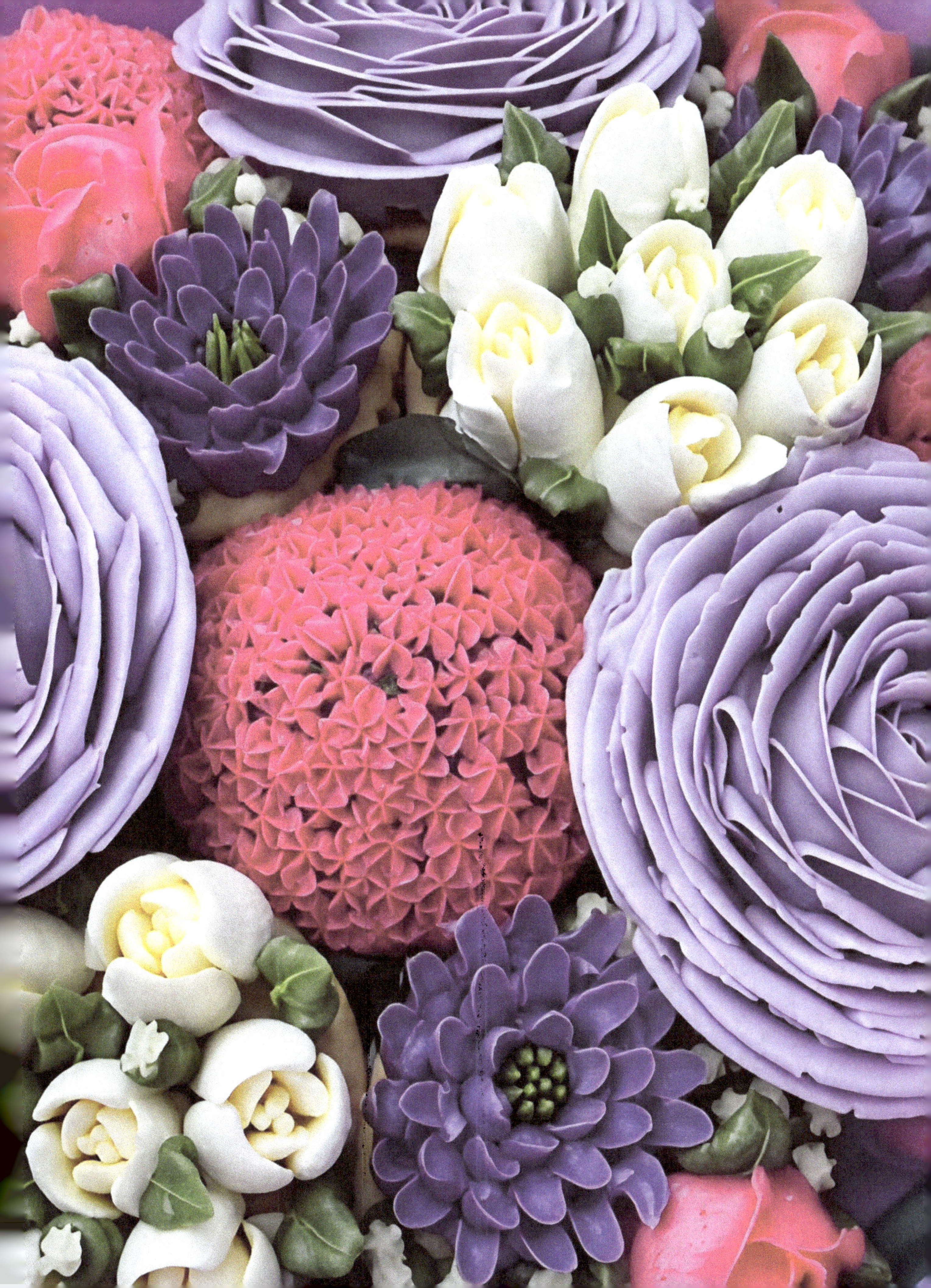

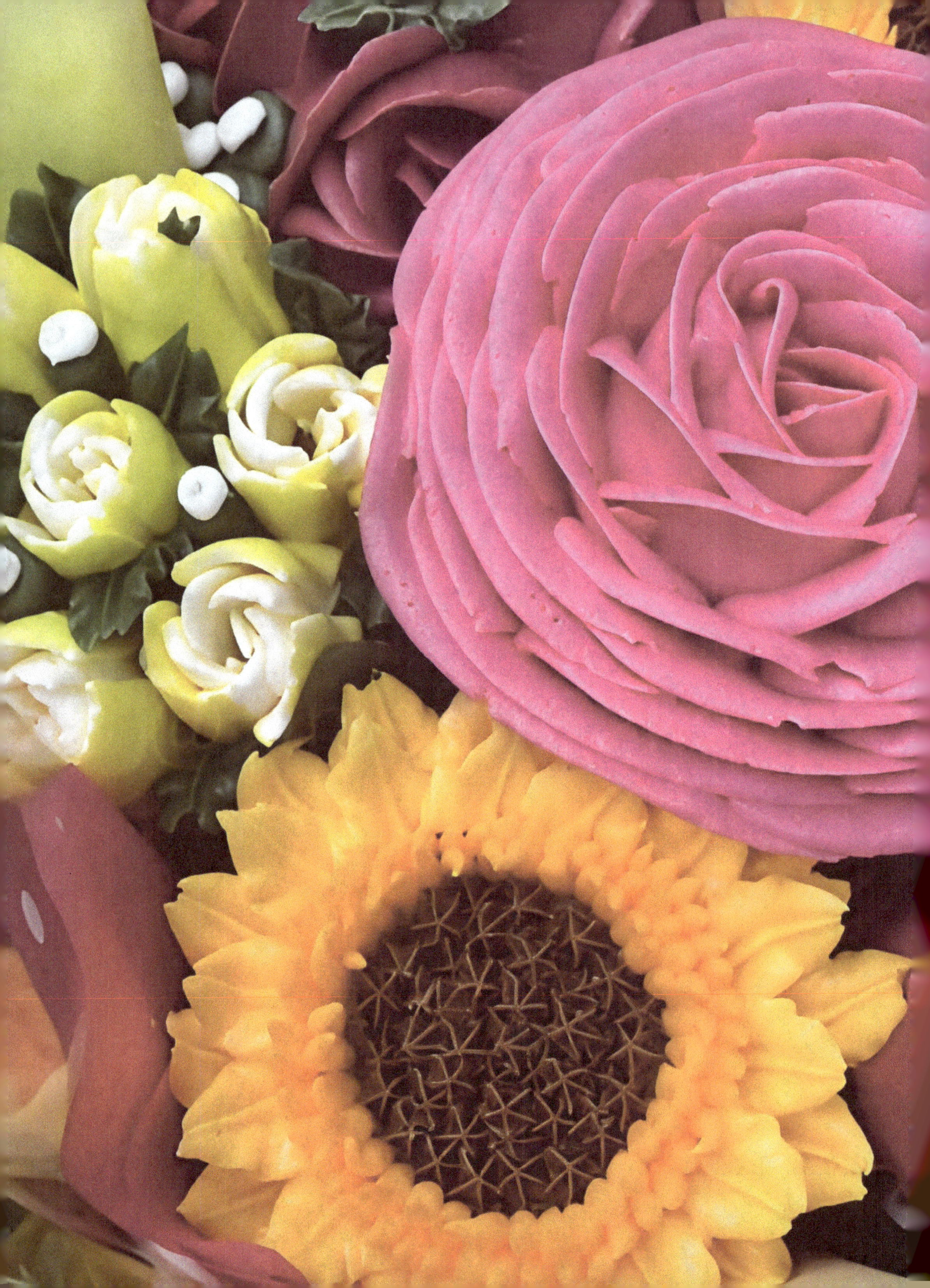

Every great artist was once an amateur. Embrace the
messiness of your first buttercream flowers—
each petal is another step towards mastering your craft!

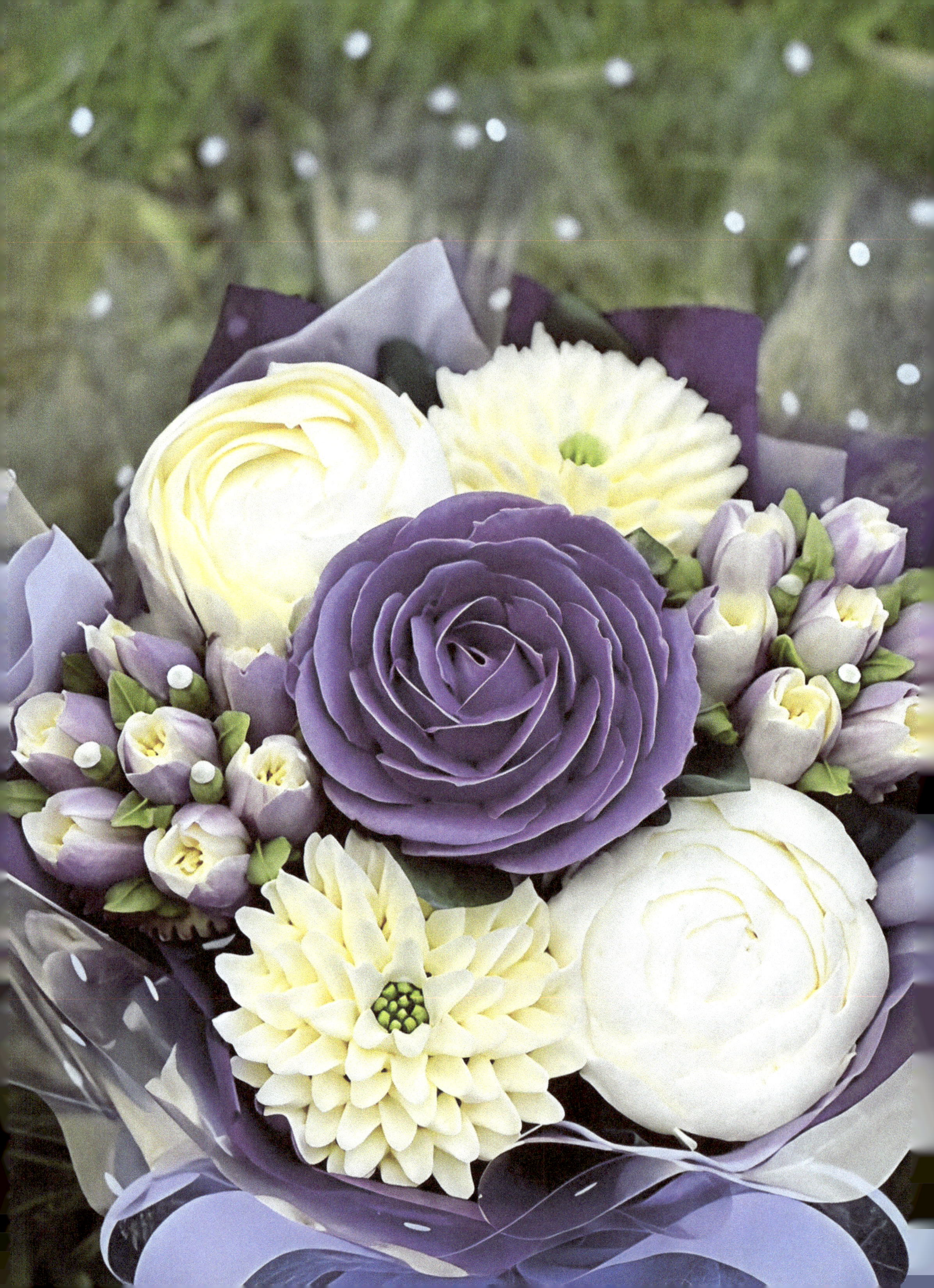

Tulip Flowers
with Leaves and Buds

Tulips were included for their quiet grace and elegant simplicity—a flower that always reminds me that beauty doesn't need to shout to be seen. It speaks to the calm confidence I hope to bring into both my baking and my life.

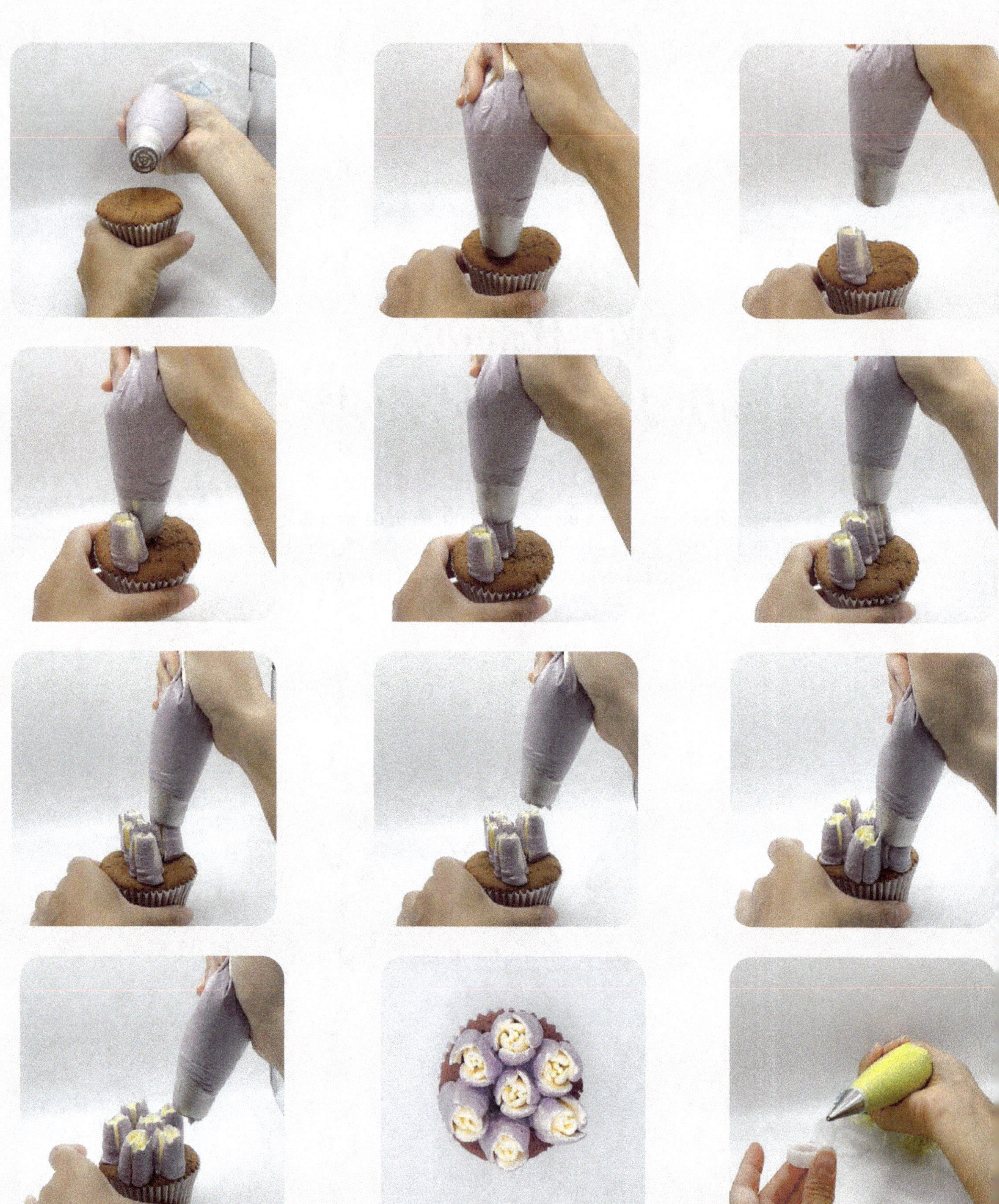

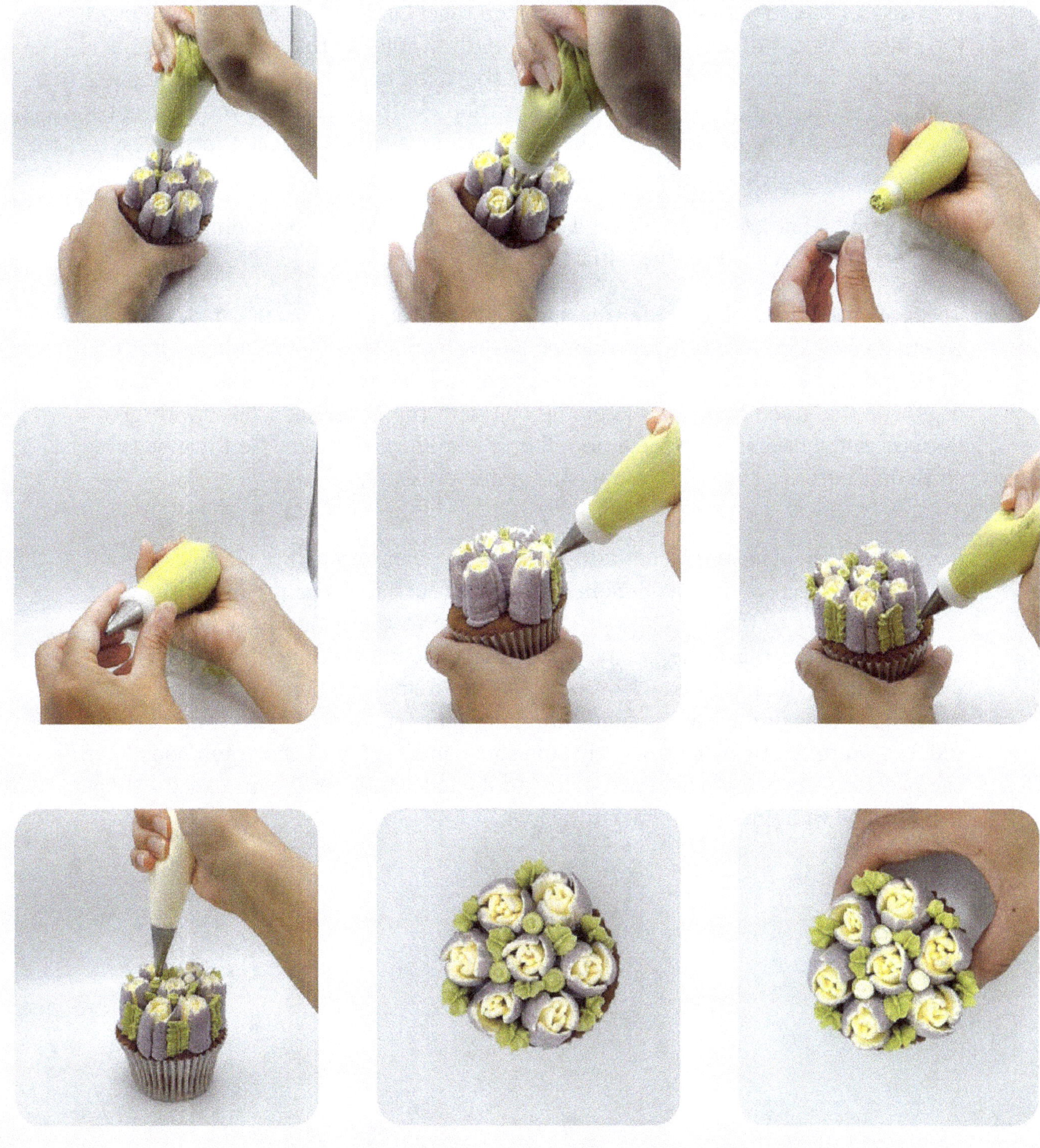

Instructions

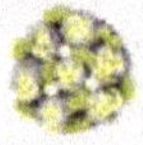 Fill a piping bag fitted with a Russian nozzle with your choice of buttercream. Here, I've used a two-tone buttercream, combining Progel Lilac and cream colours. Ensure the buttercream is of medium consistency—not too soft—so that the petals will hold their shape. Position the piping bag directly above the cupcake at a 90-degree angle. Holding the bag tightly, apply firm pressure, and gently squeeze as you lift the bag away. Stop when your flower reaches the desired height. Repeat the process to create two more tulip flowers across the cupcake.

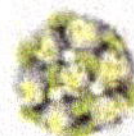 After piping a line of three tulips, fill the rest of the cupcake by adding four more tulips— two on each side of the initial line.

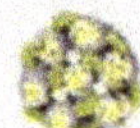 To fill in the gaps between the tulips, add some green buds in the middle of the cupcake using Tip No JEM 7. I recommend using a coupler in your piping bag as this allows you to easily switch between multiple nozzles without needing to change bags. For the green buds, fit the piping bag with the nozzle and fill it with green buttercream. I have used Progel's gooseberry colour for this step. Gently pipe three small dots between the tulips by applying gentle pressure.

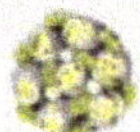 Remove the coupler attachment and replace the piping tip with a leaf tip – No 67, then securely screw the attachment back on. Ensure that the piping bag is tight, then position the piping tip at a 45-degree angle to the cupcake. Gently squeeze while maintaining this angle to pipe six leaves outside of the tulips, as shown in the illustration. Next, pipe three leaves between the tulips to fill any gaps. Finally, add white buds to your cupcake by filling another piping bag with a small round tip, Tip PM 3 in white or cream icing. Gently pipe small dots on top of the green buds from the previous step. Now, you have a beautiful cupcake adorned with elegant tulips and finished with greenery for a natural look.

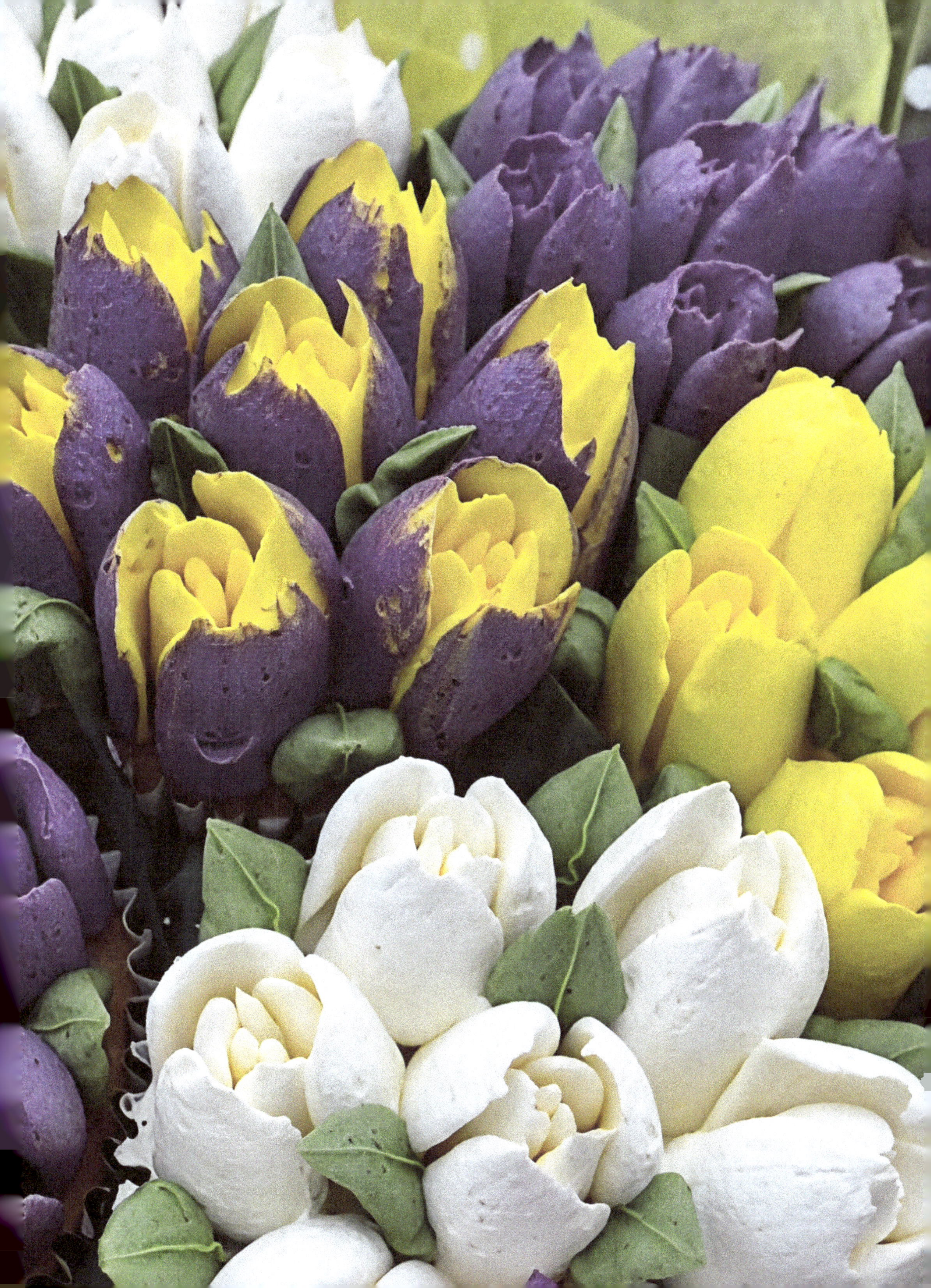

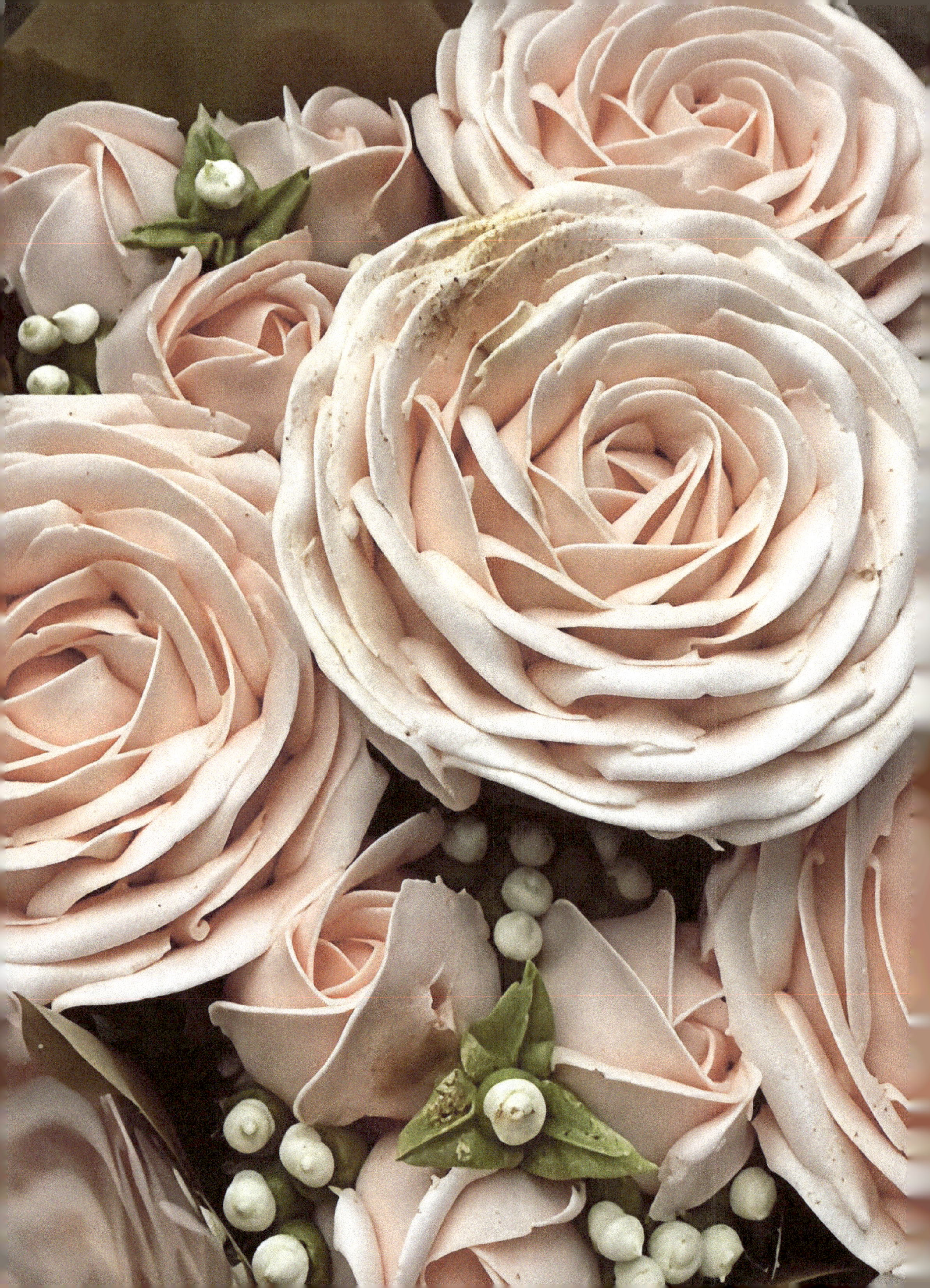

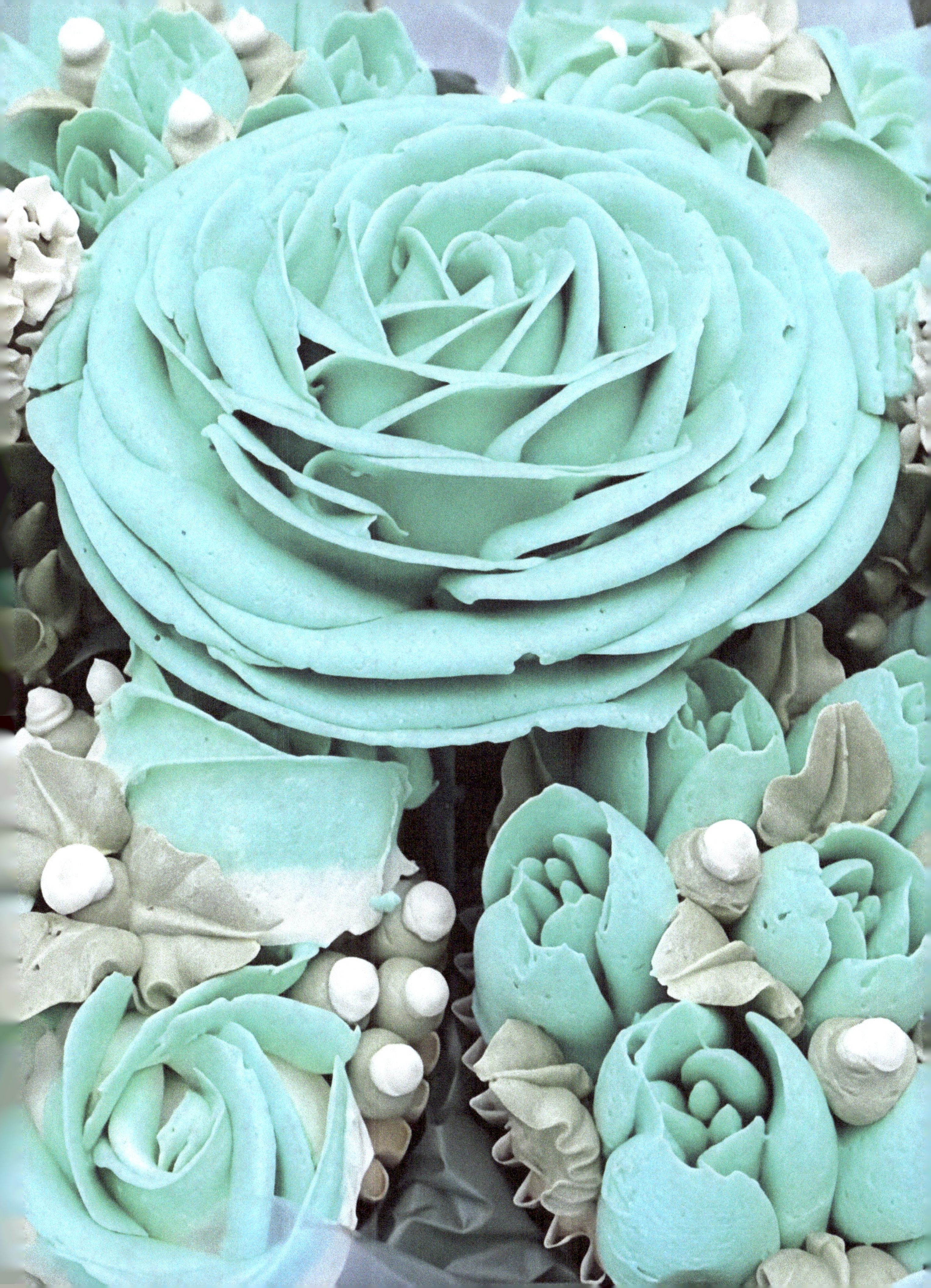

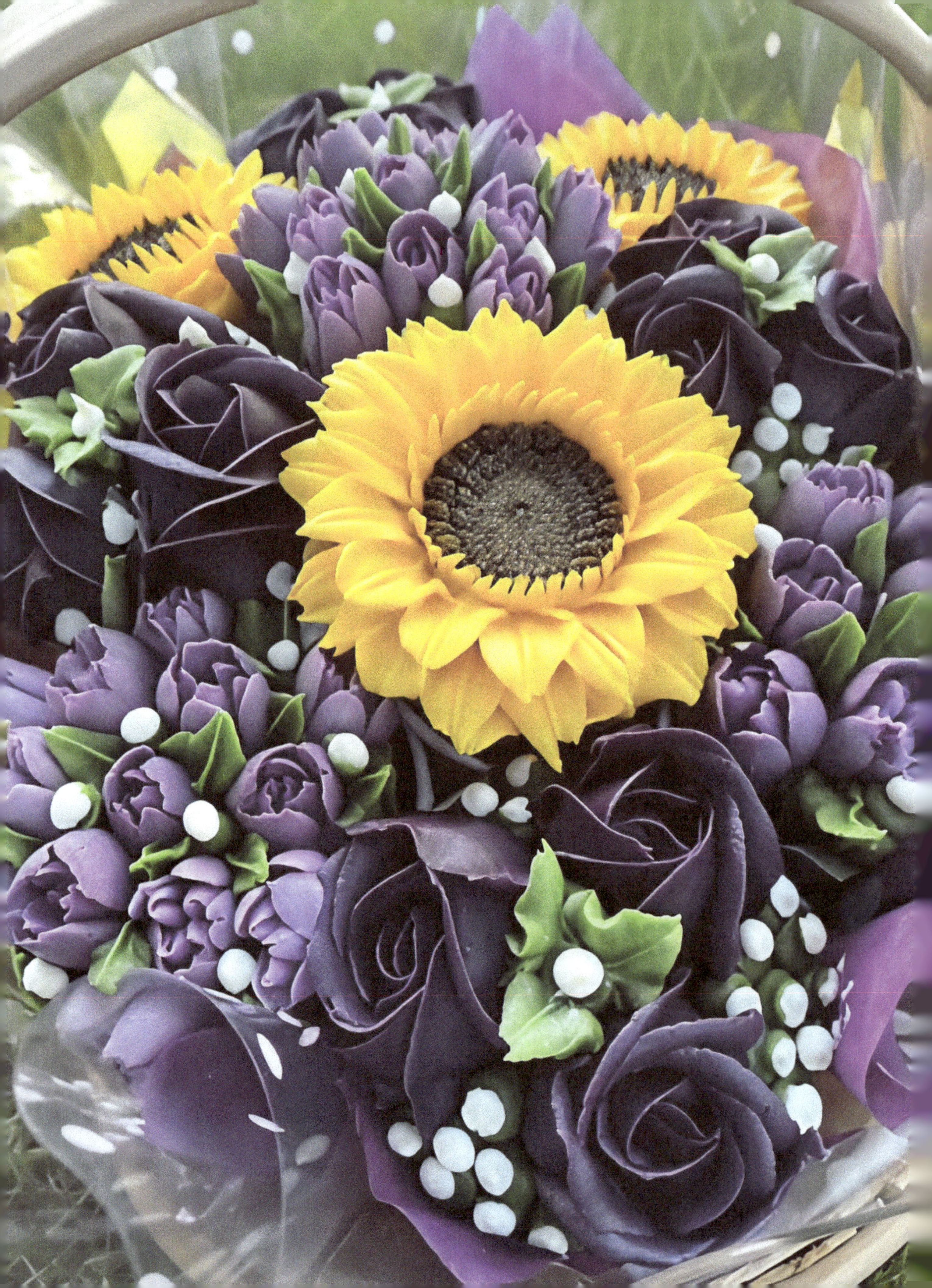

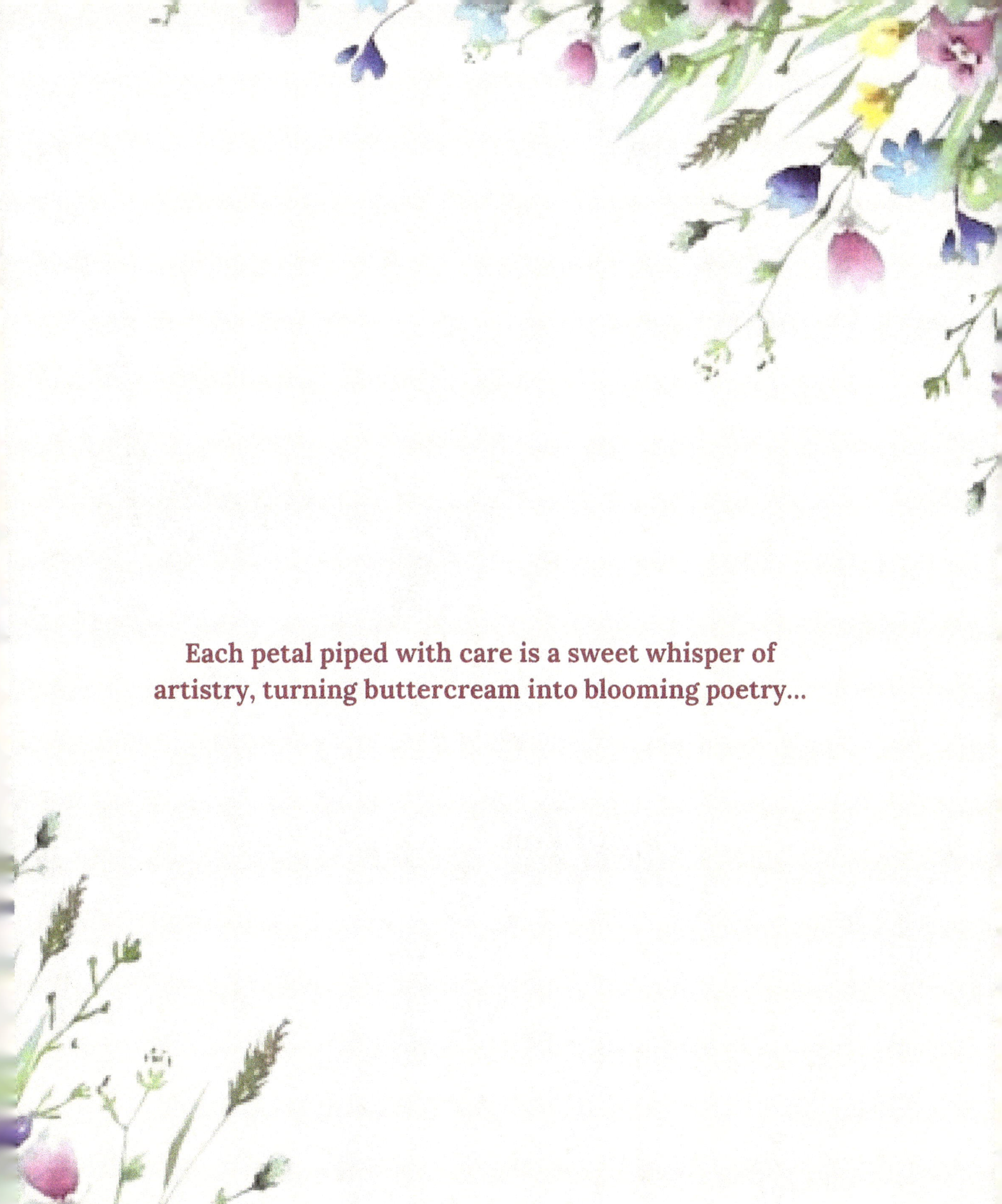

Each petal piped with care is a sweet whisper of
artistry, turning buttercream into blooming poetry…

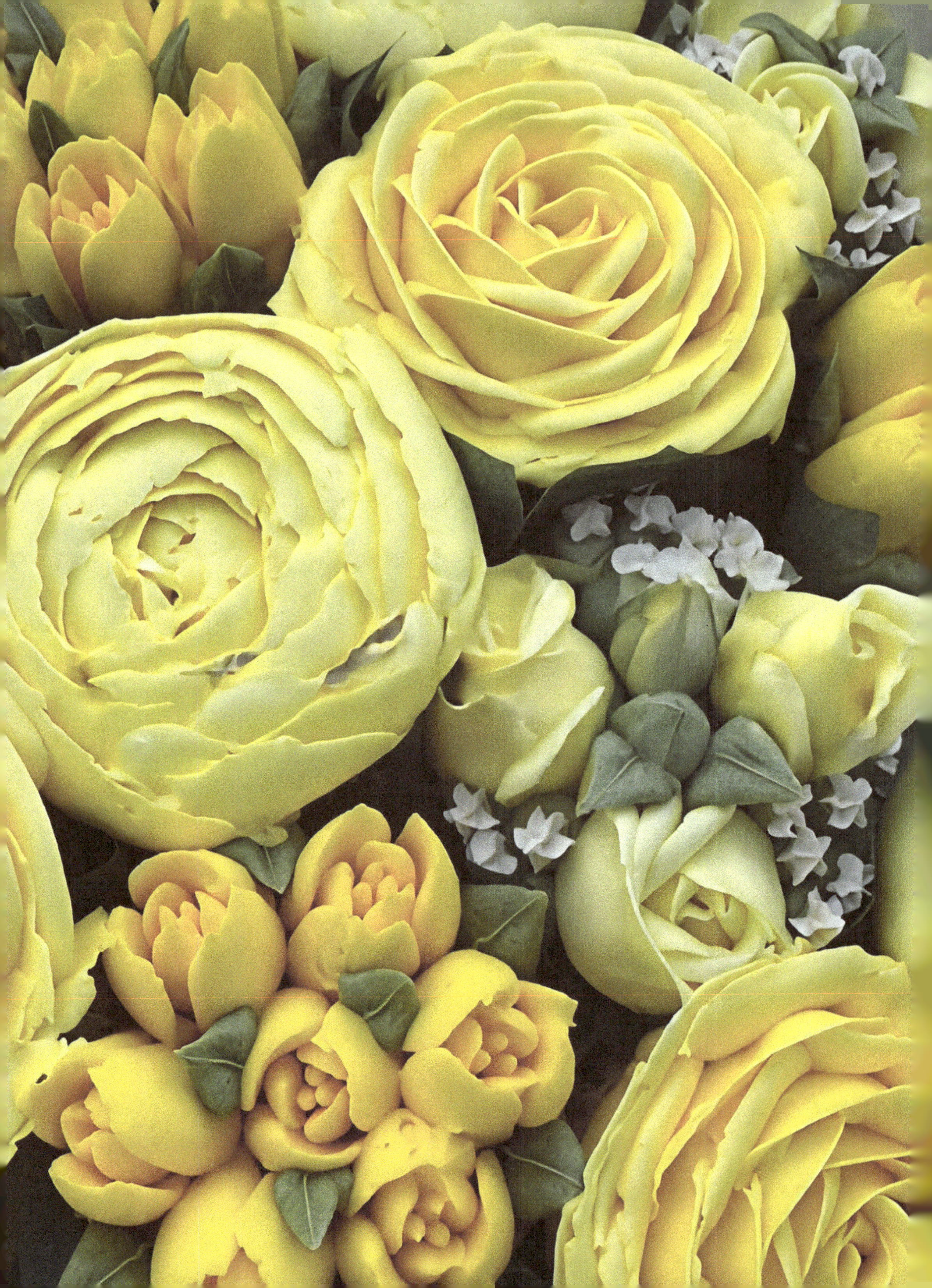

Peony Flowers

I included the Peony because it reminds me of the beautiful bouquets my husband would surprise me with—always with peonies tucked in. I loved watching them bloom, petal by petal, just like the quiet unfolding of cherished moments.

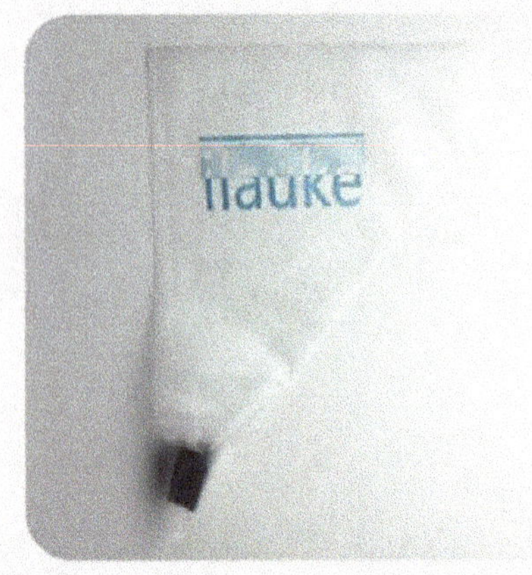
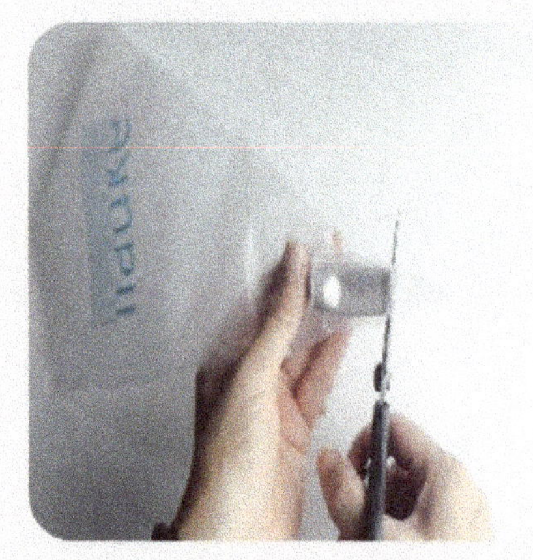
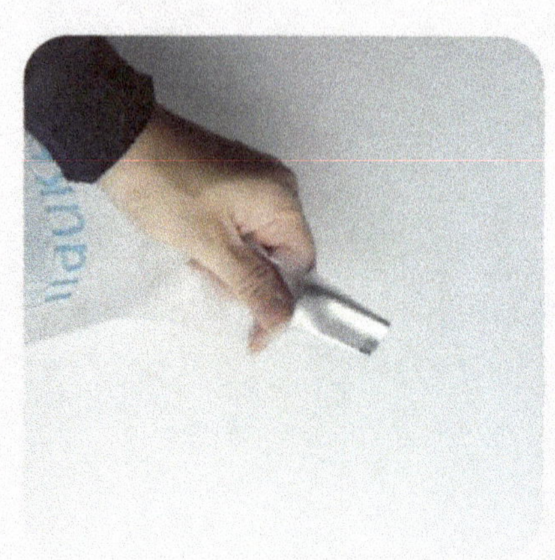
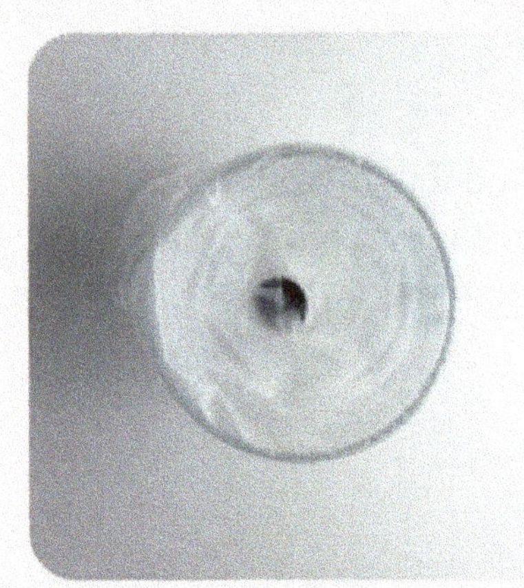
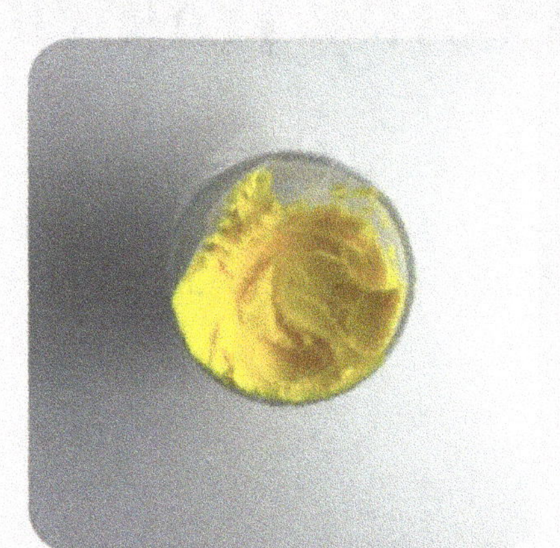
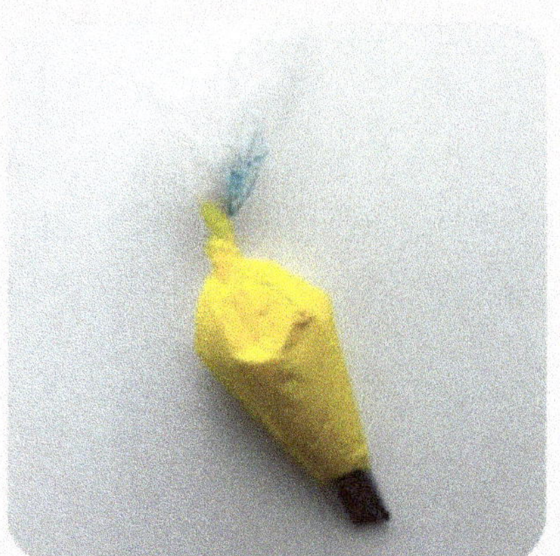
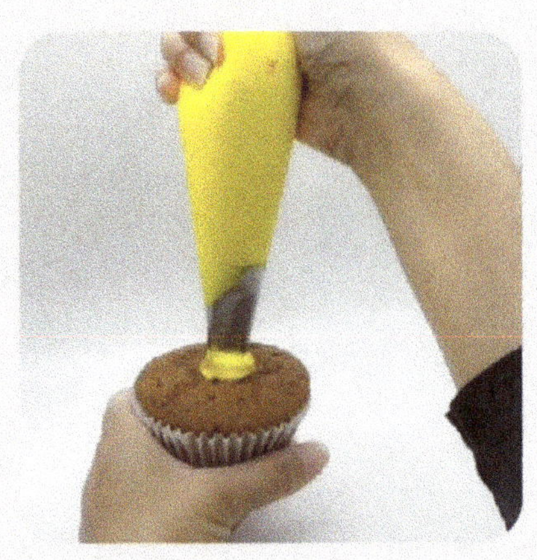
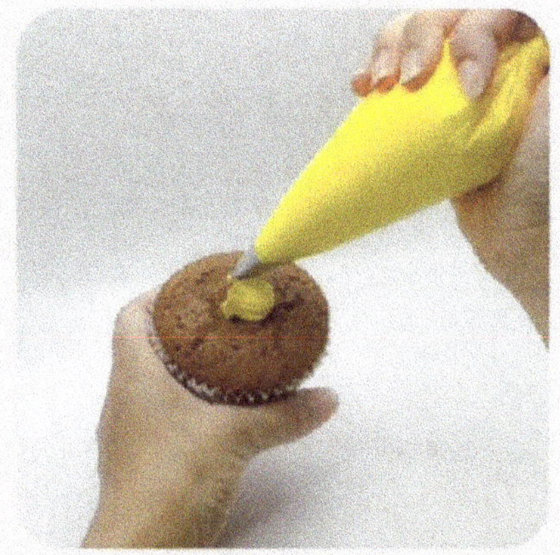
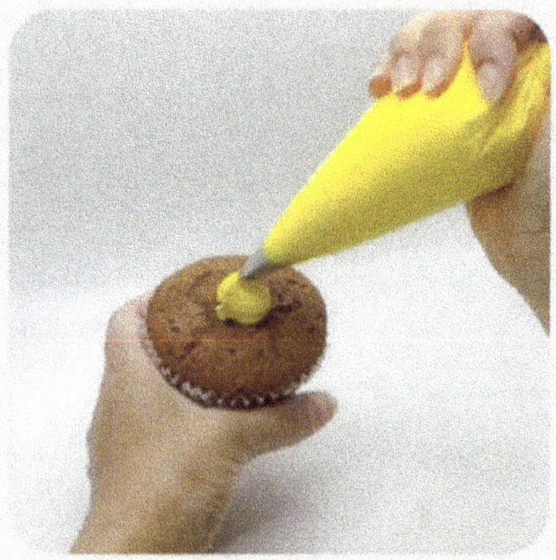

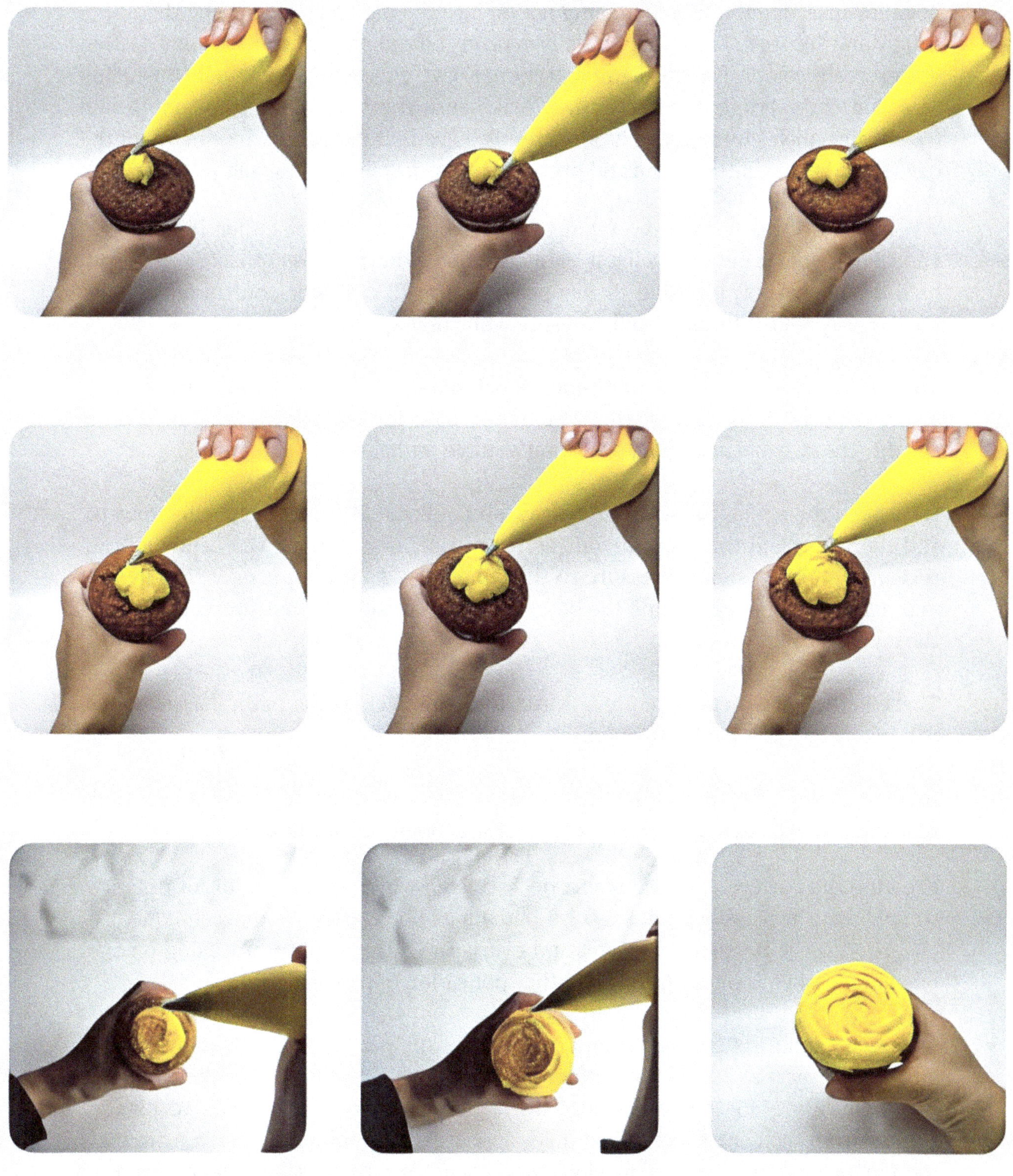

Instructions

Begin by inserting the JEM 123 piping nozzle into the piping bag, ensuring that it fits snugly and securely. Once the nozzle is in place, fill the piping bag with your desired buttercream colour. For this demonstration, I have chosen a vibrant yellow which I, achieved using Progel food colouring. Make sure the buttercream is smooth and free of air bubbles by pressing it down firmly as you fill the bag. Twist the top of the bag to secure the buttercream and prevent any from spilling out while you pipe.

When you are ready to begin piping, you have the option of either holding the cupcake in your hand or placing it on a stable work surface. Personally, I prefer to hold the cupcake in my hand as this position provides greater control and allows me to easily adjust the angle and pressure while piping.

To start creating the peony, first pipe a small mound of buttercream in the centre of the cupcake. This mound will serve as the base for your flower and should be roughly the size of a small pea, providing a stable foundation for the petals.

Next, hold the piping bag with the narrow end of the JEM 123 nozzle facing upward and the wider end touching the buttercream base. Begin piping the centre of the peony by applying steady pressure to the piping bag. As you pipe, move the nozzle in a tight spiral motion around the base, carefully layering the buttercream to form the inner petals.

These petals should curve gently inward, closely mimicking the natural appearance of a peony bud as it begins to open.

By maintaining a steady hand and consistent pressure, you will create a beautiful, realistic peony centre that will serve as the focal point of your flower.

Creating the buttercream peony is a delicate step which requires a bit of practice to achieve a professional look, so be patient as you perfect your technique. To ensure that the petals form neatly and overlap slightly, begin by focusing on the positioning of your piping nozzle and the application of pressure.

As you start moving outward from the centre of the peony, gradually increase the size of the petals. To do this effectively, angle the nozzle slightly outward at approximately a 45- degree angle. This adjustment allows the petals to extend further from the centre, creating a fuller appearance. Continue piping in a circular motion around the centre, making sure each new petal slightly overlaps the previous one. This overlapping technique helps to create a natural, layered effect typical of a real peony flower. The petals should gradually open up more as you work outward, contributing to the flower's characteristic blooming look.

When you reach the outer layers of the peony, adjust the angle of the nozzle even further outward, aiming for an angle between 60 and 75 degrees. This wider slanted angle will help you create larger, more open petals that give the peony its voluminous appearance.

Additionally, apply slightly more pressure to the piping bag to ensure that the buttercream flows out more freely, allowing the outer petals to be more pronounced and distinct.

Pipe each outer petal individually, ensuring they overlap slightly with the preceding petals to maintain a cohesive and realistic flower shape. Continue this process until the peony reaches your desired size and fullness.

Remember, piping a realistic peony can take time and practice. Do not be discouraged if your initial attempts do not turn out perfectly. Consistent practice will improve your technique and results. Additionally, to enhance the realism of your peony, consider blending two or more colours in your piping bag to create a gradient effect on the petals.

This technique adds depth and dimension, mimicking the natural colour variations found in real peonies.

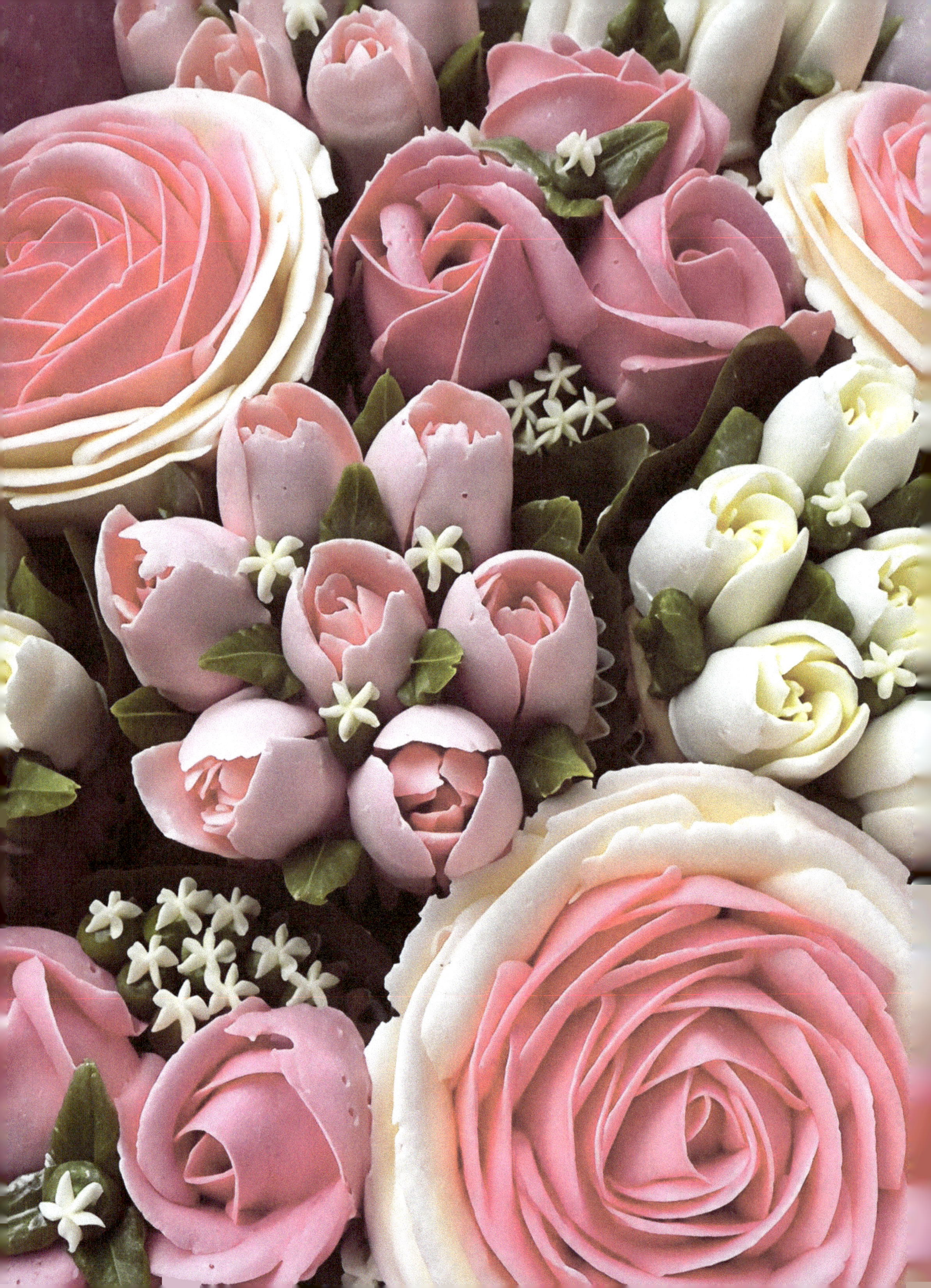

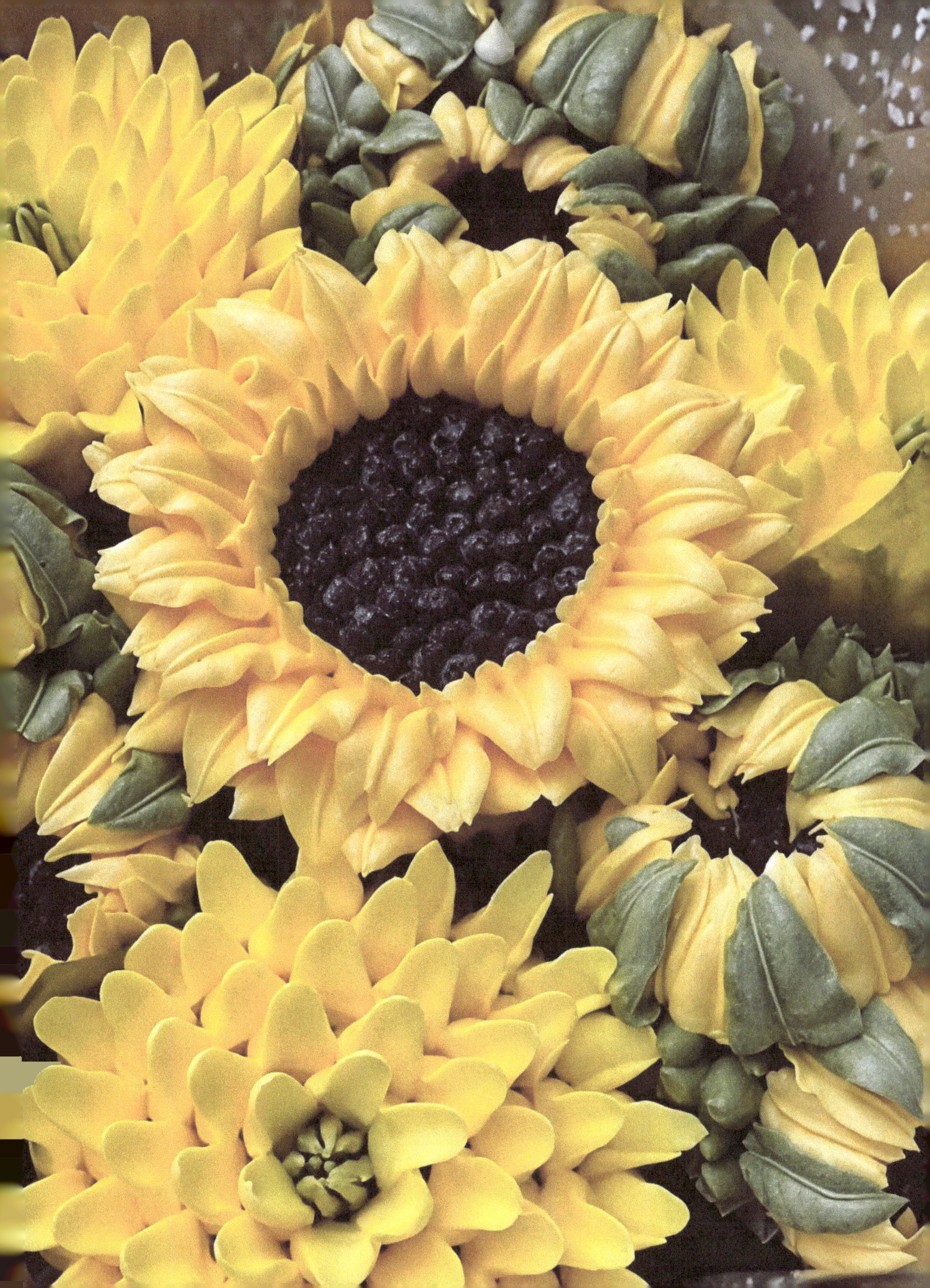

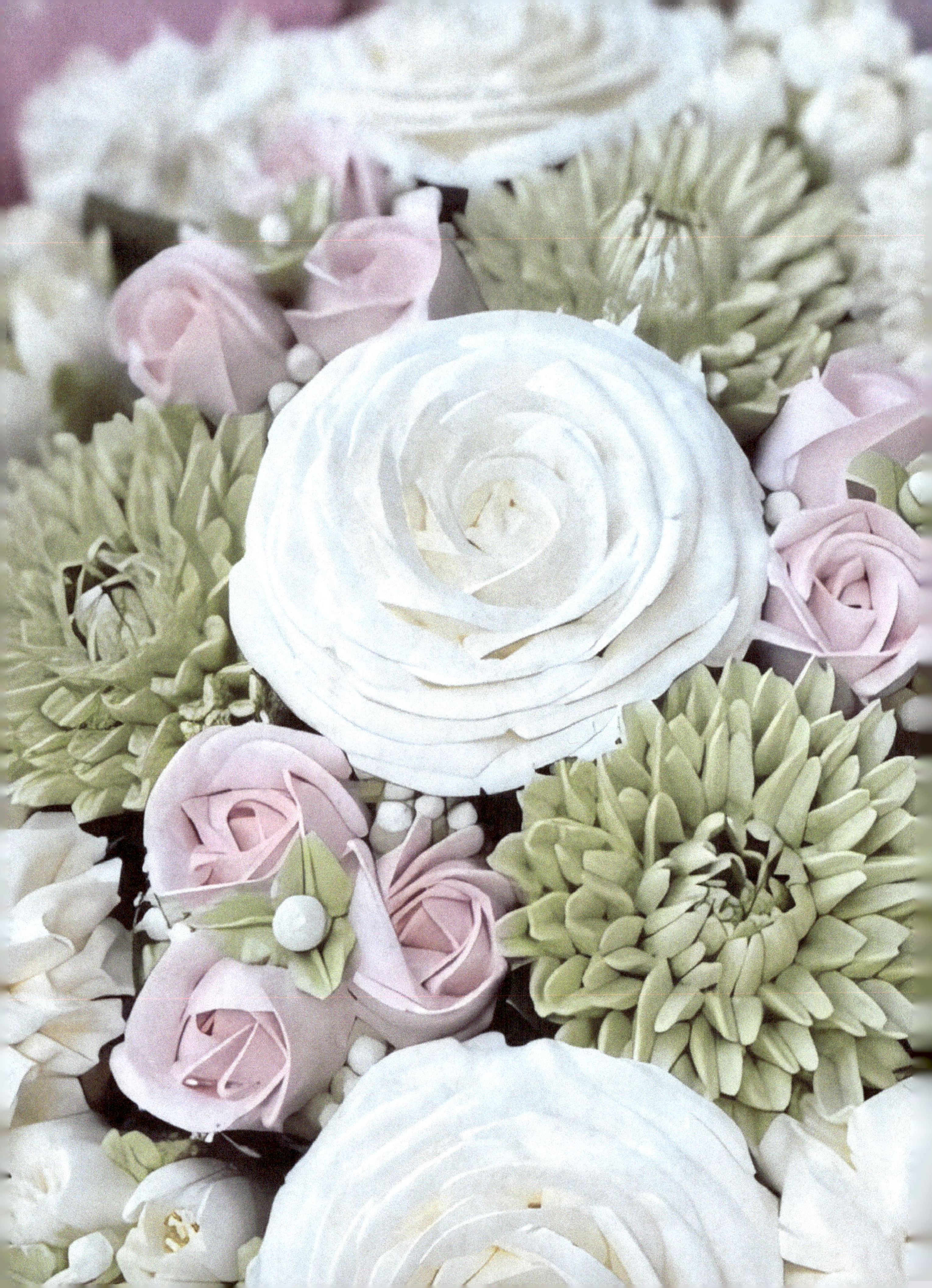

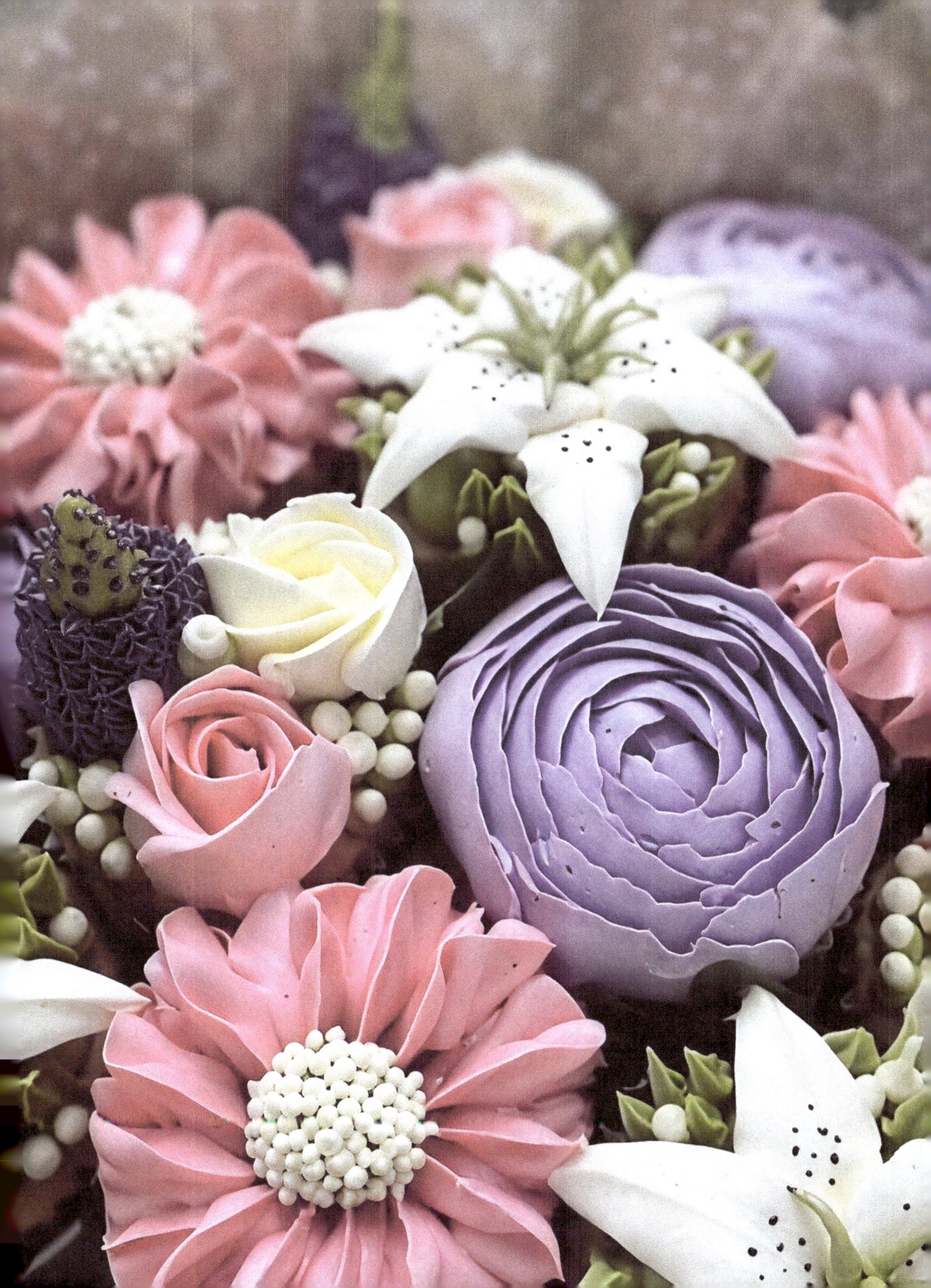

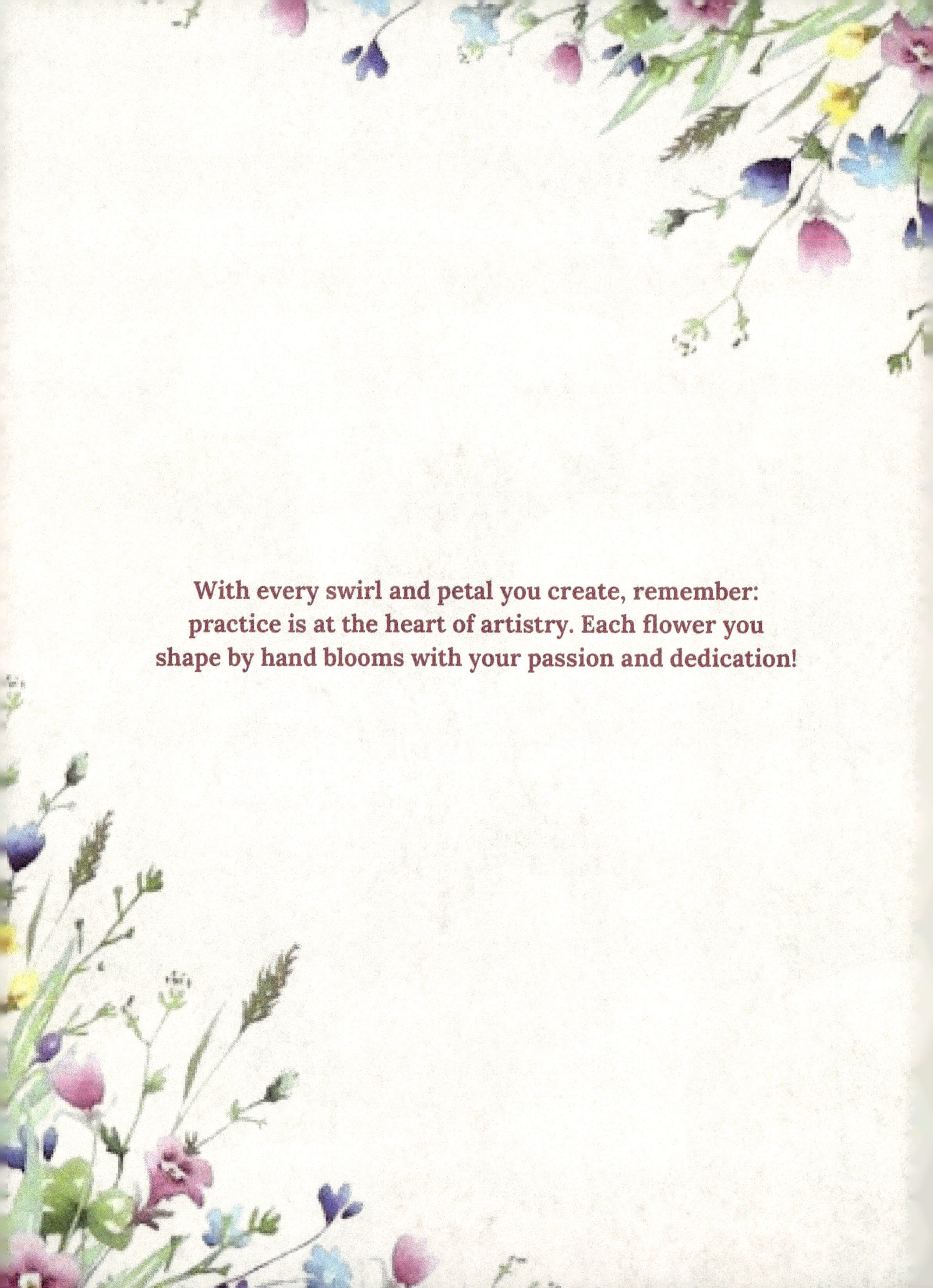

With every swirl and petal you create, remember:
practice is at the heart of artistry. Each flower you
shape by hand blooms with your passion and dedication!

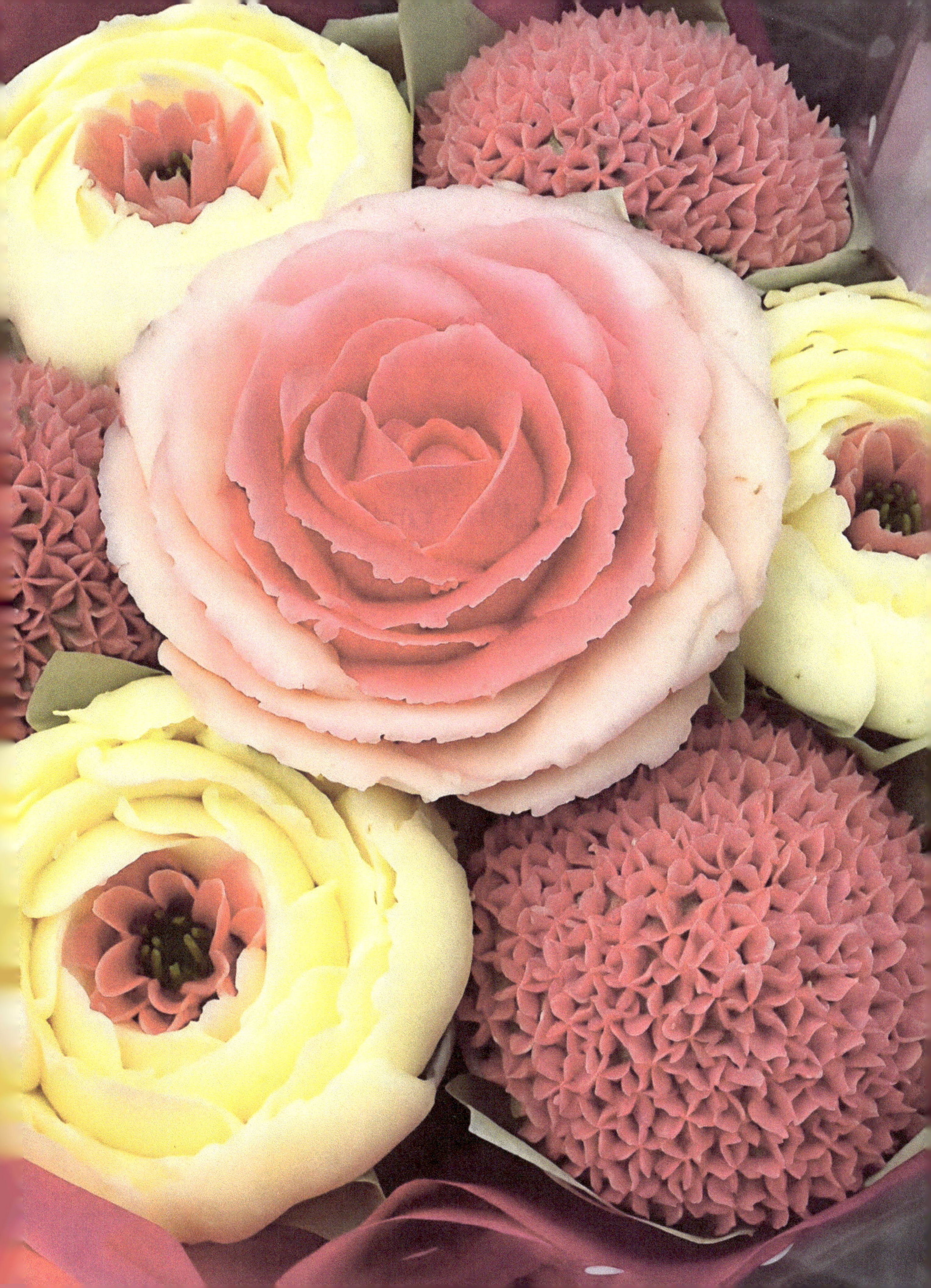

Allium Flower

I chose the Allium for its unique shape and quiet charm—it always stood tall and proud in the gardens I admired, a gentle reminder that beauty often lies in the unexpected and the wonderfully different.

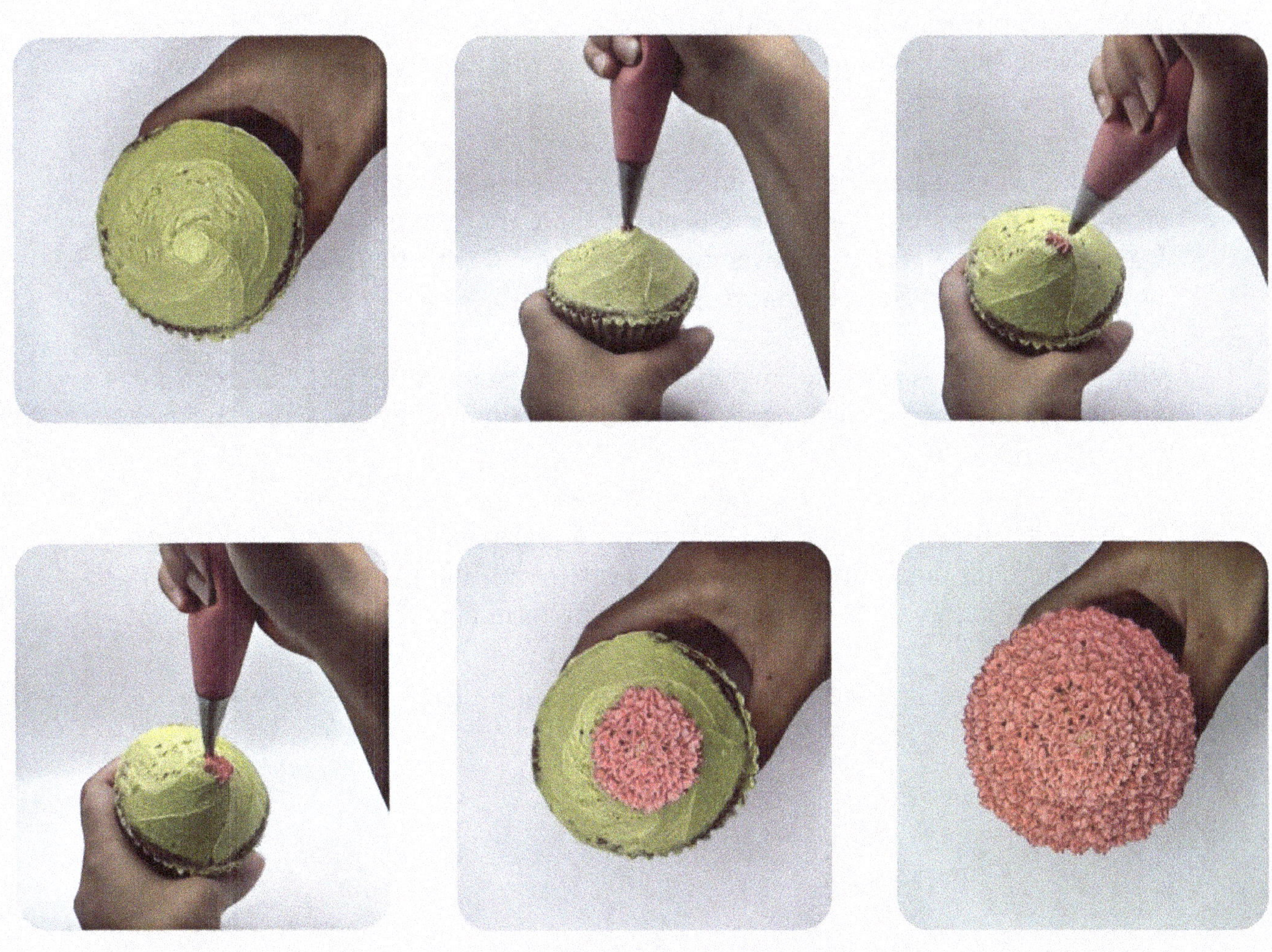

Instructions

- Begin by applying a generous layer of green buttercream icing to the cupcake or use a Wilton No 12 tip to pipe the icing. Use an offset spatula or a butter knife to spread the icing evenly over the surface of the cupcake, shaping it into a smooth mound. Ensure that the icing covers the entire top of the cupcake, extending all the way to the edges. Aim for a smooth and even finish, as this will provide a clean base for the decorative elements.

- Next, prepare your piping bag with a small star-shaped nozzle - No 24 Tip - and fill it with your chosen coloured icing. For this step, you can use a contrasting colour to the green buttercream to make the stars stand out.

- Position the piping bag above the mound of green icing and gently squeeze to pipe small star shapes onto the surface. Begin at the top of the mound and work your way outward. The goal is to cover the entire mound with these tiny star-shaped flowers, creating a delicate and textured appearance.

- You have some flexibility in how you arrange the stars. You can pipe them in a circular pattern around the mound, or you might prefer to form a vertical line from top to bottom.

- In this case, I chose to pipe the stars in a circular motion around the mound, continuing until the entire surface was covered with miniature, delicate flowers. This method ensures that the cupcake has a uniform appearance with an elegant, floral finish.

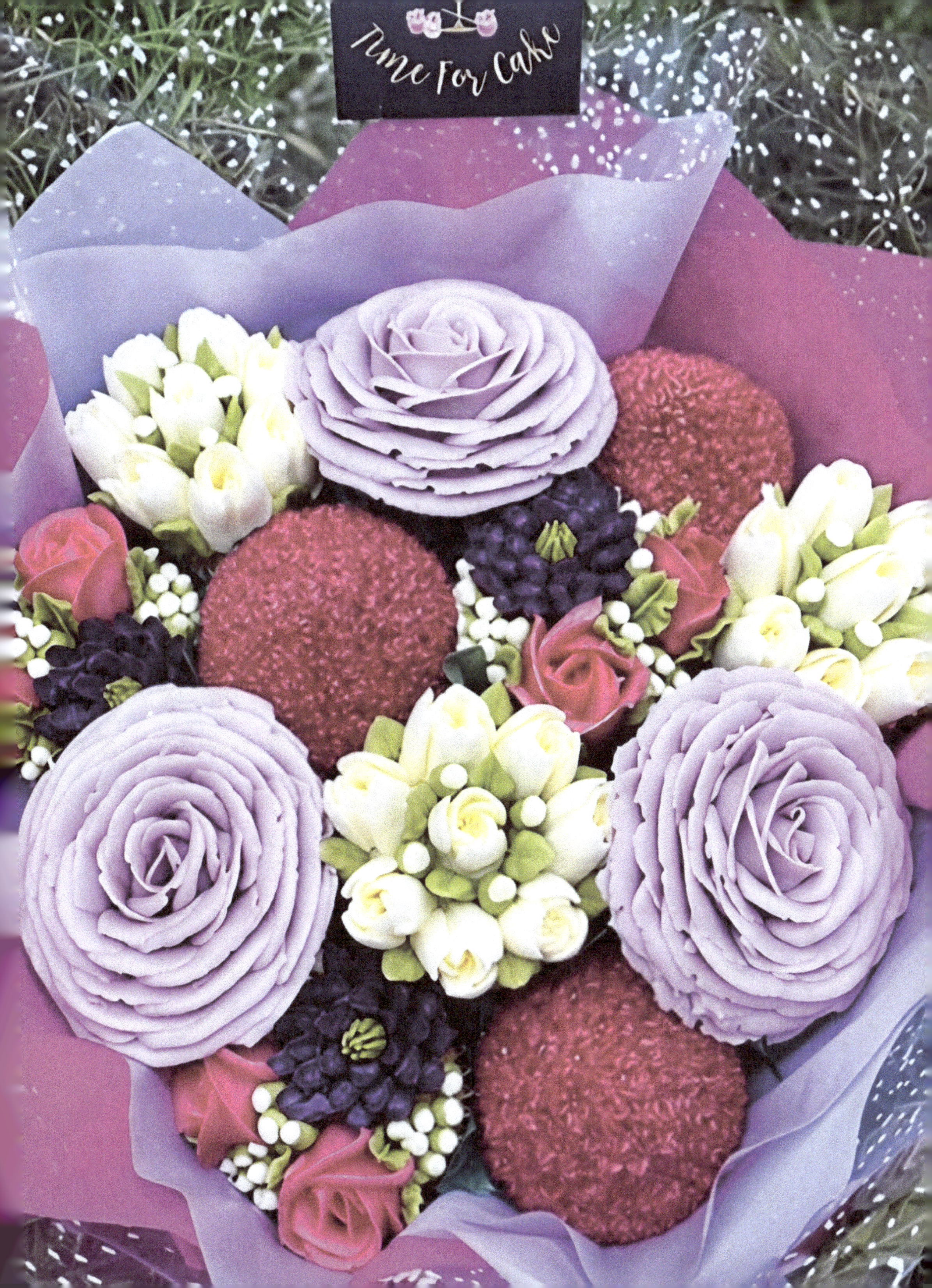
Time For Cake

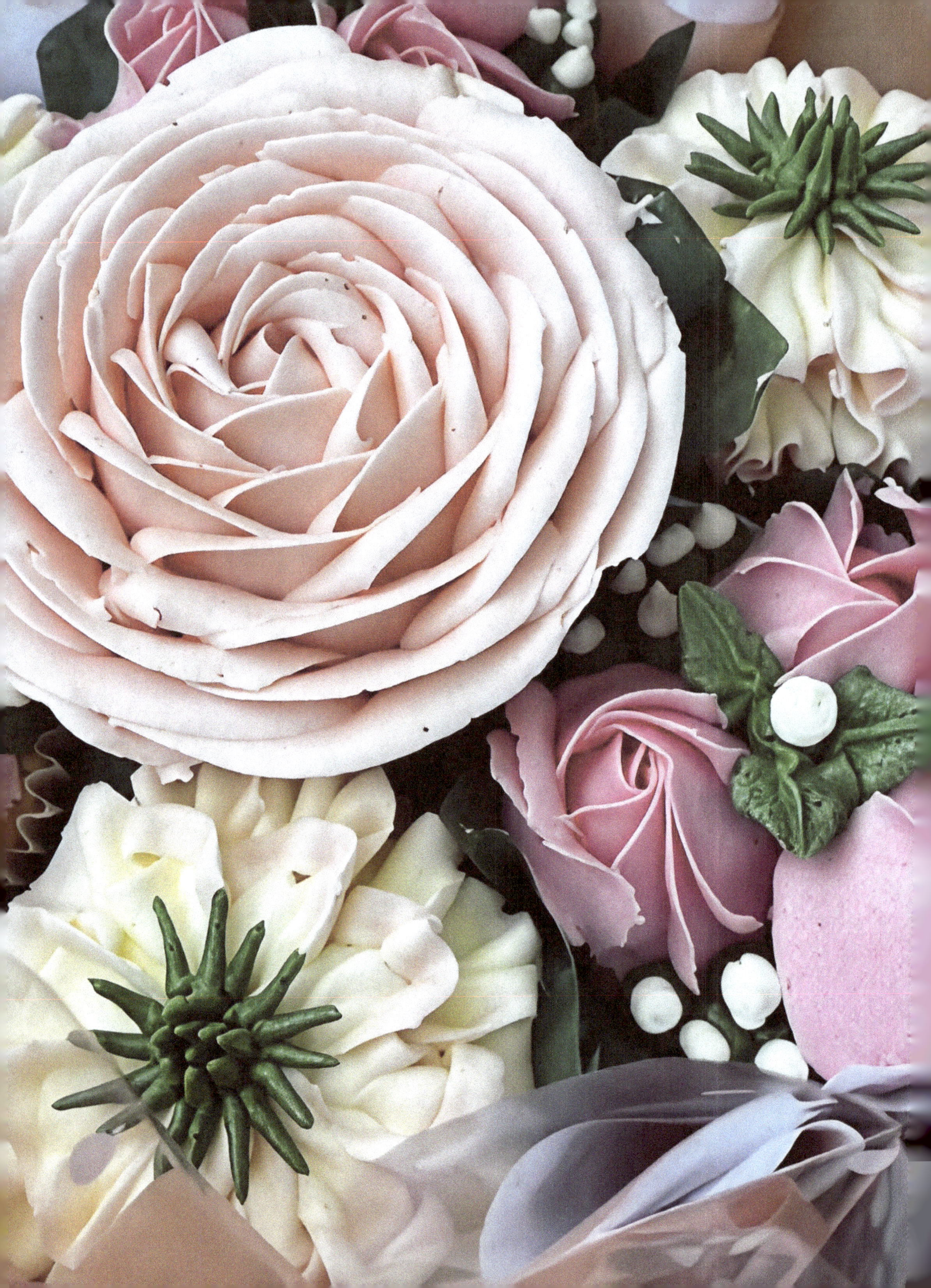

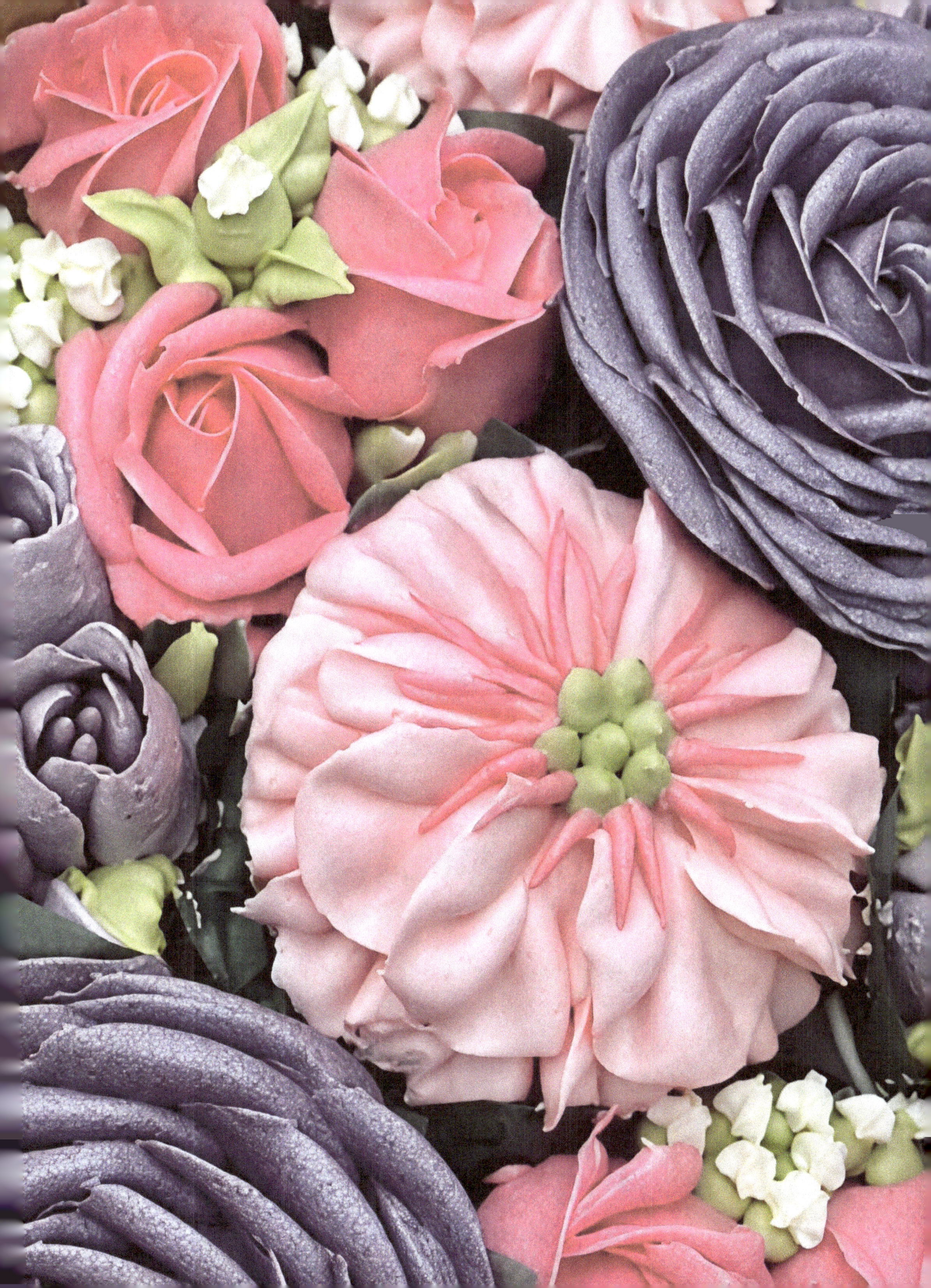

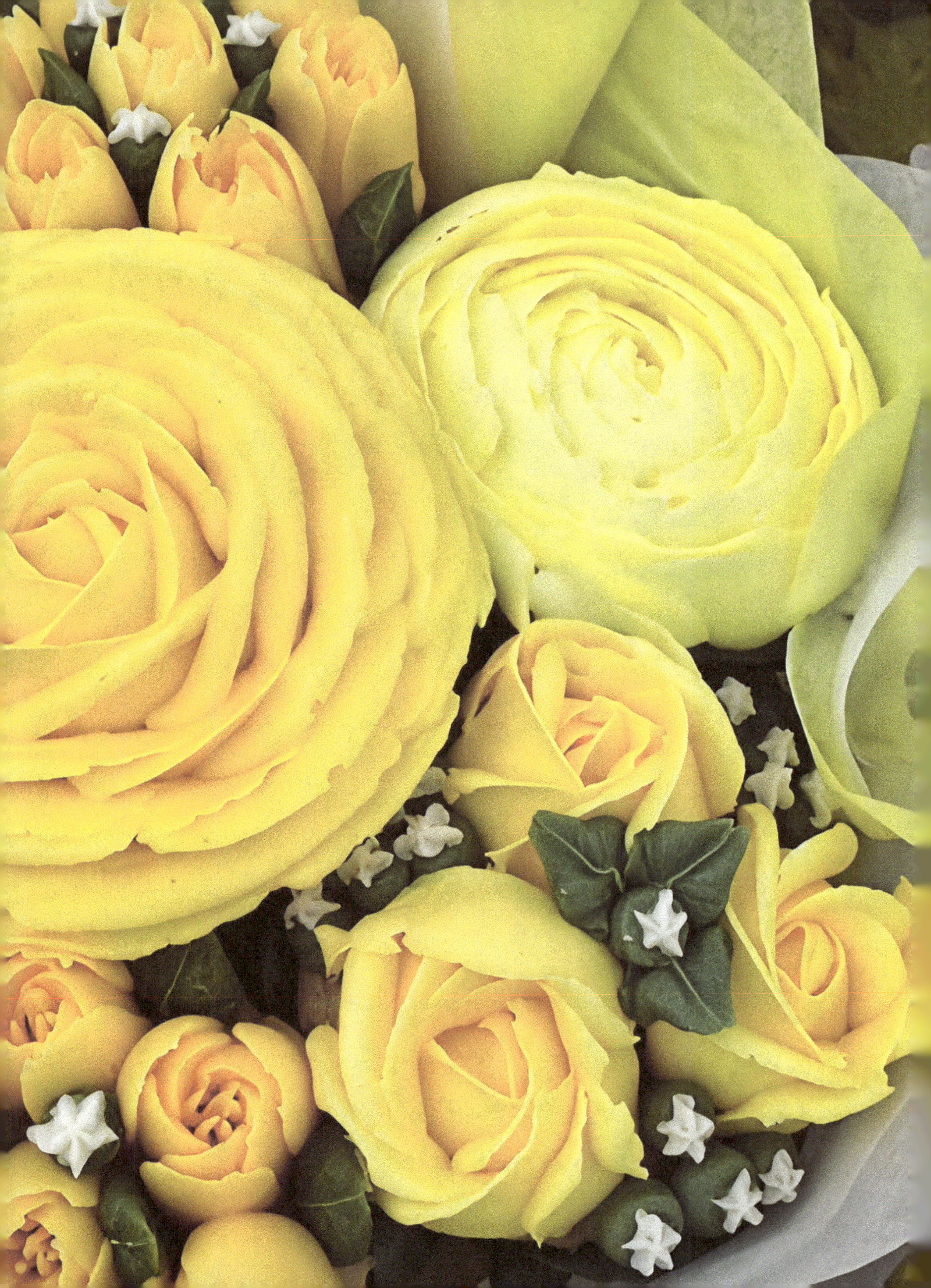

Hand-piped buttercream flowers are the edible
marriage of patience and passion - and every petal
whispers a story of love and dedication...

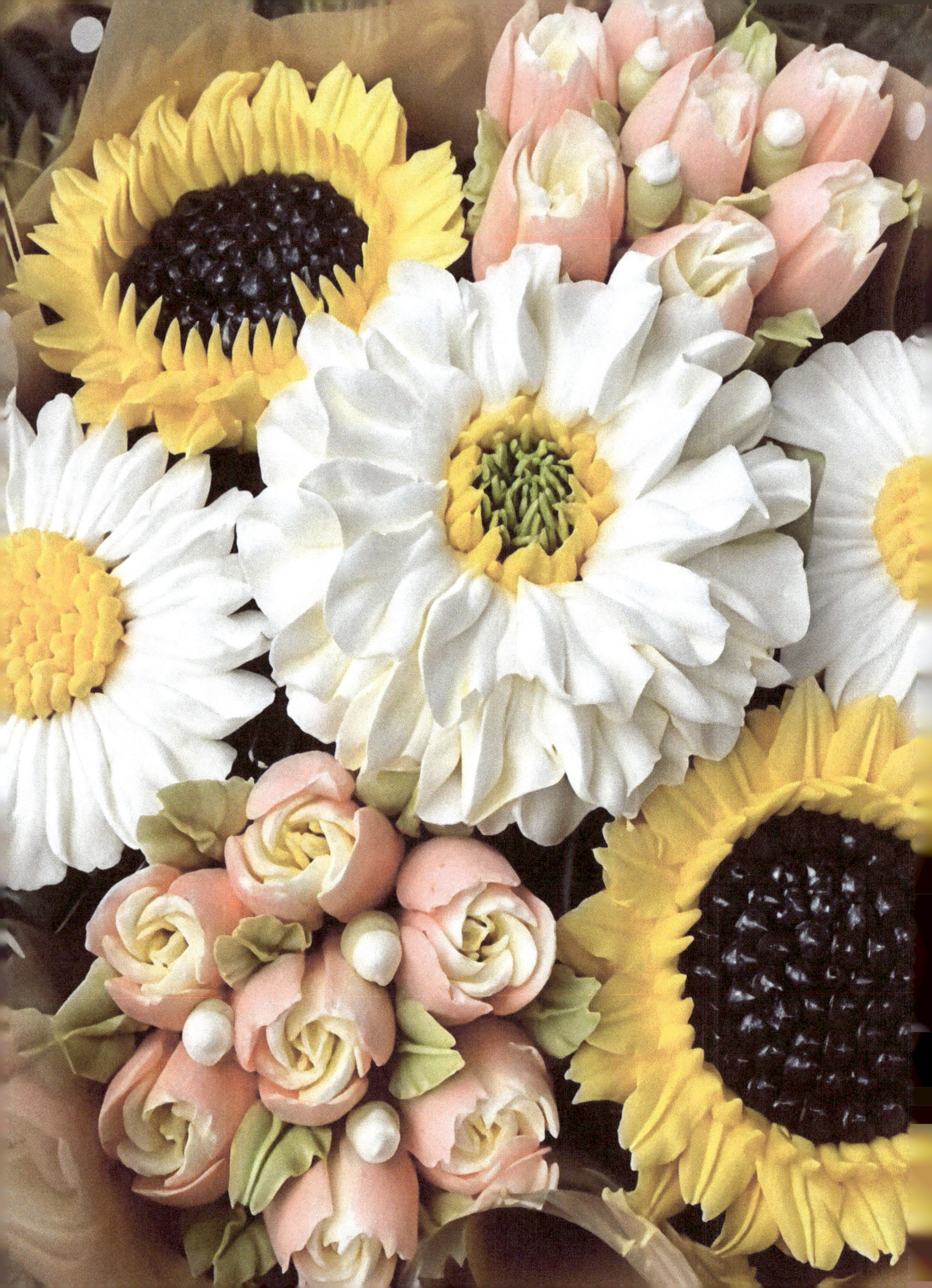

Daisy Flower

I included the Daisy because it reminds me of my daughter's tiny hands picking them on the way to nursery—simple little blooms that carried so much love and joy in their innocence.

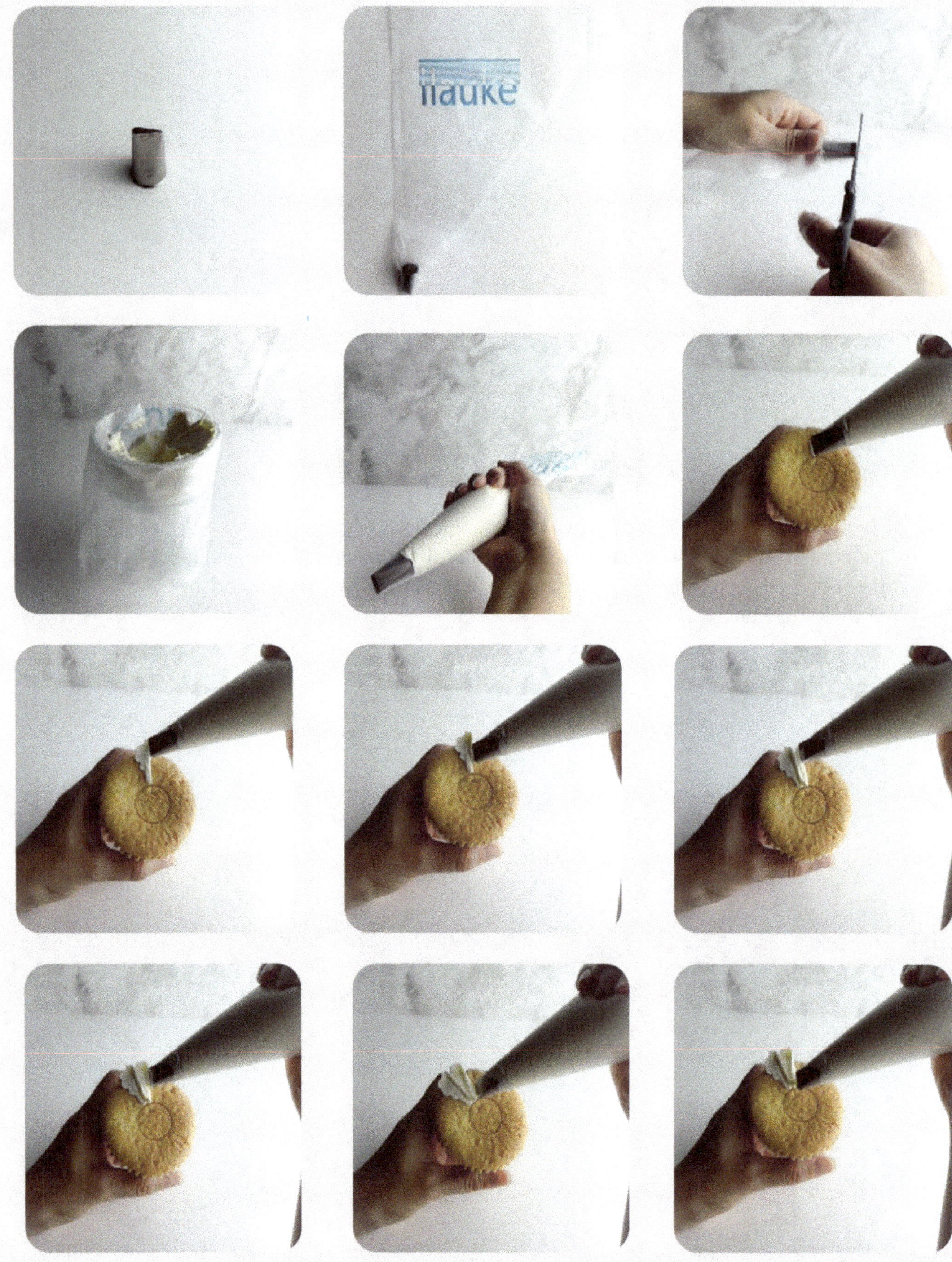
Hauke

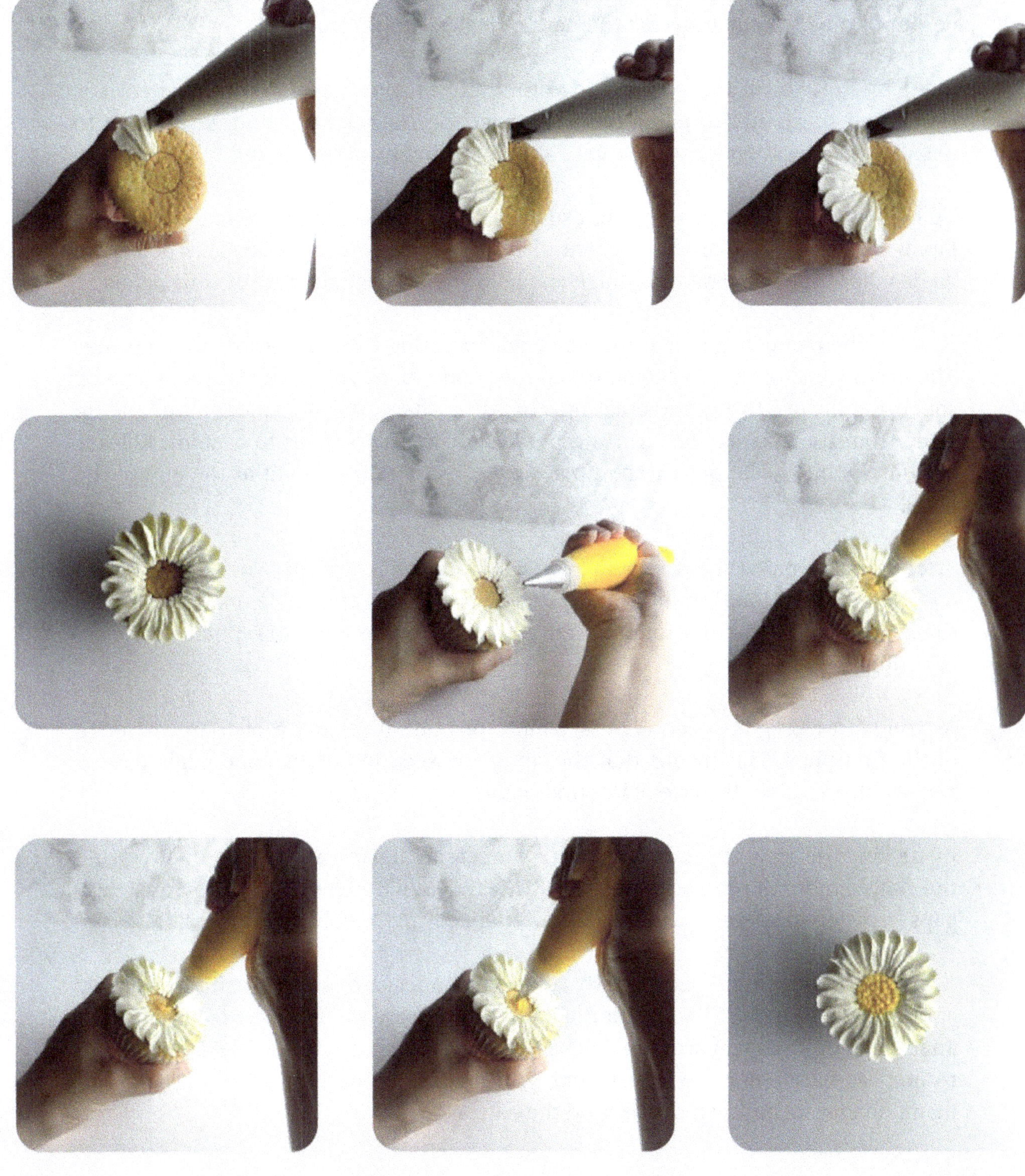

Instructions

Take your piping bag and insert the petal tip - Jem 104 - into the end. Cut the corner of the piping bag so that the nozzle fits well and is snug.

Use a spatula to fill the piping bag with white buttercream, stopping when it is about two-thirds full to allow room to twist the top. Gently squeeze the bag to push any air out, then twist the top to keep the icing from oozing out.

To help keep your petals uniform, use a small piping nozzle or the end of a round piping tip to lightly mark the centre of the cupcake with a circle. This point will guide where you will pipe the centre and help you manage the size of your petals.

Position the piping bag at a 45-degree angle, pointing the tip towards the cupcake. The narrow end of the tip should touch the round mark you have created. Begin by squeezing the bag firmly and creating a teardrop shape. As you squeeze, pull the tip away from the cupcake to form the petal, allowing it to taper to a point. Release pressure gently while pulling the tip away to create a clean point at the end of the petal.

After you have piped the first petal, you will want to ensure that your second petal complements it. Hold the piping bag steady at a 45-degree angle, maintaining the same pressure as you did for the first petal. This angle helps the petals stand up beautifully.

As you start piping the second petal, aim to position it so that it overlaps the edge of the first petal. This means that the tip of the second petal should begin at - or just slightly - inside the base of the first petal.

By tucking the second petal underneath, you create a natural layering effect, giving the flower more depth and dimension. This technique helps to hide any unsightly gaps between the petals, making the flower appear more cohesive and full.

After piping the second petal, gently rotate the cupcake to a new position, typically about a quarter turn. This rotation allows you to view the cupcake from different angles and ensures you are placing the next petal in a balanced way. Each time you rotate, take a moment to adjust your grip on the piping bag. This will help you maintain control as you move around the cupcake.

Continue piping additional petals in this manner. Each new petal should be tucked slightly underneath the previous one, creating that desired layered effect. Aim for a natural look— do not worry about making each petal identical; a little variation can enhance the flower's charm - just like a real thing!

Aim for a total of 18-22 petals. The exact number will depend on the size of your cupcake and how full you want your flower to be. For larger cupcakes, you might want to add a few more petals, while smaller ones may require fewer. As you pipe each petal, use the circular guide that you marked at the beginning as a visual reference. This circle will help you to maintain a consistent shape and size for your petals.

Try to keep each petal approximately the same length and width to create a harmonious look. If you find that some petals are larger or smaller, adjust your pressure and technique slightly. It is helpful to periodically step back and view the cupcake from a distance to assess the overall balance and symmetry.

Take a clean piping bag and fit it with a small round tip. Here, I have used PME 3.

Fill the bag with the yellow buttercream, stopping when it is about halfway full. Twist the top of the bag to keep the icing contained and to maintain control while piping.

Look at your cupcake where you previously marked the centre with a piping nozzle or a light dot. This guide will help you determine where to pipe the yellow buttercream.

Hold the cupcake or flower cupcake steady on your work surface, ensuring that it's easy to reach.

Grip the piping bag with a firm yet gentle hold, positioning it directly above the centre of the daisy. The tip of the bag should be just above the surface of the cupcake, ready to pipe.

Begin by gently squeezing the piping bag to release the buttercream. Start with a small dot at the marked centre point. For the first dot, squeeze lightly for a second or two, allowing the buttercream to build up slightly before lifting the tip away. This will create a nice rounded dot that resembles the centre of a flower.

Continue piping additional dots around the first one, forming a cluster or circle. To achieve a fuller centre, aim for small, even dots that slightly overlap each other. This overlapping effect will create a more textured, vibrant look. As you pipe, you can vary the size of the dots a little for added interest but keep them relatively uniformed for a polished appearance to your beautiful finished daisy.

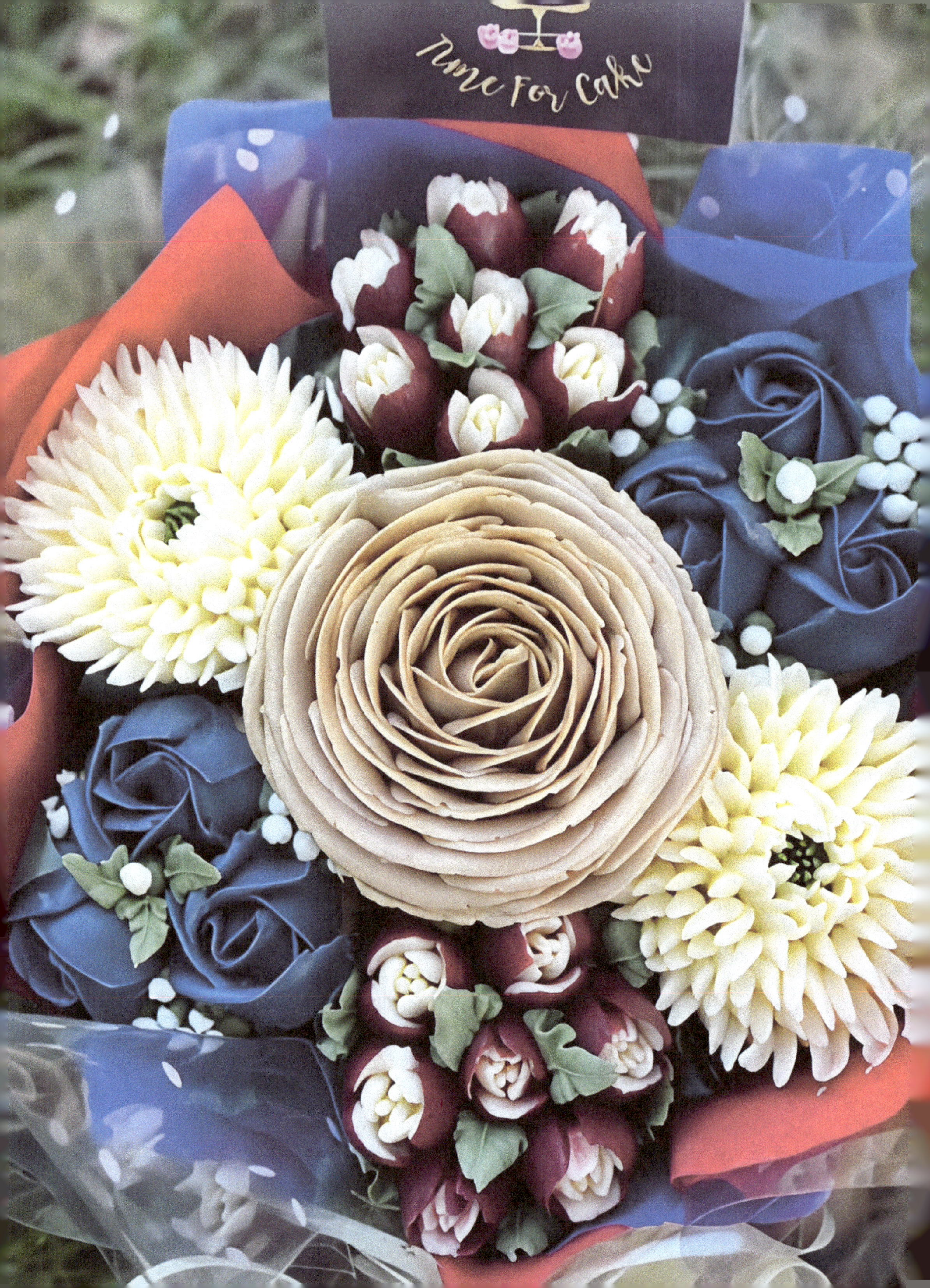

Time For Cake

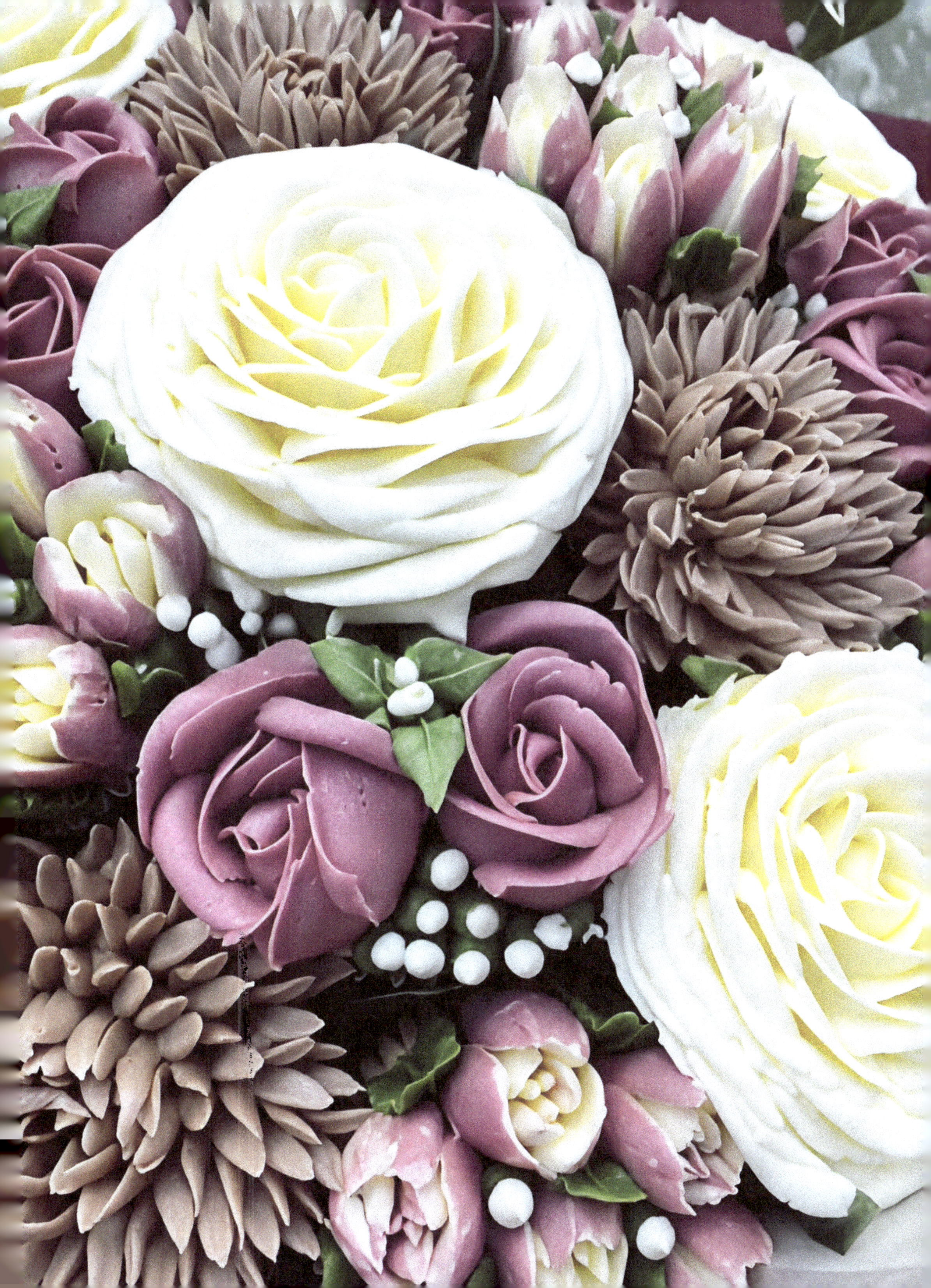

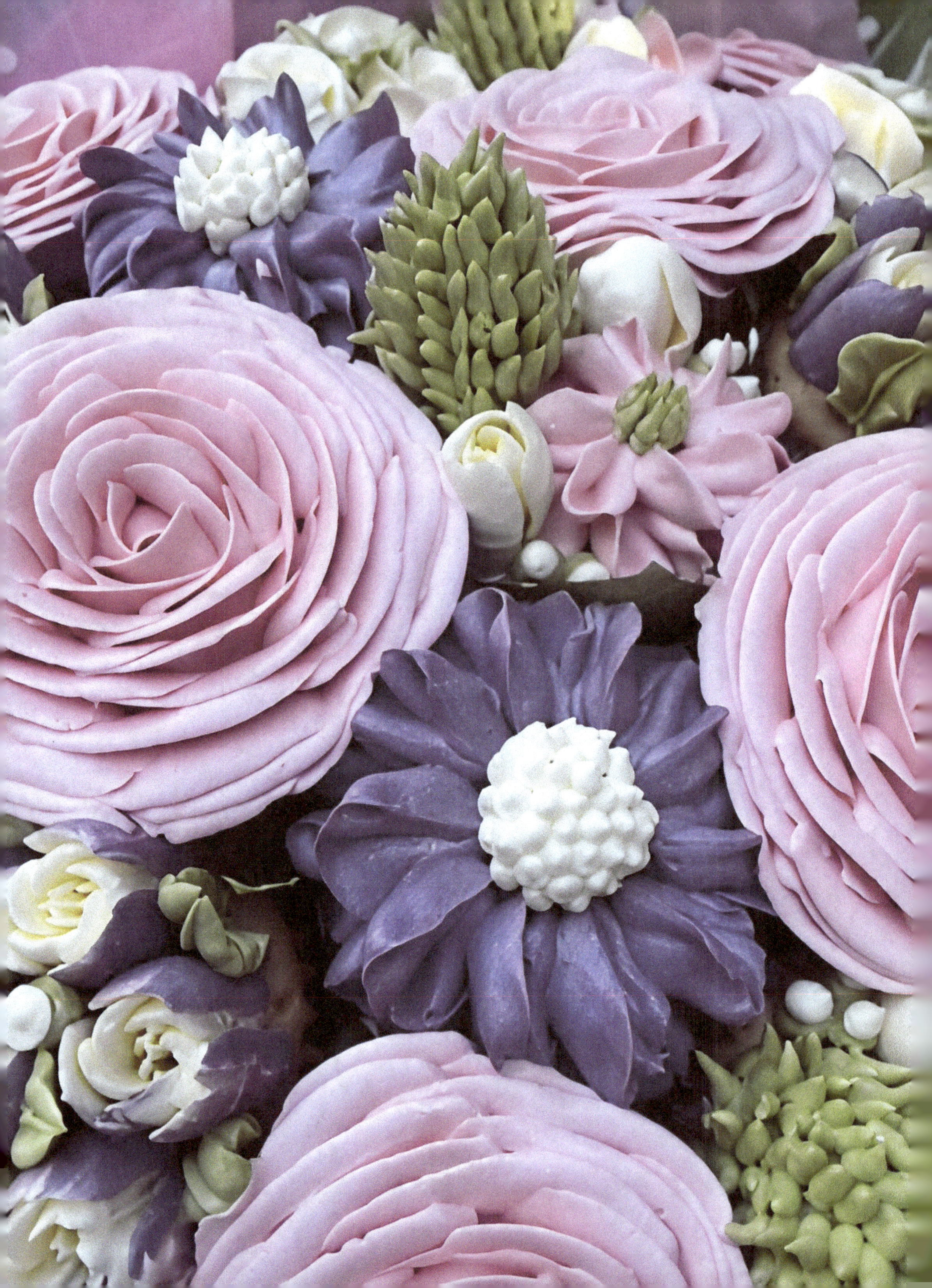

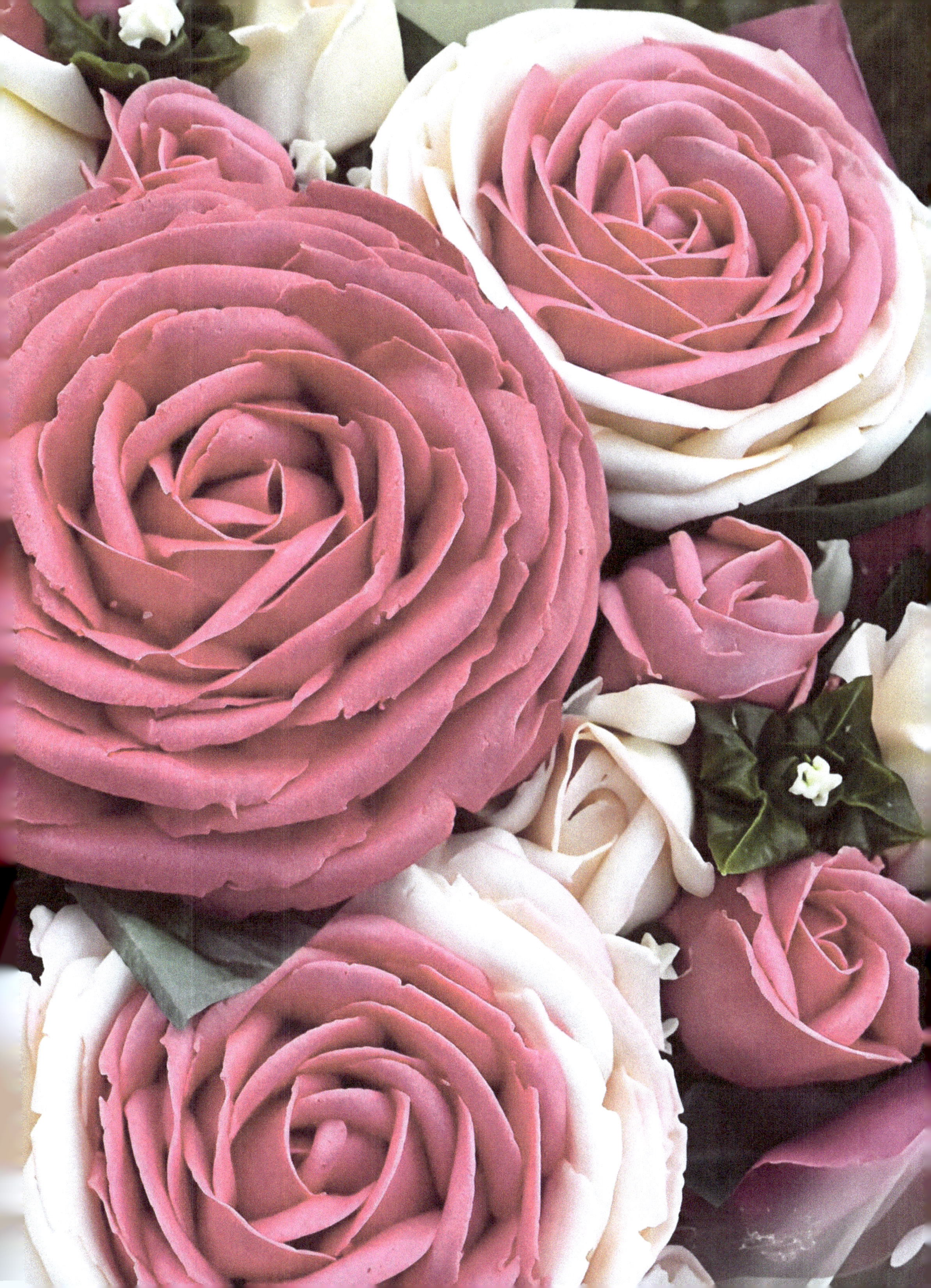

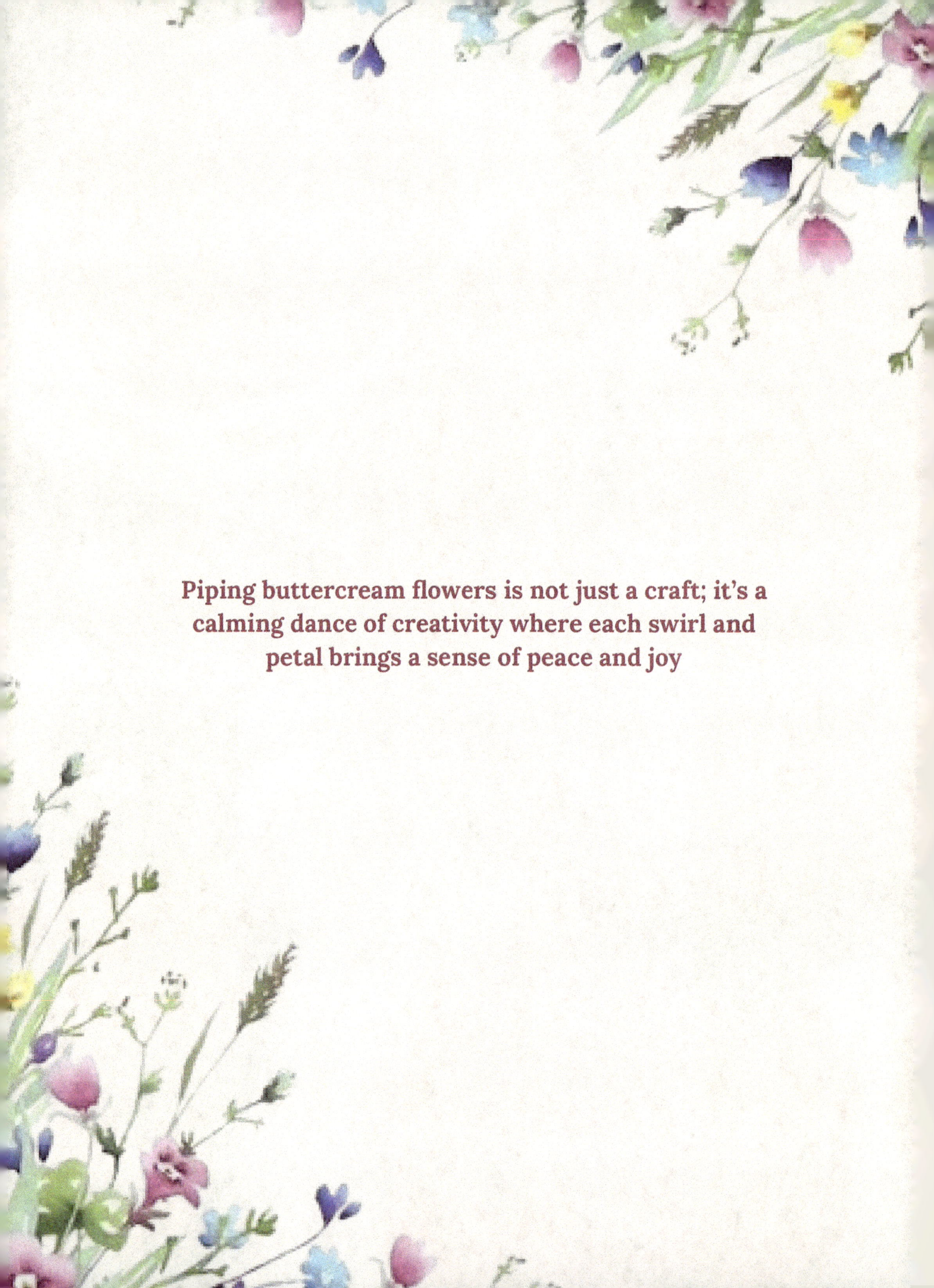

Piping buttercream flowers is not just a craft; it's a calming dance of creativity where each swirl and petal brings a sense of peace and joy

Scabiosa Flower

I included the Scabiosa for its soft, delicate beauty—often quietly nestled among bolder blooms, yet always capturing my heart with its gentle charm, much like the quiet moments in life that leave the deepest imprint.

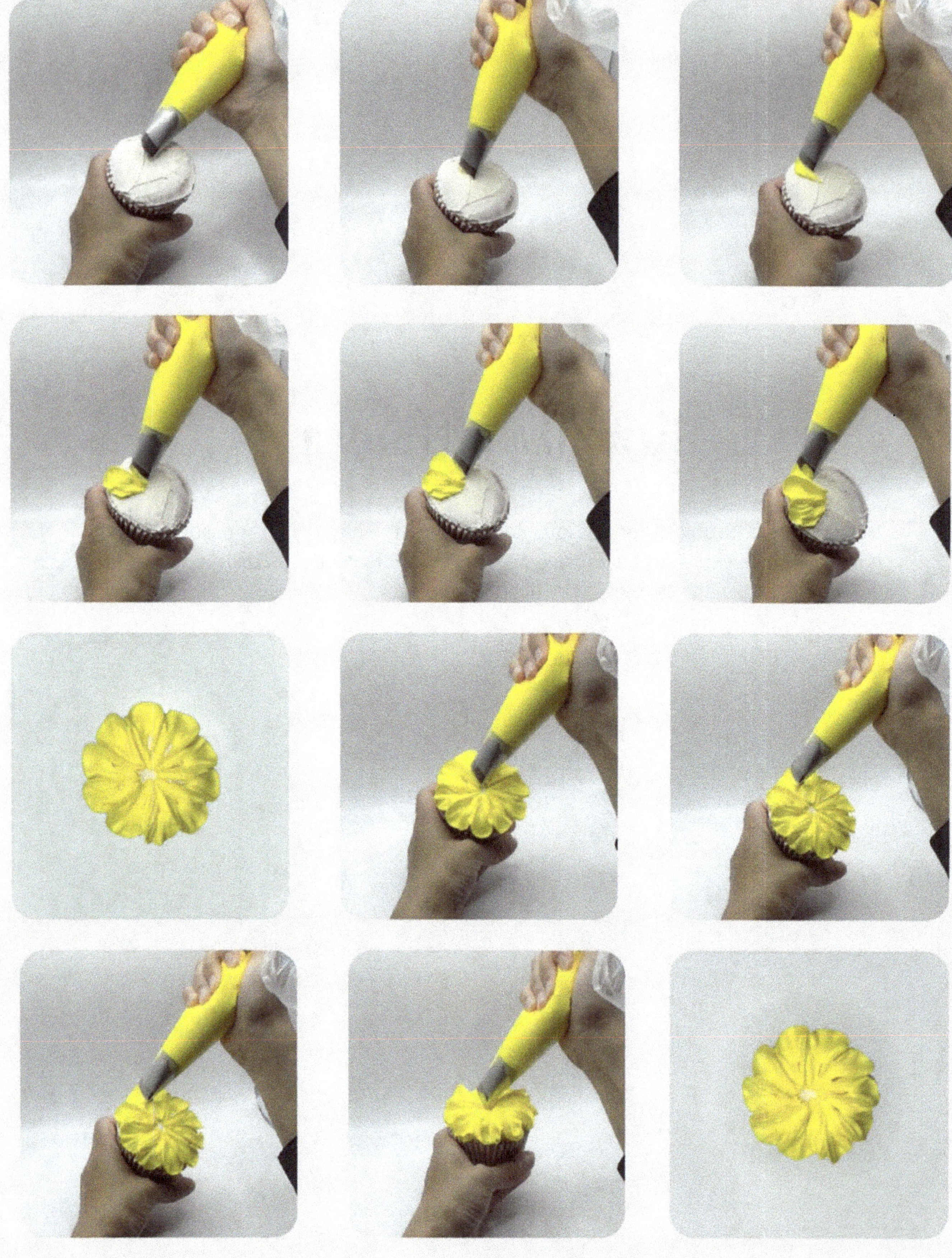

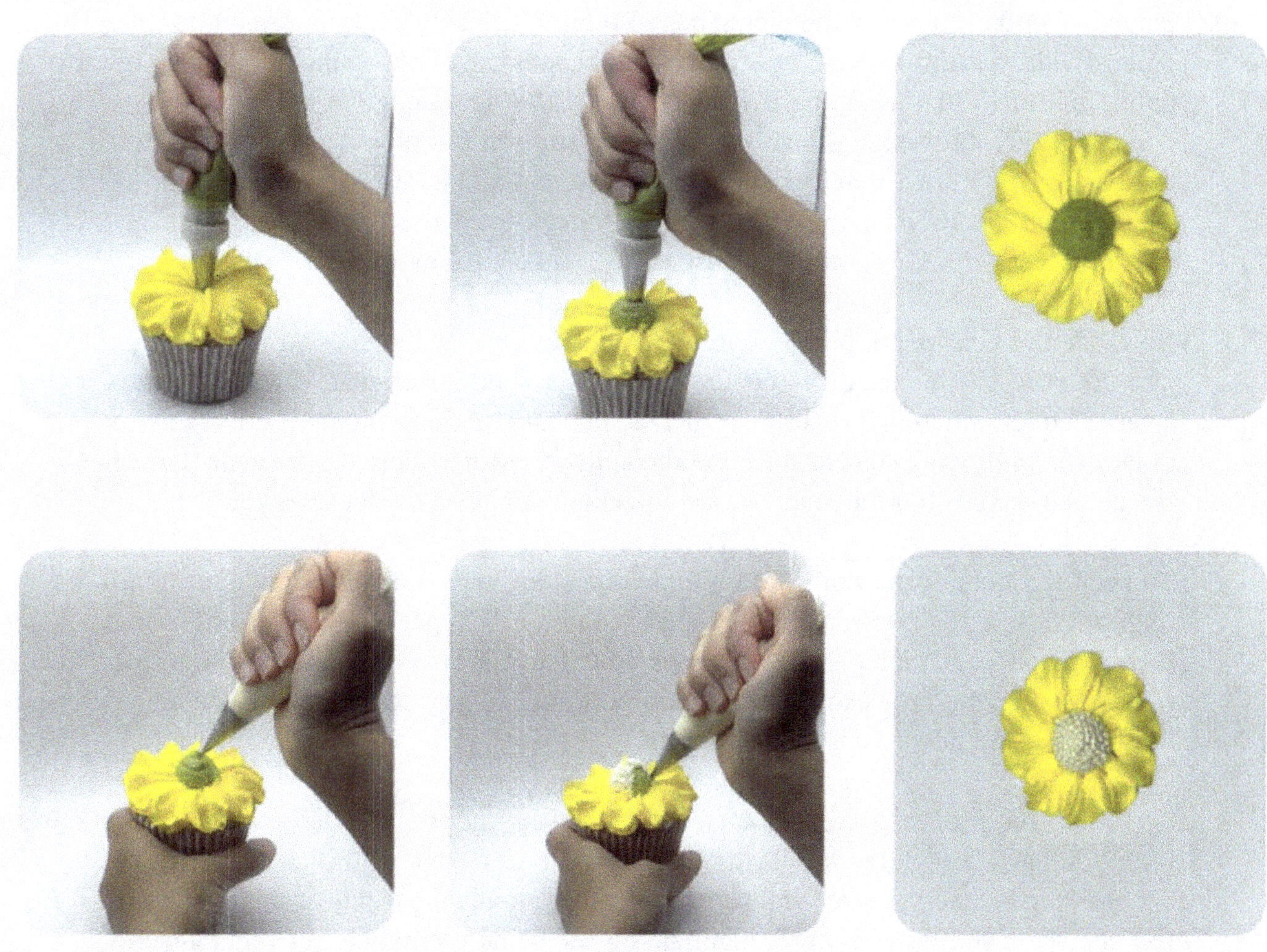

Instructions

You must hold your piping bag at a 45-degree angle to the surface of the cupcake. This gradient will give you the best control and allow for smooth, even petal shapes. Ensure that the narrow end of your petal tip is facing outward, away from the cupcake's centre. This is what helps create the delicate, thin edge of each petal while the wider end will form the thicker, more stable base.

Begin by gently squeezing the piping bag to release the buttercream. As you do this, pipe a wide teardrop shape starting from the centre of the cupcake. Move the piping tip outward, stretching the petal toward the outer edge of the cupcake. As you reach the outer edge, slowly ease the pressure on the piping bag to create the thin, tapered end of the teardrop. To complete the petal, stop squeezing entirely while simultaneously pulling the piping bag away from the cupcake to smoothly finish the petal tip. This gradual release is key to getting a natural, clean edge.

Now, for the next petal, position your piping bag so that the second petal begins just underneath the edge of the first one. This slight overlap creates a natural layered effect, much like real flower petals. Repeat the same piping motion as you did for the first petal: start at the base and apply pressure to create the wide part of the petal, then stretch the petal toward the edge, releasing pressure as you finish.

To keep the petal formation smooth and consistent, use your non-dominant hand to gently rotate the cupcake as you pipe each petal. This prevents you from having to reposition your piping bag and keeps your hand in a comfortable position for piping. Rotate the cupcake slowly as you continue to add more petals, keeping a steady pace and flow to ensure uniformity.

Continue this process, layering each petal slightly underneath the previous one, until you have completed a full ring around the outer edge of the cupcake. If you are working on a multi-layered flower, you can gradually pipe smaller petals toward the centre as you move inward, maintaining the same technique but reducing the size of the petal by controlling the pressure of the piping bag.

After piping 9 or 10 evenly spaced petals onto the surface of the cupcake, you will have a beautiful first layer that wraps around the top; leaving a noticeable hole in the centre. This first layer is the foundation of your buttercream flower and will already start to reveal its shape and form.

Now it is time to add the second layer of petals, which will add both depth and dimension, making your flower more lifelike. Pick up the cupcake gently in one hand, holding it steady, and take your piping bag in the other. With the piping tip at a slight angle, begin to pipe the second layer of tear-drop shaped petals directly on top of the first row.

You have two options when it comes to placement: you can either begin piping the second layer in the same spot where you started the first, or you can start from any petal around the first layer. I personally prefer to begin piping right over the first petal I piped in the previous layer. This method not only creates a lovely, uniform look, but it also helps build the symmetry of the flower as you continue adding petals.

As you pipe each petal, slightly overlap the edges with the previous row, ensuring that the new petals sit nicely on top, creating a full, multi-dimensional appearance. Do not worry if the hole in the middle remains—it's supposed to be there for now. We will fill this in during the next step, and that final touch will really bring your buttercream flower to life.

To create a large bud in the centre of your design, start by preparing your icing. For this, you will need green-coloured icing, although you can use any shade that complements your overall design.

There are two ways to set up your piping bag. You can either fit the nozzle directly into the bag or use a piping bag fitted with a coupler. A coupler is a handy tool that allows you to switch between different nozzles without needing to change the bag. This can be especially useful when you are piping multiple elements like buds and leaves in one go.

For this step, I recommend using a piping bag fitted with a coupler, as I have done here. I am using Wilton Tip No. 12, which is ideal for creating a large bud in the centre. This round tip allows you to build a smooth, domed bud, which will serve as the focal point for the rest of your flower design.

Now, when you are ready to pipe, you can either hold the cupcake in your hand or place it on a flat surface. If you are new to piping, setting the cupcake on a flat surface may give you more stability and better control, especially for this central bud. Having a solid surface also makes it easier to apply consistent pressure to your piping bag, which is key to achieving a clean, smooth bud.

To create the bud, position the nozzle directly above the centre of your cupcake. Apply gentle pressure to the piping bag and slowly squeeze out the icing. As you squeeze, form a mound that is large enough to serve as the base for the rest of your flower. The size of this mound will depend on how prominent you want the centre bud to be, but it should be a substantial enough height to stand out once you begin piping the petals around it.

Continue applying pressure until the mound reaches the desired size, then release the pressure and lift the piping bag away. You should now have a smooth, rounded bud in the centre of your cupcake, ready for the next steps in your floral design!

For the next step, we will add tiny white dots to the bud to enhance its texture and detail. You can use any colour of your choice for these dots, but, for me, white creates a beautiful contrast, giving the flower a delicate, realistic look.

Begin by filling your piping bag with white icing and fitting it with a PME No. 3 nozzle, ideal for fine detailing. You can work with the cupcake in your hand for more control or leave it on a work surface—whichever feels more comfortable for you.

Using a steady hand and plenty of patience, carefully pipe small dots all over the green bud. Take your time to ensure even spacing and consistent sizing. To create more depth, you can choose to cover the entire bud with dots or just a portion of it, depending on the look you are going for. The choice is entirely yours, allowing for creative freedom.

With practice, you will find that these techniques become second nature, and soon you will develop your own unique designs, adding a personal touch to each flower you create.

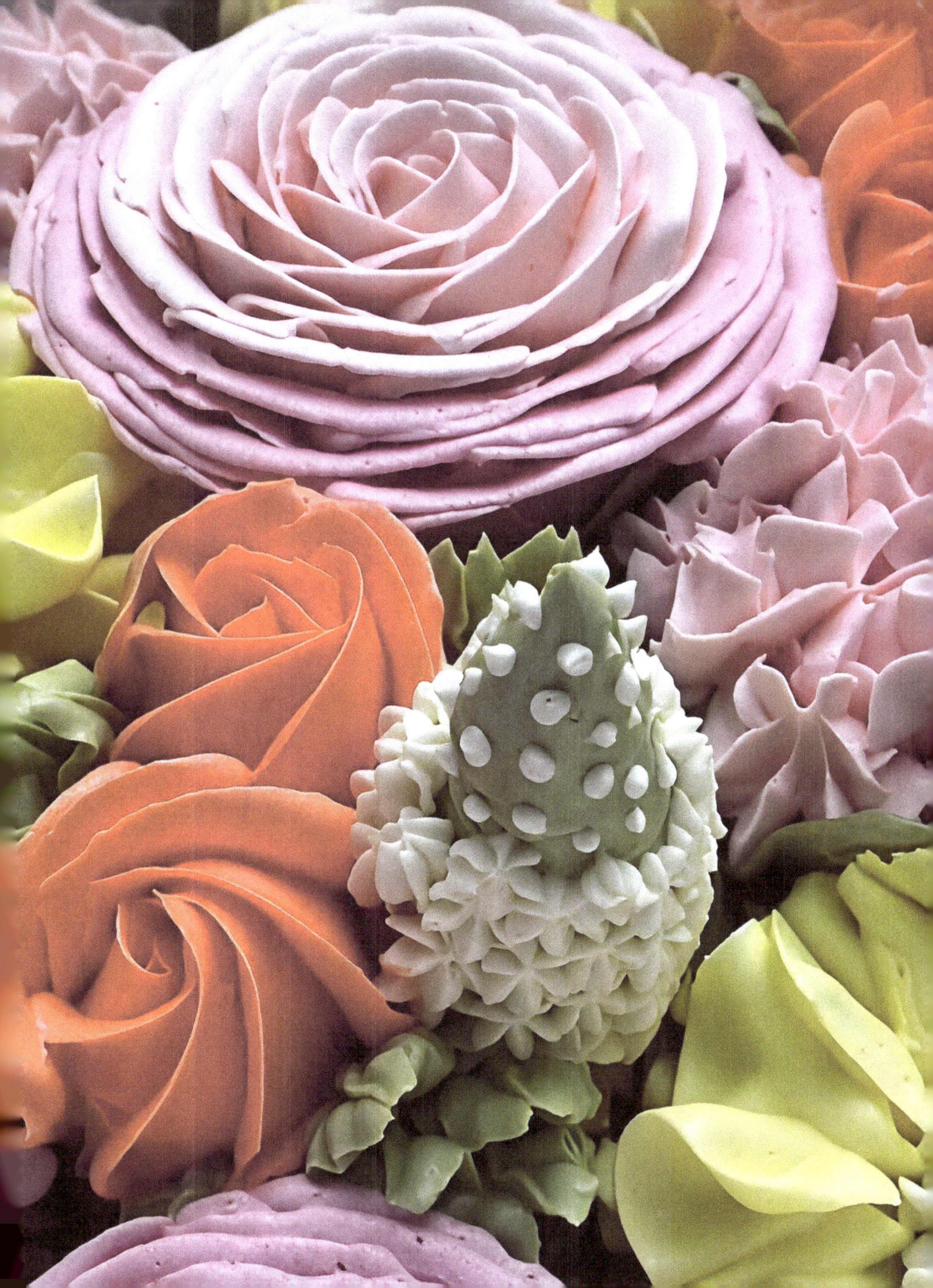

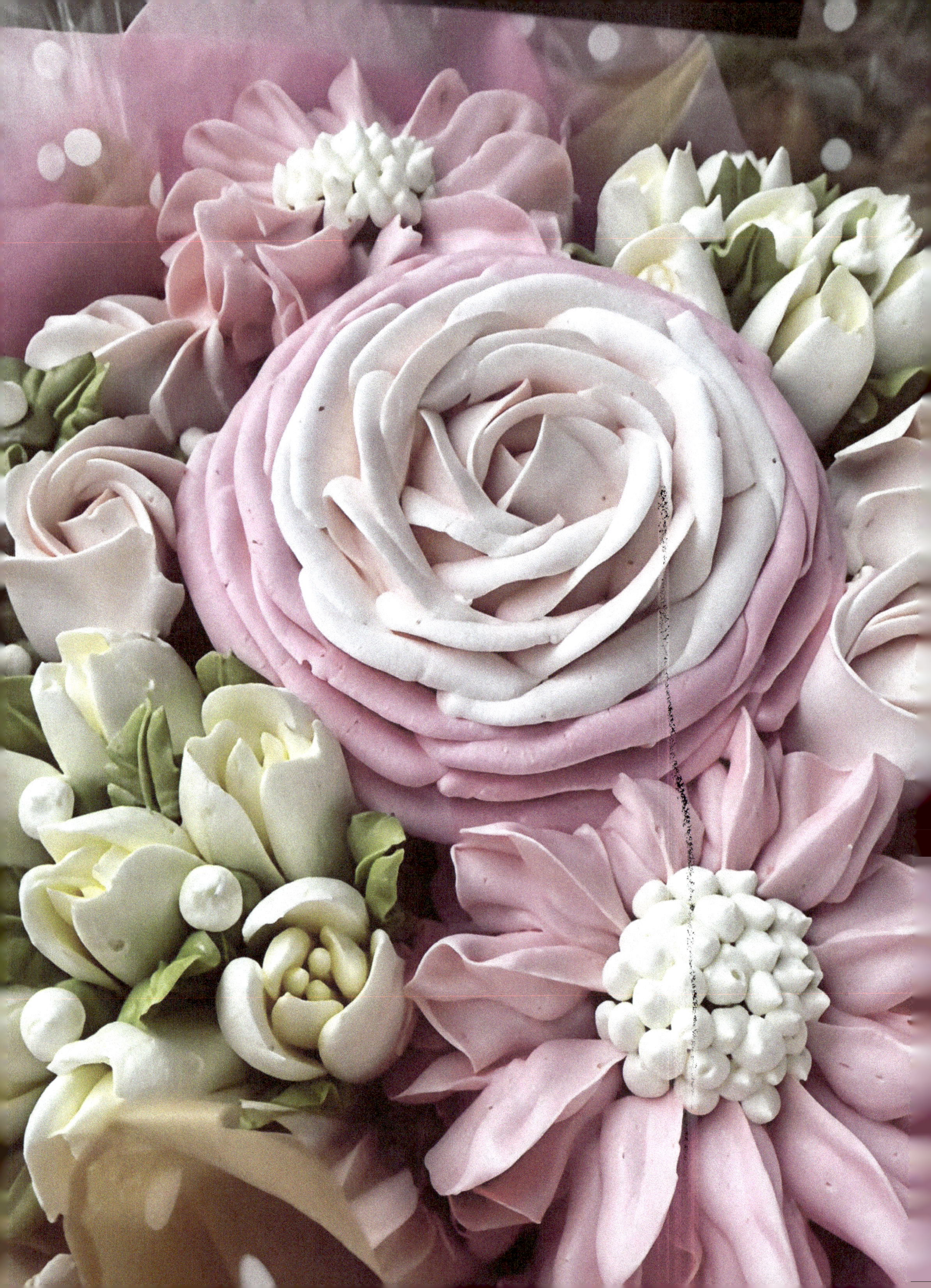

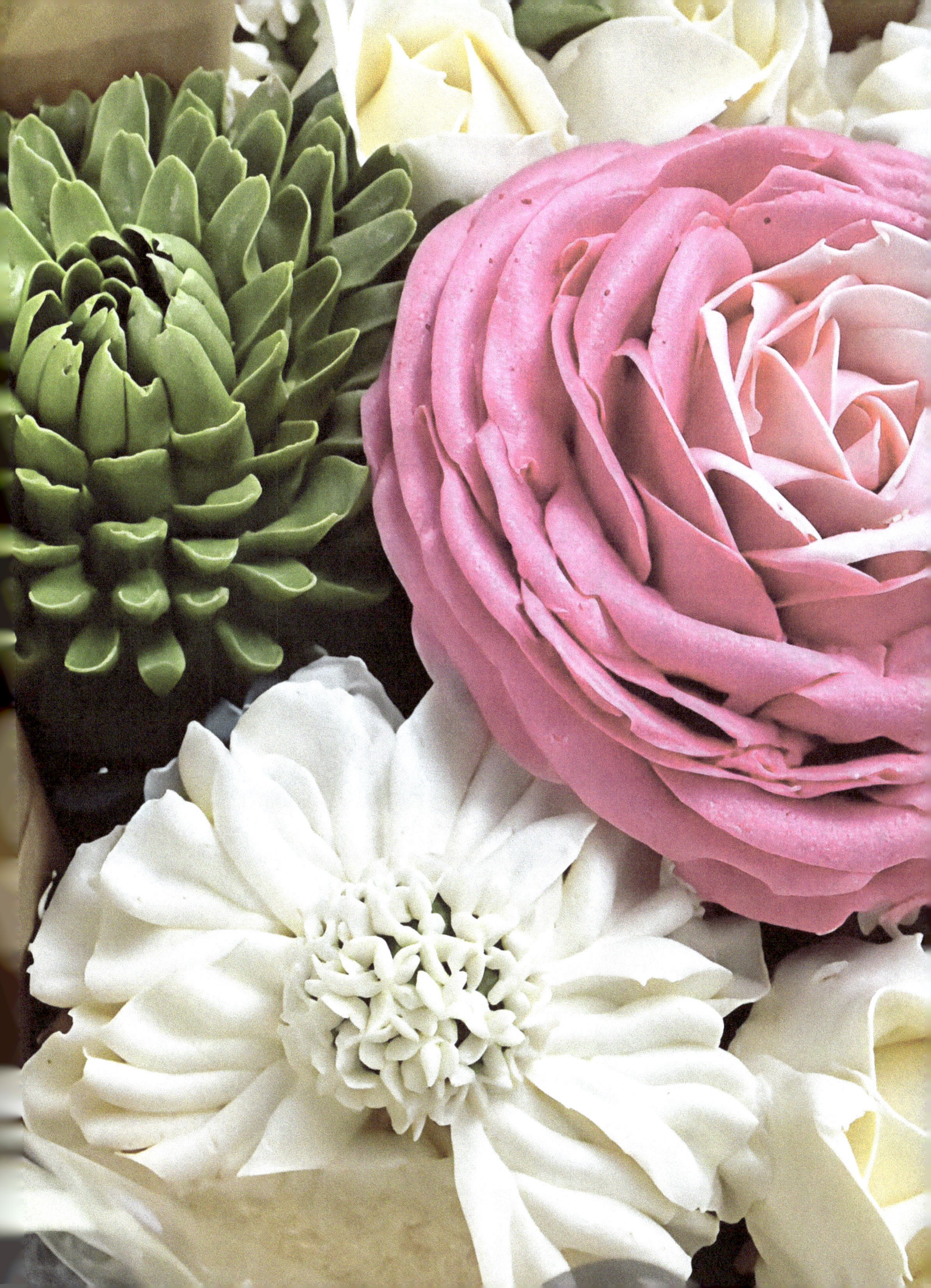

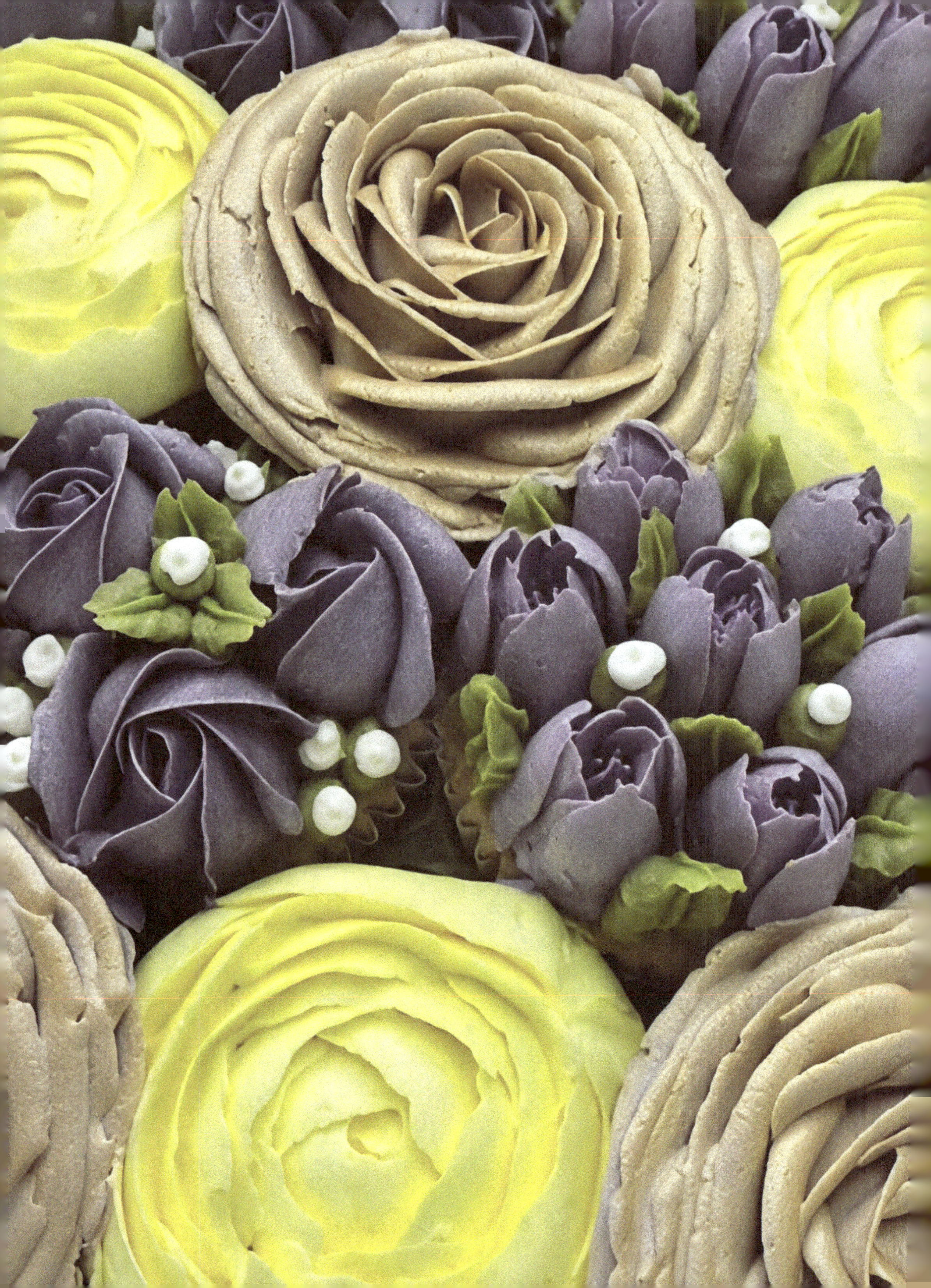

Hand-piping intricate buttercream flowers is like
painting with sweetness—each delicate petal is a
joyful masterpiece waiting to be shared..

Rosette Flower

I included the Rosette because it holds the memory of my beginnings—when I spent hours perfecting this simple swirl. It was the first step on a journey that blossomed into a love for intricate floral piping and the foundation of everything that followed.

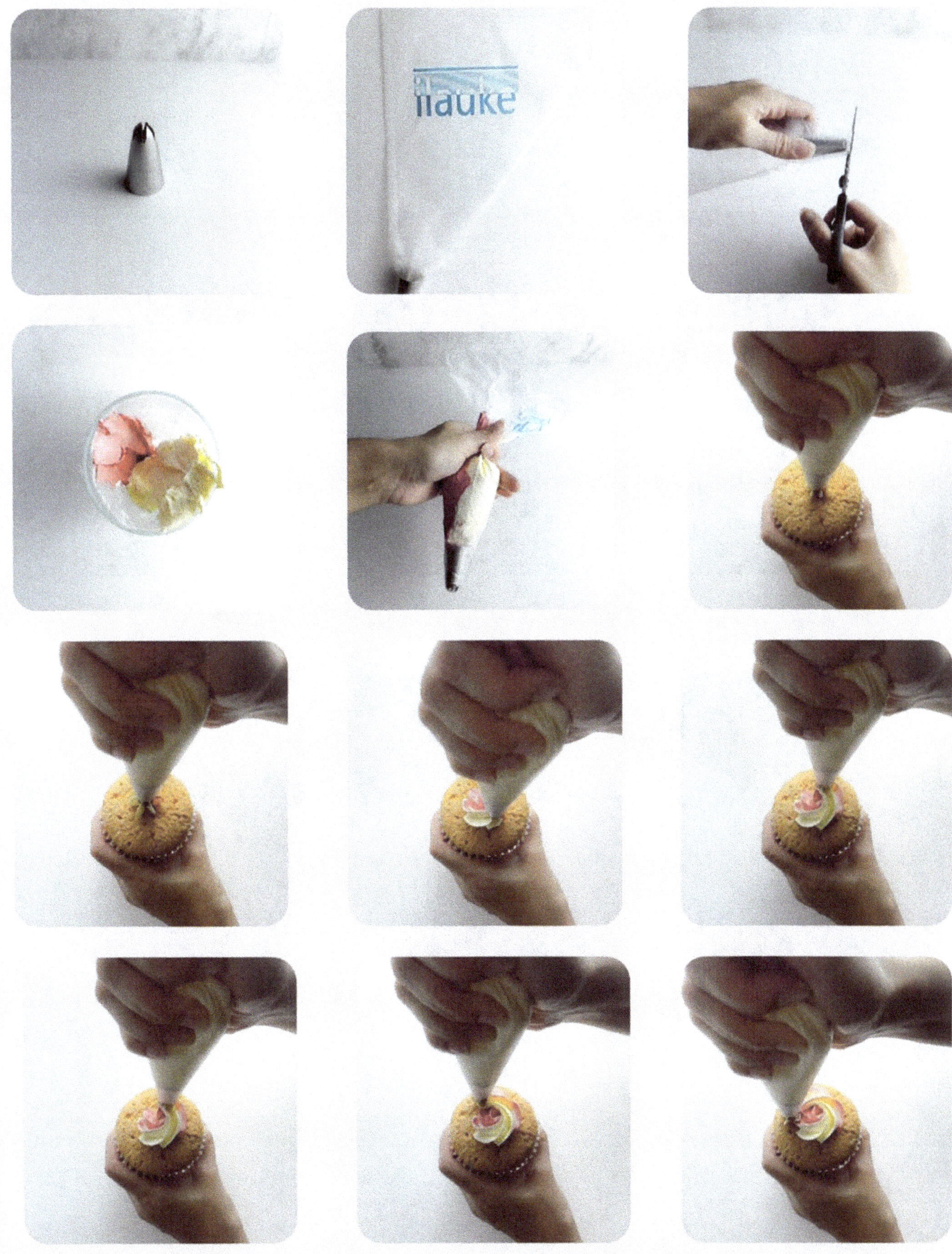
hauke

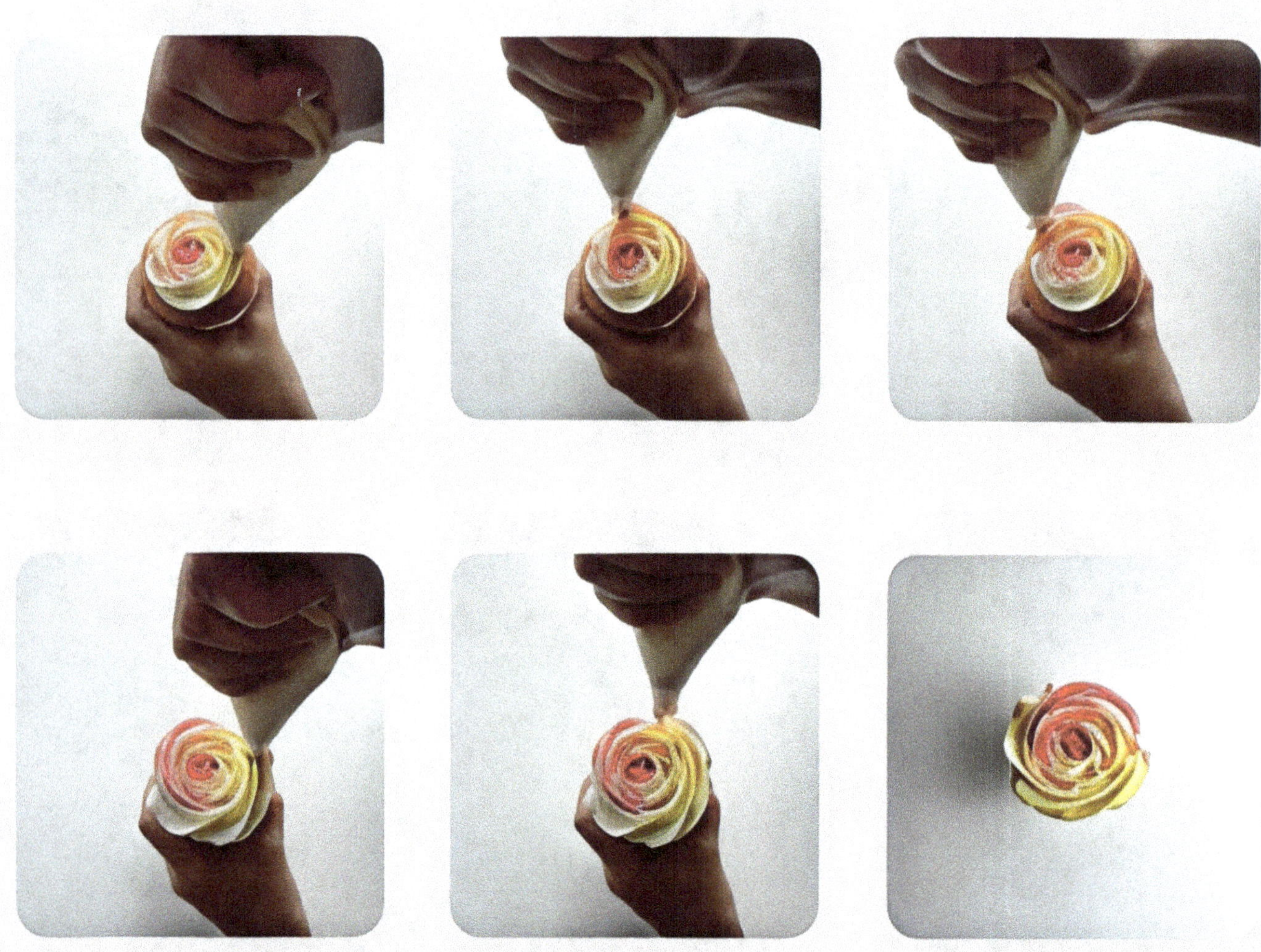

Instructions

The hand-piped buttercream rosette is a timeless and elegant flower; perfect for adding a touch of beauty to cakes and cupcakes. With its swirling petals that mimic the delicate unfurling of a rose, it is a popular choice for both beginners and experienced decorators. Hand-piped rosettes are versatile—they can be made in a variety of sizes and colours, making this an essential technique for creating stunning floral arrangements in buttercream.

To create a beautiful and simple rosette, we will be using the Wilton 2D piping nozzle, which is perfect for achieving those lovely, textured petals.

Take the Wilton 2D nozzle and insert it into the open end of the piping bag. Ensure that you push the nozzle all the way to the tip of the bag, allowing it to rest snugly against the end.

To properly prepare a piping bag, assess where to cut its tip to fit the nozzle securely. Hold the bag upright and make sure that the nozzle slightly extends out without being unstable. Trim the tip carefully with sharp scissors, starting with a small cut. Reinsert the nozzle to check the fit, trimming more if needed until it's snug for precise piping without gaps.

With the nozzle properly fitted, your piping bag is now ready to fill with buttercream and create stunning rosettes!

To begin the process of piping, take your piping bag and insert the chosen piping nozzle into the bottom. Then, place the entire piping bag with the nozzle into a tall glass. This will provide stability while you fill the bag. Next, carefully fold the wider end of the piping bag over the rim of the glass. This step is crucial as it creates a seal around the glass, preventing any icing from spilling out while you're filling the bag.

For creating a rosette, you have the option to use either a single colour or a combination of colours. In this instance, we will be piping a beautiful pink and white rosette. To achieve this two-tone effect, grab a simple kitchen butter knife. With the knife, scoop out some pink icing and carefully spread it along one side of the piping bag, ensuring that it is packed in securely. Then, fill the remaining space in the bag with white icing; making sure to push it down gently to eliminate any air pockets.

Once you have filled the bag, lift it out of the glass, ensuring that the icing is pushed down toward the piping nozzle. After the icing has settled, twist the top of the piping bag to tighten it, which will give you better control while piping.

Now you are ready to pipe your rosette! If this is your first time, you may find it easier to place your cupcake on a flat work surface. This provides stability and allows you to focus on your piping technique. Alternatively, if you feel comfortable, you can hold the cupcake in one hand while gripping the piping bag in the other.

Position the piping bag vertically above the centre of the cupcake. Squeeze the bag firmly to start piping a star shape at the centre where you want the rosette to be. This star will serve as the base of your rosette, providing a lovely focal point for the flower.

To begin creating your buttercream rosette, first raise the piping tip slightly above the surface of your star-shaped base. This slight elevation will allow for better control as you pipe. With a steady hand, start by piping a line of icing towards the top of the star, making sure to maintain even pressure to ensure a consistent flow of icing.

Next, initiate the circular piping motion. Imagine you are forming a lowercase "e" as you pipe around the star. This motion should be fluid and gentle, allowing the icing to form a tight circle that elegantly wraps around the star's edges. As you pipe, keep your wrist relaxed and use your fingers to guide the piping bag, rather than applying excessive pressure, which can lead to uneven icing.

Continue this circular motion, gradually working your way around the cupcake. Maintain a slow and steady pace, ensuring that each rotation of icing is smooth and uniform. This will help in creating a beautifully defined rosette that complements the base star.

As you near the end of your piping, it is crucial to control the pressure on the bag. To finish the rosette - and avoid the formation of an unwanted tip at the end - gradually decrease the pressure as you approach the point where you started. Just before you connect the final piece of icing to the base, stop squeezing entirely. Instead of dragging the tip along, gently pull the piping tip away from the cupcake. This technique will give your rosette a clean, polished look, completing your beautiful decoration.

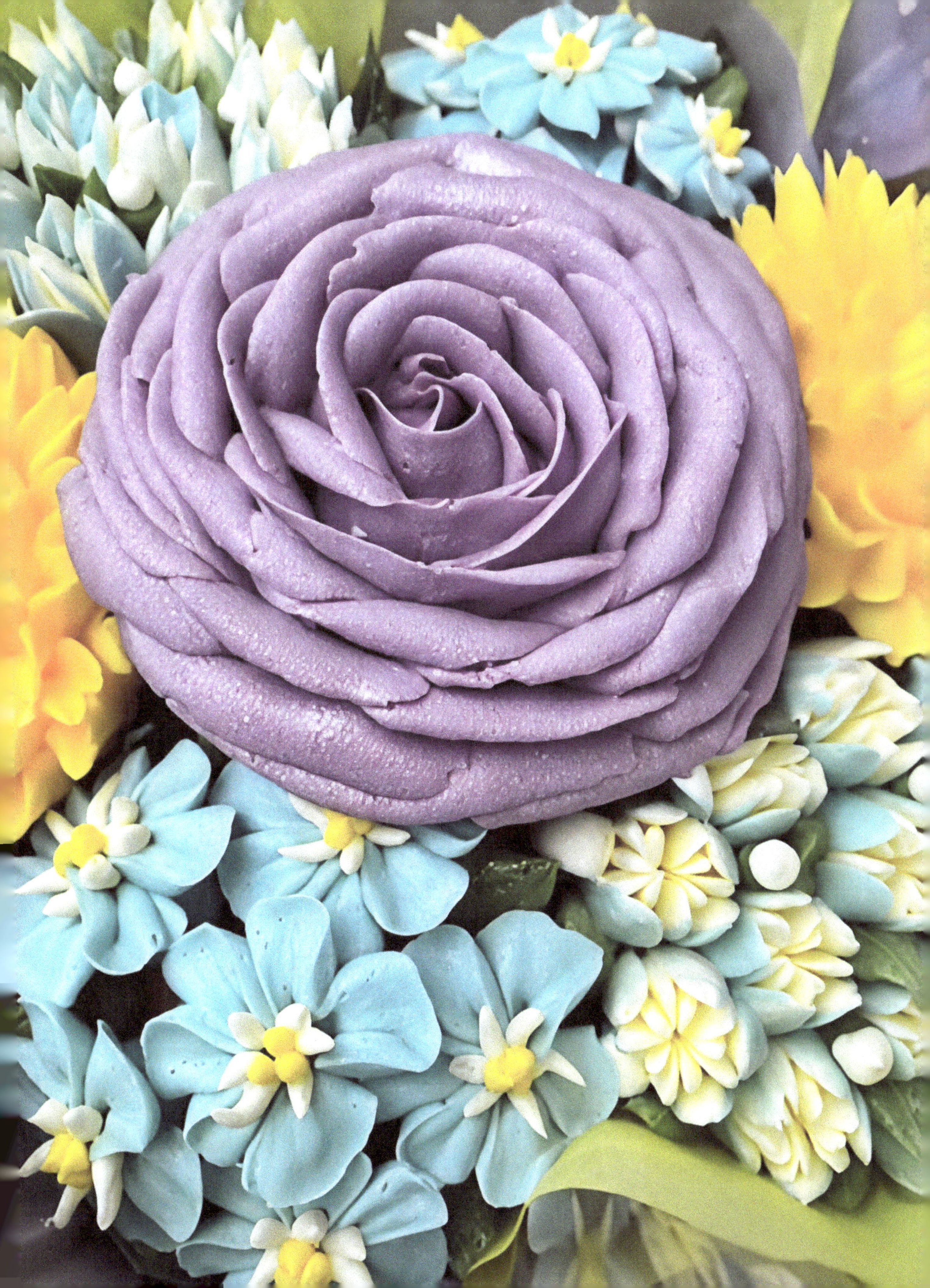

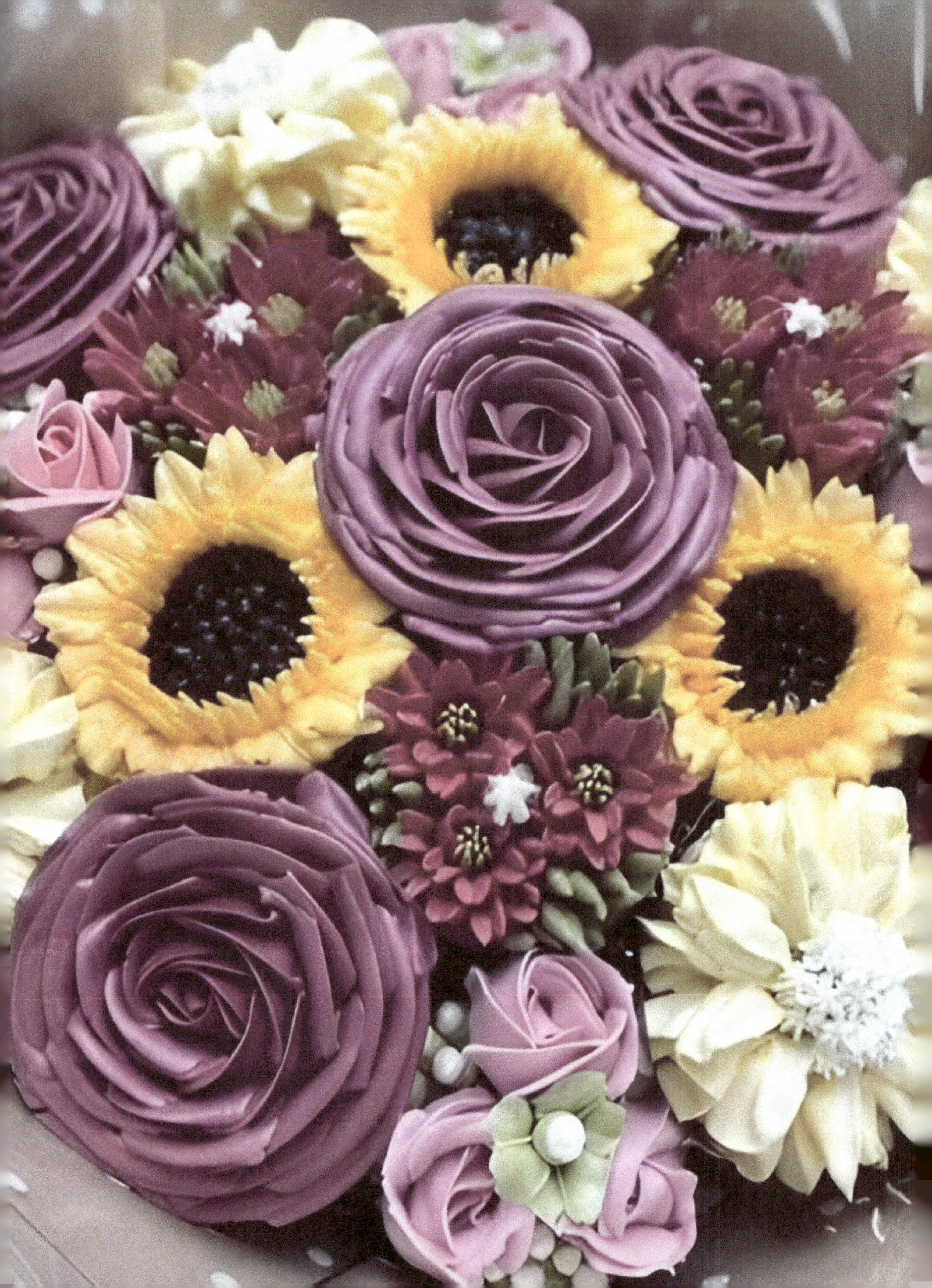

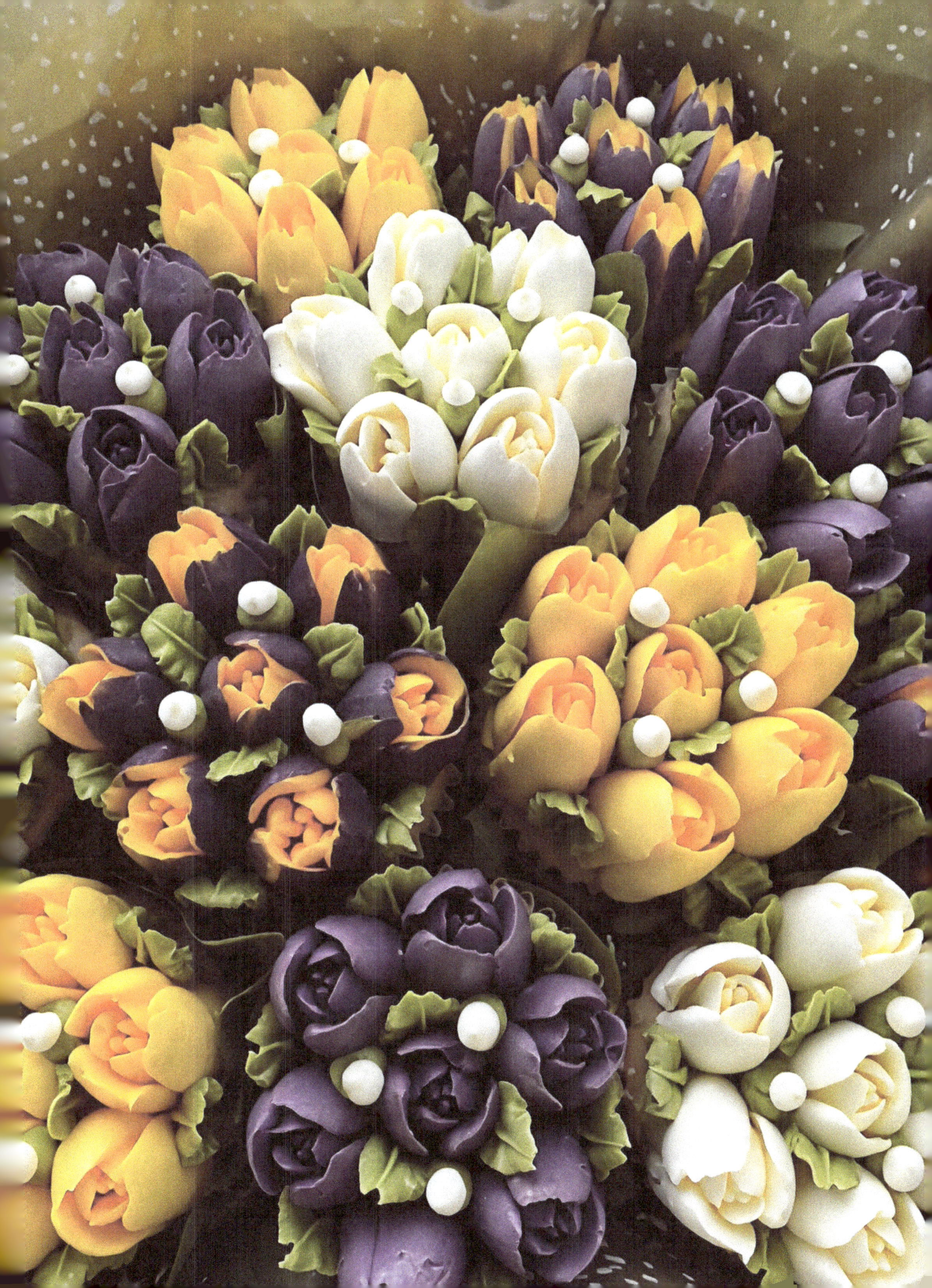

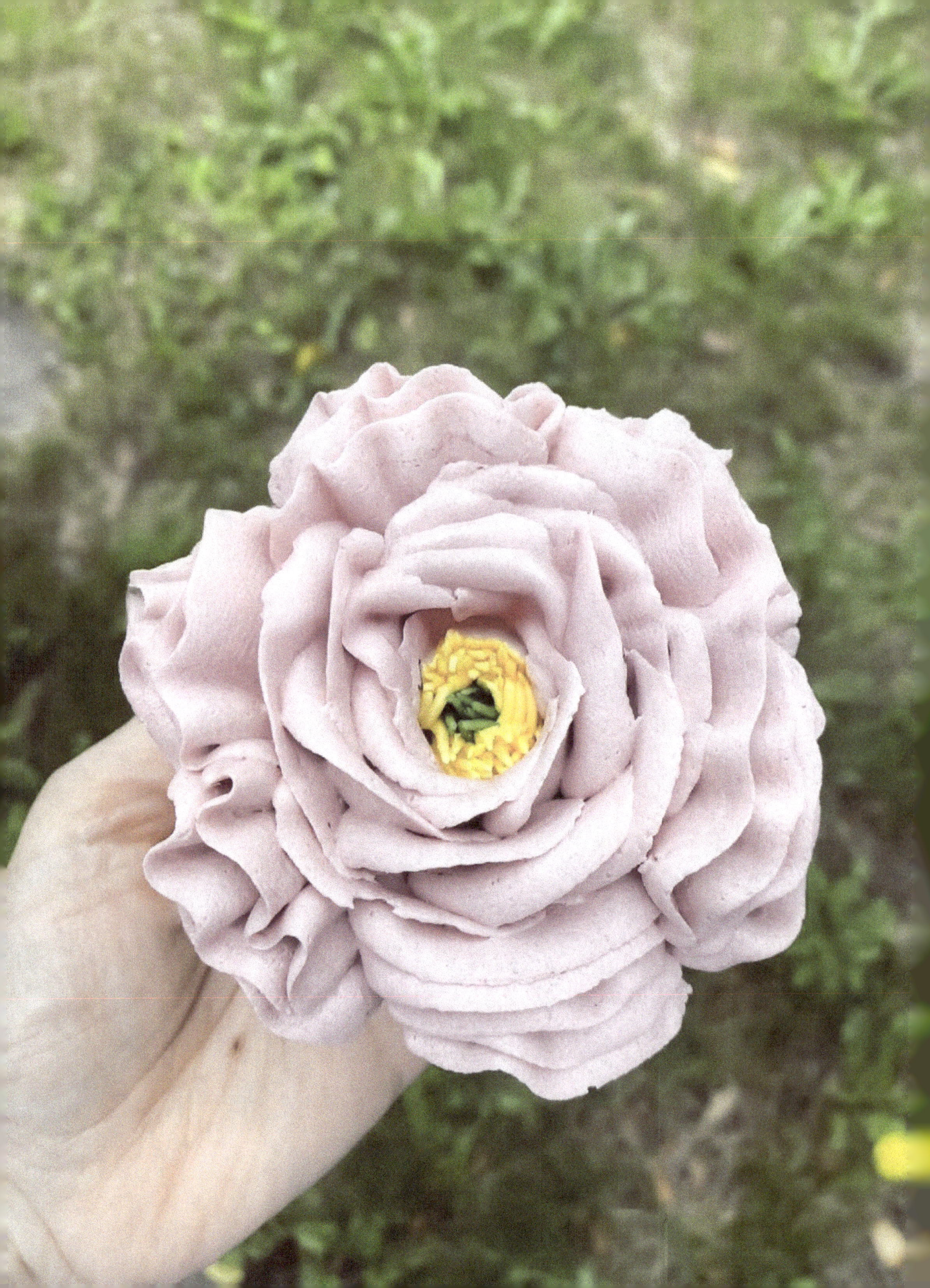

Every expert was once a beginner. Embrace the journey,
keep practicing, and soon your buttercream flowers
will bloom beautifully!

CHALLENGE FLOWER

A mini floral garden

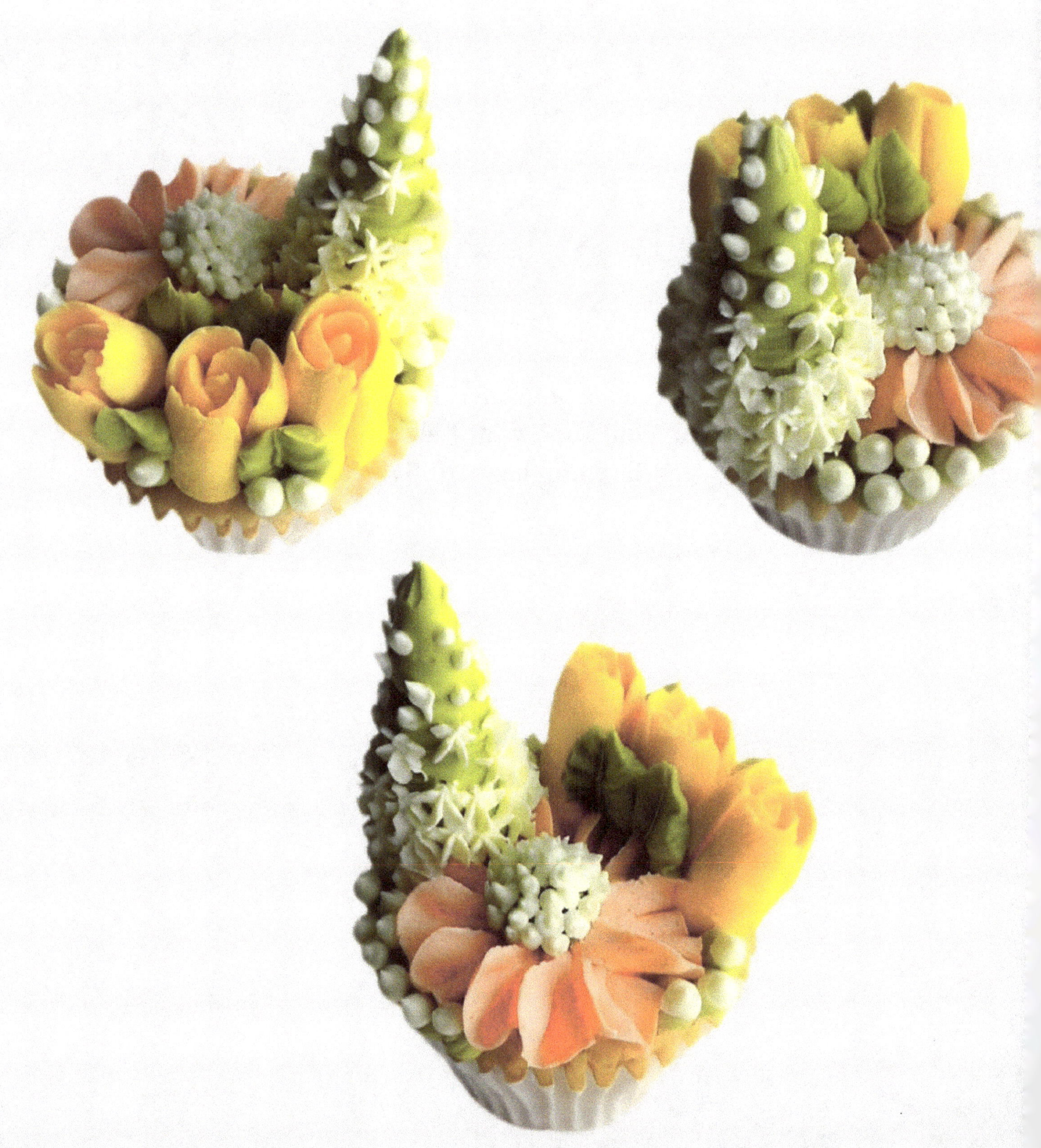

You have come so far in your journey; now, it's time to take on an exciting challenge that will showcase everything you have learned! This beautiful arrangement—featuring a delicate mini scabiosa flower, tall veronica flowers with both bloomed and un-blossomed buds, accompanied by three elegant tulips—is a wonderful way to assess your skills. To finish, you will add lush leaves and a mix of green and white buds for a harmonious, fresh touch.

Remember, piping these intricate elements may feel daunting at first, but do not give up! Every stroke and swirl is a testament to your progress. Patience and practice are your greatest allies, and with each attempt, you will get closer to mastering the art. Take pride in how far you have come, and trust that persistence will bring out the beauty in every flower.

Keep going—you are capable of more than you know!

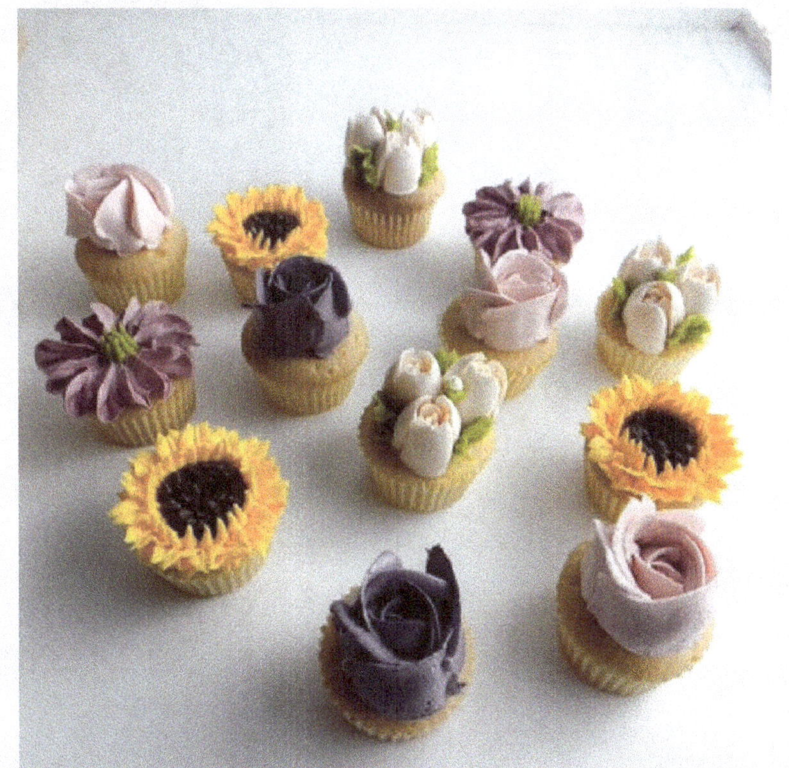

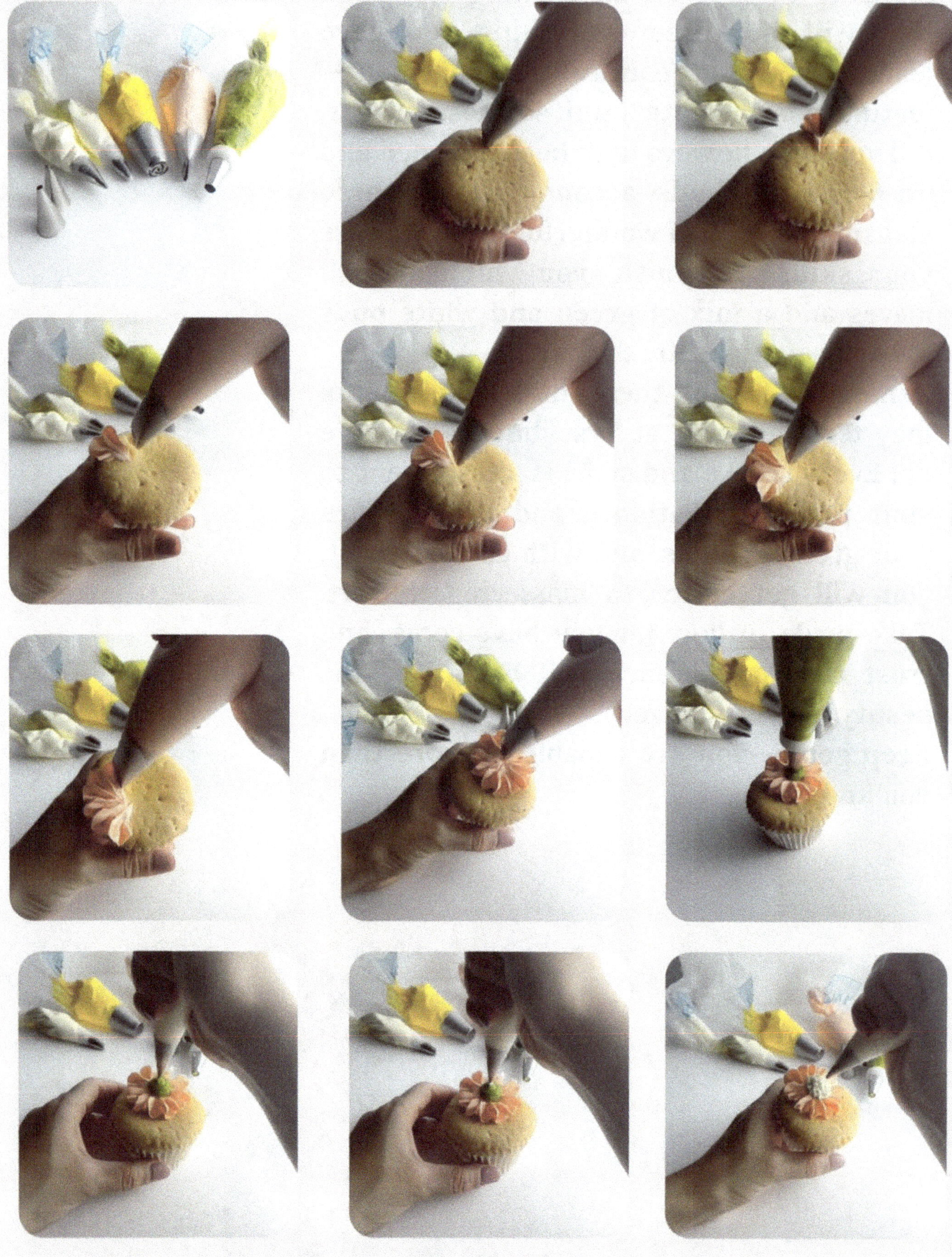

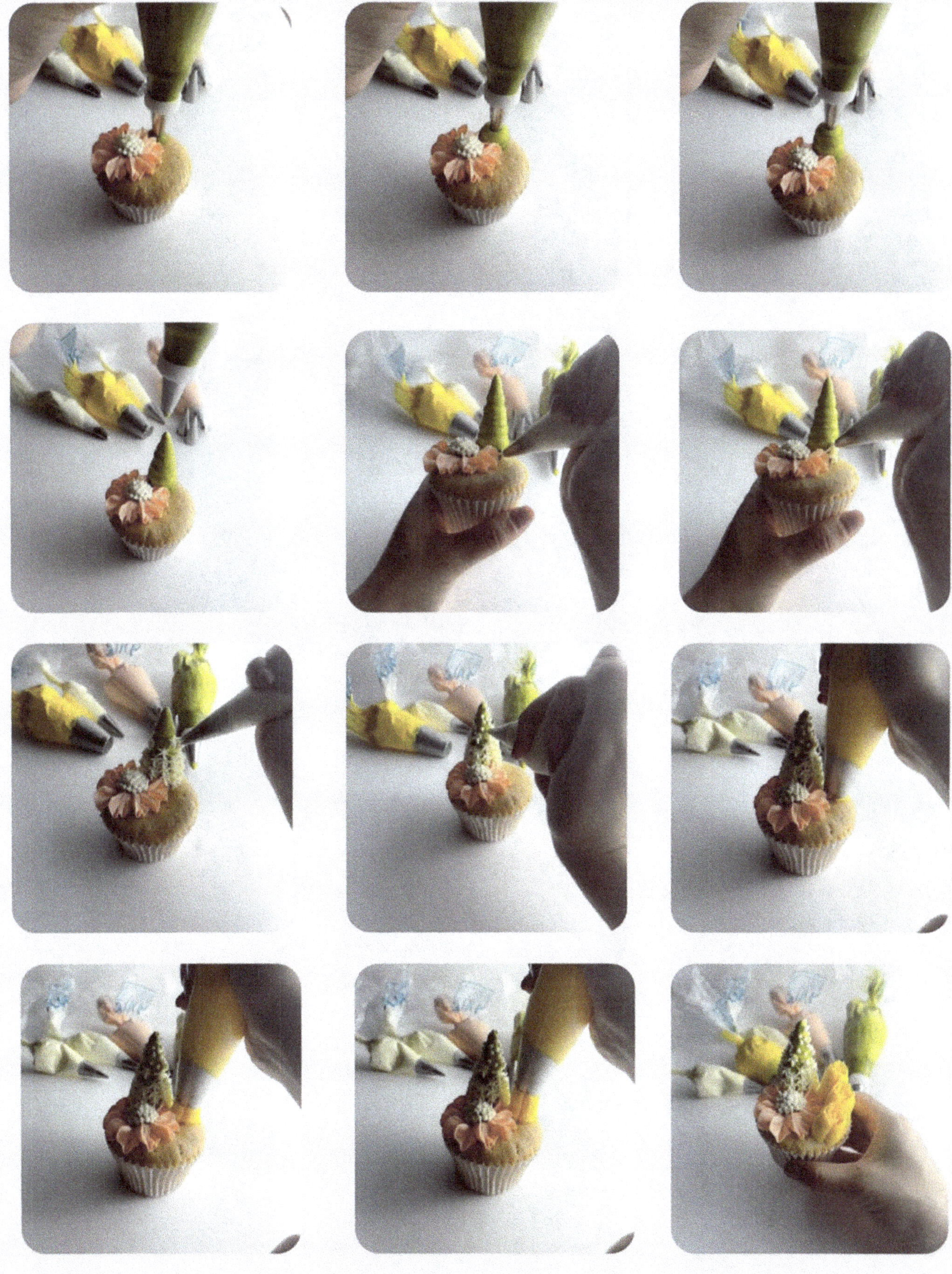

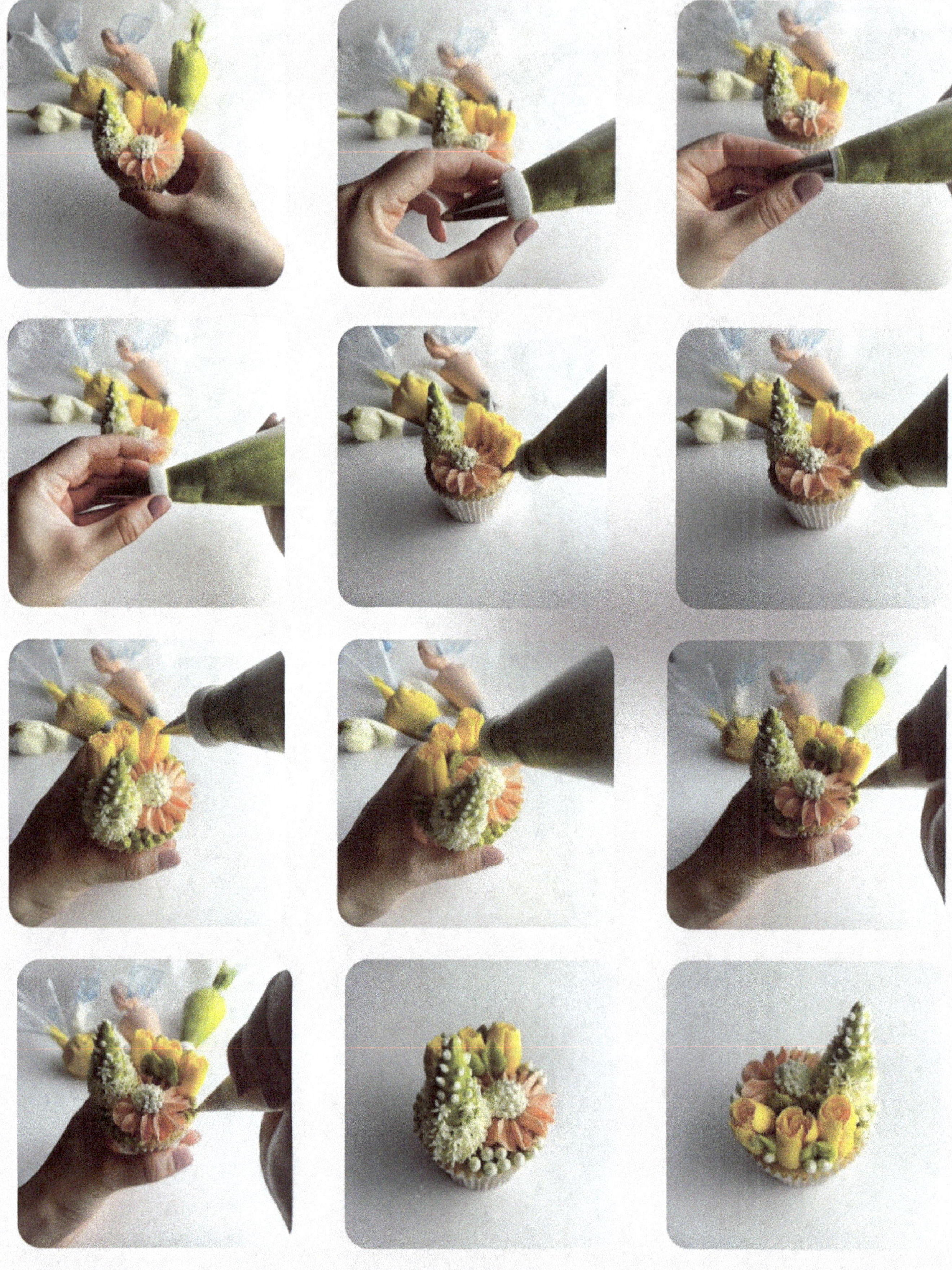

Instructions

For this final flower design, I thought it would be a delightful idea to combine several of the flowers you have learned throughout this book and create a charming little garden on a cupcake. This project not only showcases your skills but also allows you to experiment with colour combinations and techniques, resulting in a beautifully cohesive floral arrangement.

To get started, you will need to prepare your icing bags with your chosen colours and the appropriate nozzles already fitted. It is important to have everything ready so that you can focus on the piping process without interruptions. For instance, when piping green buds and leaves, you can streamline your workflow by using a coupler in your piping bag. This way, you can easily switch between different nozzle sizes and shapes while keeping the same colour of green icing. The same technique can be applied when using white icing, whether you are creating tiny buds or delicate mini gypsophila flowers.

Let's begin with the mini scabiosa flower. For this step, you will use the same technique you have practiced earlier in the book, utilising nozzle Ateco 124K. Position the nozzle at a slight angle to the cupcake and create small petals that curve gently towards one corner of the cupcake. It is essential to maintain consistent pressure as you pipe to ensure the petals have an even shape and size.

For the scabiosa flower, I recommend using a light peach colouring gel mixed with plain white icing to achieve a soft, pastel hue. This blend will not only give the flower a lovely subtle colour but also add depth to your arrangement, making it visually appealing against the backdrop of the cupcake. But of course, it's your choice as to which colours you would like to use for your garden.

As you begin piping the mini petals onto your cupcake, it is essential to remember to turn the cupcake slowly as you work. This rotation helps ensure that each petal is evenly placed, allowing for a beautifully balanced design. Given that we are not covering the entire surface of the cupcake this time, it is important to keep the petals small. This will allow you to fit more petals onto the cupcake while maintaining a delicate and intricate appearance.

In the main tutorial for creating the scabiosa flower, we typically use two layers of petals to achieve a fuller look. However, in this garden-themed design, we are focusing on producing smaller flowers. With this approach, a single layer of petals will suffice. Each petal can be intricately defined, allowing for a stunningly detailed finish without the need for additional layers. This technique not only simplifies the process but also highlights the beauty of each individual petal; creating a vibrant and captivating floral display on your cupcake.

Once you have carefully piped all the petals for your scabiosa, the next step is to create the focal point at the centre of the flower. To do this, we will fill in the middle by piping a small green bud. For this step, you will need to use a Wilton No. 12 piping nozzle, which is perfect for creating this specific shape.

When piping the green bud, it is important to apply just the right amount of pressure. You want to ensure that the bud is defined and holds its shape without being overly large or heavy. Start by positioning the nozzle directly above the centre of the flower. With a gentle squeeze, allow the buttercream to form a small mound.

As you pipe, gradually release pressure while lifting the nozzle away to create a clean finish at the top of the bud.

Keep in mind that the green colour of the bud not only adds a beautiful contrast to the vibrant petals but also mimics the natural look of a scabiosa flower, enhancing the overall realism of your design. Take your time during this process; the delicate balance of size and detail will contribute significantly to the beauty of your finished cupcake.

Using the PME 3 nozzle, cover the green bud with small white buds all over. Start by positioning the nozzle just above the green centre. Apply gentle pressure while pulling the nozzle away to create tiny, delicate white buds that will surround the green base. Ensure that these buds are spaced evenly to create a natural, full appearance. As you work, remember to vary the size of some of the white buds to mimic the natural irregularity found in real scabiosa flowers. This technique adds depth and dimension to your flower, making it look more life-like.

Using the same vibrant green icing, we will now pipe the tall and elegant veronica flower, utilizing the Wilton 12 nozzle for this task. Before starting, I recommend placing the cupcake on a flat, stable surface. This positioning is crucial as it allows you to maintain control and avoid applying excessive pressure while creating the tall, conical mound characteristic of the veronica.

Begin by gently touching the tip of the nozzle to the spot on the cupcake where you want your veronica flower to be positioned. It is essential to start with a steady grip on the piping bag. As you start squeezing the bag, begin to lift it upwards while simultaneously applying pressure. This technique is key to achieving the desired height and shape of the flower.

Gradually raise the piping bag to your preferred height for the veronica flower, ensuring that you maintain a steady flow of icing. The goal is to create a smooth, conical shape that tapers to a point. Once you reach the desired height, slowly and carefully pull the bag away from the cupcake, releasing the pressure just as you detach the nozzle from the icing. This final movement will help to form a clean tip at the top of your flower.

Take a moment to assess the flower you have created. If the height or shape is not quite right, do not worry; practice makes perfect. With each attempt, you will gain more control over the icing and develop a better understanding of how to manipulate the piping bag to achieve the stunning, elegant look of this flower.

Using a No 24 star nozzle, pipe small white stars around the base of the green veronica flower. You can hold the cupcake in your hand or place it on a flat surface —holding it gives you more control, allowing you to easily turn the cupcake as you pipe. I like to cover the base with these small stars. However, you can either cover the entire base or pipe stars only part way up. Varying the lengths of the stars can also create a nice texture. If your piping bag has a coupler, you can switch out the nozzle for a smaller round one. For this step, I am using a PME 3 nozzle.

Next, I piped small, random dots at the tips of the veronica flower to represent un-bloomed star buds.

Now, let us dive into piping beautiful tulips! For this step, I am using a small Russian tulip nozzle, which is specifically designed to create tulip flowers with ease. Russian nozzles come in various designs, each producing unique petal shapes and sizes, so it is a matter of personal preference which design you choose for your tulip. Whether you prefer a classic tulip look or something more intricate, there is a nozzle that will suit your style.

Begin by inserting your chosen Russian tulip nozzle into a clean piping bag. Make sure the nozzle is snugly fitted at the tip to prevent any icing from leaking out.

Next, prepare your buttercream icing. For a vibrant tulip, I recommend using a bright yellow icing. You can achieve this by mixing yellow gel food colouring into your buttercream until you reach your desired shade.

Carefully fill the piping bag with the yellow icing. Do not overfill it; about two-thirds full is ideal to allow for easy handling and control.

Once filled, gently squeeze the bag to push the icing down towards the nozzle, ensuring there are no air bubbles trapped inside. Twist the top of the piping bag to secure the icing in place.

Hold the piping bag firmly at a 45-degree angle above your cake or surface where you want to create the tulip. Make sure the nozzle is positioned just above the area where you want the flower to bloom.

Apply firm pressure on the piping bag and gently squeeze as you lift the bag upward. The icing will begin to flow out, forming the petals of the tulip. Maintaining consistent pressure throughout the piping process is important to ensure even petals.

As you lift the bag, continue to squeeze until your tulip reaches the desired height. The petals will start to flare out and take shape. Once you are satisfied with the size, stop applying pressure and gently lift the bag away.

To make a beautiful arrangement, repeat the process and pipe two more tulip flowers. You can vary the height and angle slightly to create a more natural look. Feel free to experiment with different colours or nozzle designs for added variety in your floral arrangement.

To enhance the overall aesthetic of our cupcakes, we will pipe mini green buds strategically next to any empty spaces. This step not only adds a pop of colour but also gives the cupcakes a more polished and complete appearance.

For this design, I recommend using a JEM 7 nozzle, which is perfect for creating those delicate mini green buds. As I had already fitted my green icing bag with a coupler, I only needed to change the nozzle to pipe the buds. Ensure that your buttercream is at the right consistency—smooth and slightly stiff to hold its shape while piping.

Begin by holding the piping bag at a slight angle, positioned close to the surface of the cupcake where you want to add the green buds. Apply gentle, consistent pressure to the piping bag as you squeeze. As you release the pressure, quickly pull the nozzle away to form the bud shape. Aim to create several mini buds around the cupcake, filling in any empty spaces. The key here is to maintain a light touch and allow the buds to be varied in size to mimic the natural look of fresh greenery.

Once you have piped the mini green buds, it is time to add a touch of foliage. Using the same green-coloured buttercream, replace the JEM 7 nozzle with a leaf nozzle. For this project, I opted for a No. 67 leaf nozzle, known for its ability to create beautifully shaped leaves. However, feel free to use any leaf nozzle that suits your preference or is available to you.

To pipe the leaves, position the piping bag at a 45-degree angle to the cupcake. Start at the base of where you want the leaf to be and squeeze gently while pulling the bag outward and upwards to form the leaf shape. Release pressure as you reach the tip of the leaf and lift the nozzle away to create a clean finish. Continue this process, adding leaves around the mini green buds to enhance the overall design and create a vibrant, garden-like effect on your cupcakes.

I completed the finishing touches on our garden-themed cupcake by delicately piping a small white bud on top of the previously piped green buds. I used a gentle pressure technique, allowing the white icing to bloom gracefully, creating a stunning contrast against the lush green base. The overall effect is a beautiful interplay of colours and textures, transforming a simple cupcake into a delightful work of art.

The cupcake is not just visually appealing; it boasts an impressive array of textures and intricate designs that invite closer inspection. Each element has been thoughtfully crafted, with the delicate white buds adding a layer of sophistication and elegance. This cupcake truly embodies the essence of beauty, evoking a sense of joy and satisfaction for anyone who lays eyes on it.

However, it is essential to remember that achieving this level of detail takes time and practice. If you are new to piping, it is easy to feel frustrated when things do not turn out as expected. I encourage you to embrace the learning process and take your time with each piping session. With each attempt, you will gain more confidence and skill, I promise.

One crucial tip to keep in mind is to avoid overfilling your piping bag with icing. If your bag is too full, the warmth from your hands can cause the icing to soften, resulting in floppy, less-defined petals that lack the desired structure. Instead, fill your piping bag just enough to allow for control and precision while piping.

Do not hesitate to experiment with different colours and designs as you develop your unique style. Play around with various techniques and let your creativity flow. Discovering your niche will not only enhance your piping skills but also bring you immense joy in the decorating process. Enjoy the journey and have fun creating your own beautiful edible garden!

Understanding Colour Theory

Before diving into colouring, it's essential to understand the basics of colour theory. The colour wheel is a useful tool, showing primary, secondary, and tertiary colours and how they relate to each other. By mixing primary colours (red, yellow, and blue), you can create secondary colours (green, orange, and purple) and even more complex hues.

Understanding complementary colours (those opposite each other on the wheel) can help you to create visually striking combinations, while analogous colours (those next to each other) offer a more harmonious look.

Types of Colouring Agents

•Gel Colours: Highly concentrated and ideal for buttercream, as they do not alter the consistency.

•Liquid Colours: More diluted and can affect the texture of the buttercream if used excessively.

•Powdered Colours: Great for achieving intense hues without affecting consistency.

•Natural Colours: Derived from fruits, vegetables, or spices, offering a more muted palette but a healthier option.

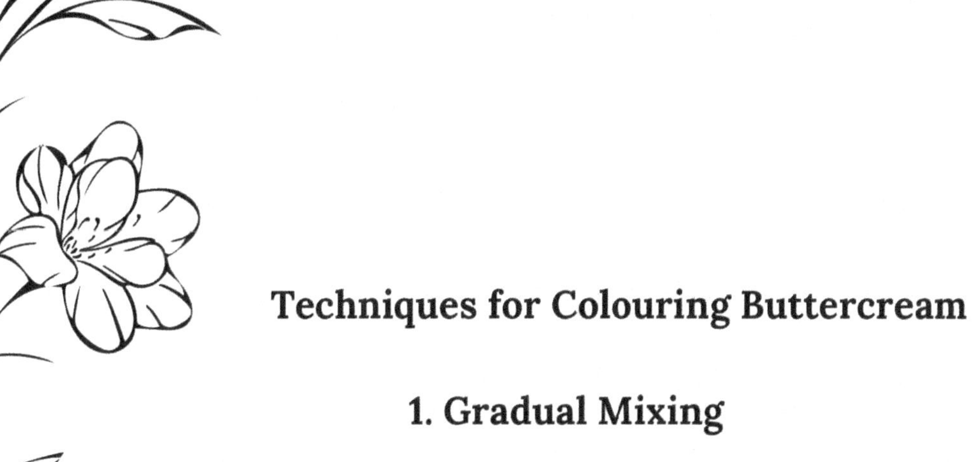

Techniques for Colouring Buttercream

1. Gradual Mixing

Start Small: Begin by adding just a small amount of food colouring to your buttercream. Using a toothpick or the tip of a spatula, add the colouring agent gradually. This allows you to have better control over the intensity of the colour.

Mix and Assess: Mix the buttercream thoroughly after each addition, making sure the colour is evenly distributed. It is important to remember that buttercream colours naturally deepen as they sit, so it is wise to pause and let the buttercream rest for about 10-15 minutes before deciding if more colour is needed.

Avoid Oversaturation: By adding colour gradually, you reduce the risk of oversaturating the buttercream. Oversaturated buttercream can become too intense, potentially affecting both the appearance and taste. If the colour becomes too dark, it can be difficult to lighten without altering the buttercream's consistency by adding more uncoloured buttercream.

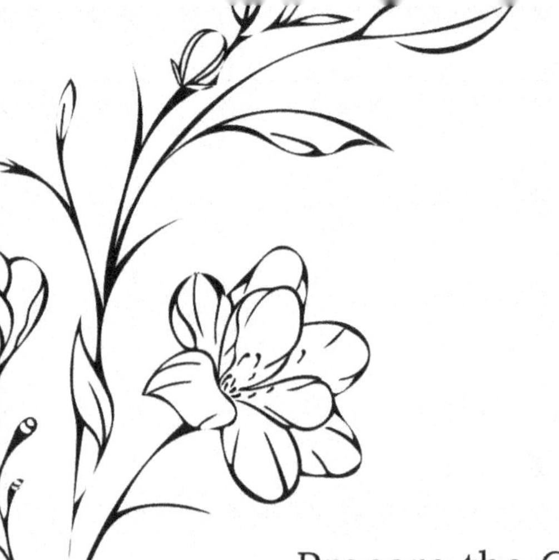

2. Marbling

Prepare the Colours: Choose two or more colours that you would like to marble together. Prepare separate bowls of buttercream for each colour, making sure they are vibrant but not overly mixed or dark.

Light Mixing: Spoon the different coloured buttercreams into a single bowl. Using a spatula, gently fold the colours together. Be careful not to overmix; you want to create a streaky, marbled appearance where the colours blend partially but still maintain their distinct lines.

Pipe Carefully: When you pipe the buttercream, the marbled effect will translate beautifully into your flowers, creating a stunning, natural-looking blend of colours. This technique works exceptionally well for petals that require a more organic, varied appearance, such as roses or peonies.

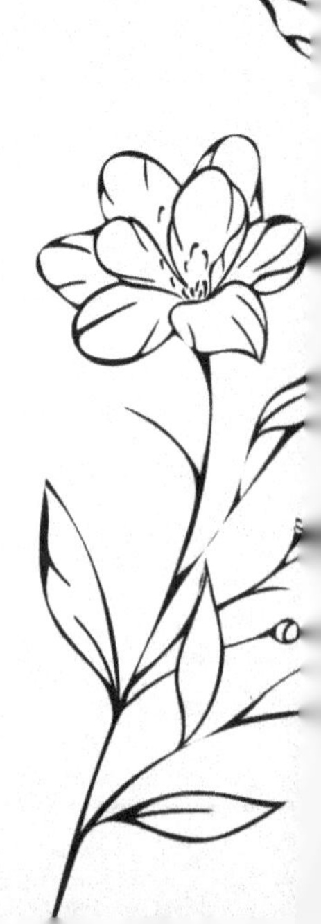

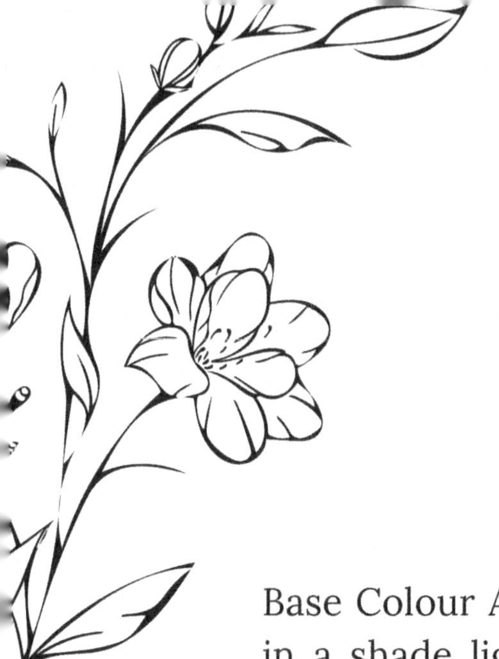

3. Layering

Base Colour Application: Start by applying a base layer in a shade lighter than your chosen colour. This will serve as the foundation for your buttercream flowers.

Add Depth with Darker Shades: Once the base layer is applied, gradually add darker shades of the same colour. This can be done by mixing in a small amount of a darker hue into your existing buttercream. Use a piping bag fitted with a small nozzle to apply these darker shades to specific areas of the petals where natural shadows would fall.

Blend and Refine: For a more natural look, blend the edges of the darker shades into the lighter base colour using a small brush or a spatula. This layering technique adds depth and dimension to your buttercream flowers, making them appear more realistic and visually appealing.

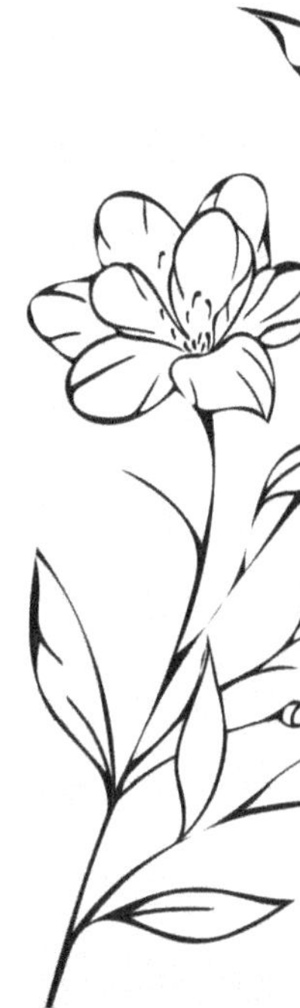

Do's

Do Use High-Quality Colouring Agents

 When it comes to buttercream, the quality of your colouring agents can significantly impact the final result. High-quality gel or paste food colours offer vibrant, consistent hues that will not alter the consistency of your buttercream. These products are concentrated, allowing you to achieve rich colours without thinning out the buttercream, which is essential for creating sharp, defined petals and details in your floral designs.

Do Allow Time for Colours to Develop

One of the secrets to perfect buttercream colouring is patience. Buttercream colours tend to deepen and become more vibrant over time. After mixing in your colour, allow the buttercream to sit for at least 30 minutes, preferably longer, before making any further adjustments. This waiting period ensures that the final colour is true and prevents you from accidentally adding too much colouring agent.

Do Experiment with Small Batches

Before committing to a full batch of buttercream, it is wise to test your colours in smaller quantities. This approach allows you to experiment with different shades and intensities without risking an entire batch. Mix small portions of buttercream with your chosen colours, observe how they develop, and then decide if you need to tweak the formula before scaling it up.

Don'ts

Don't Overmix

Overmixing buttercream can lead to a soft, overly airy texture that is challenging to work with, especially when piping intricate flowers. A softer buttercream will not hold its shape well, resulting in droopy petals and blurred details. Mix just enough to incorporate your colours and achieve a smooth texture, stopping as soon as you reach the desired consistency.

Don't Add Too Much Colour at Once

When adding colour to your buttercream, start with a small amount and gradually increase it as needed. Adding too much colouring agent at once can result in overly dark or vibrant shades that are difficult to correct. It is much easier to build up colour slowly than to lighten an intensely coloured batch, which might require adding more uncoloured buttercream, potentially altering the texture.

Don't Forget About Natural Light

The lighting in your workspace can dramatically affect how your buttercream colours appear. Artificial lighting may skew colours, making them appear different from how they will look in natural light. Always check your buttercream in natural daylight to ensure that the colours are accurate and meet your expectations. This step is crucial, especially if the final product will be displayed or photographed in natural light.

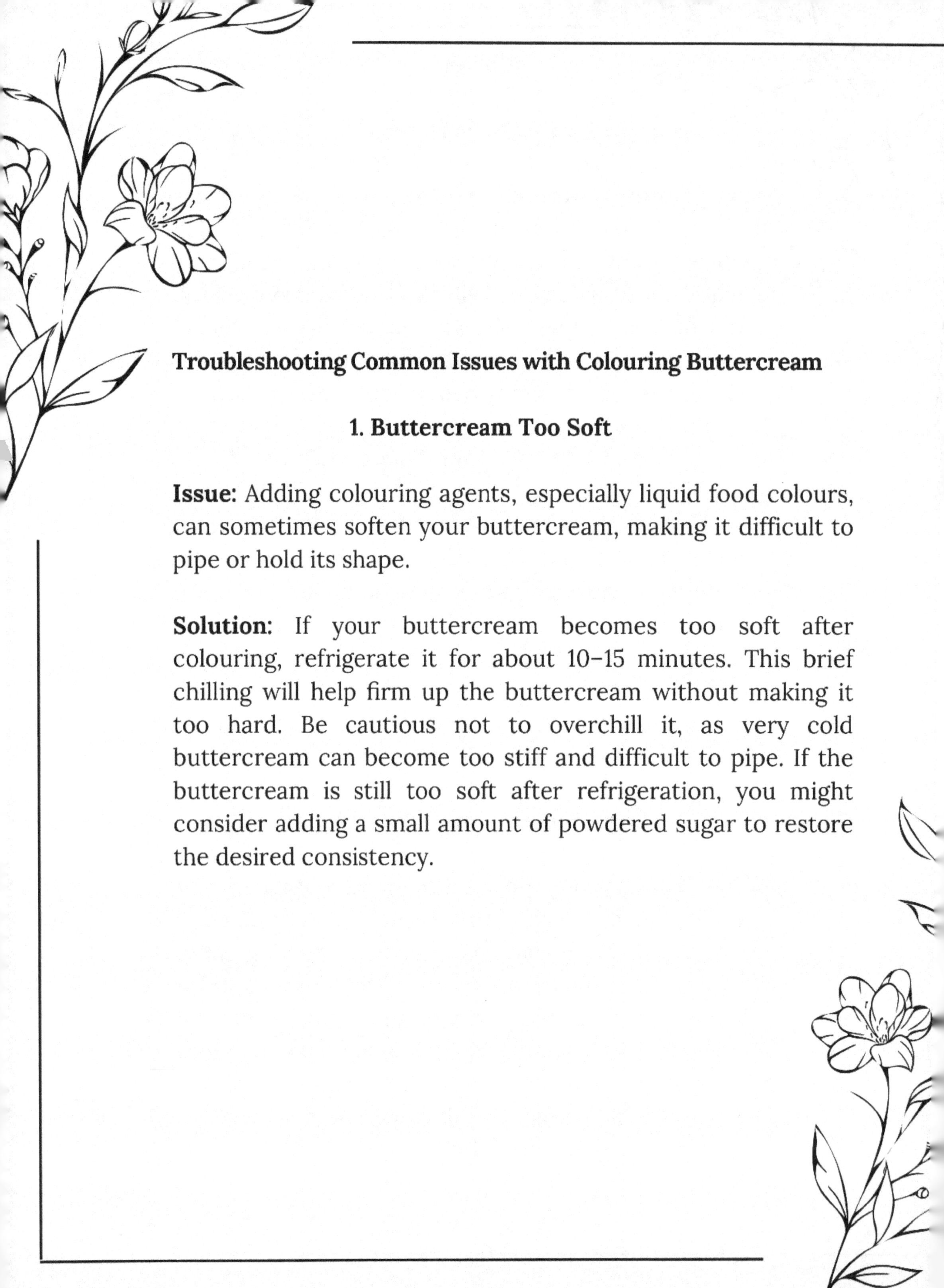

Troubleshooting Common Issues with Colouring Buttercream

1. Buttercream Too Soft

Issue: Adding colouring agents, especially liquid food colours, can sometimes soften your buttercream, making it difficult to pipe or hold its shape.

Solution: If your buttercream becomes too soft after colouring, refrigerate it for about 10–15 minutes. This brief chilling will help firm up the buttercream without making it too hard. Be cautious not to overchill it, as very cold buttercream can become too stiff and difficult to pipe. If the buttercream is still too soft after refrigeration, you might consider adding a small amount of powdered sugar to restore the desired consistency.

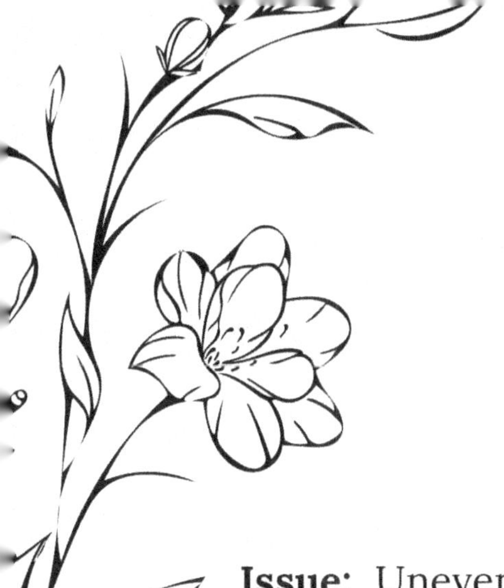

2. Uneven Colour Distribution

Issue: Uneven or streaky colours can occur when the buttercream is too cold or the colouring is not properly mixed.

Solution: Always make sure that your buttercream is at room temperature before adding colour. Cold buttercream can cause uneven mixing, leading to streaks. When you add colouring, stir slowly and thoroughly to ensure the colour is evenly incorporated. Using gel or paste food colours also helps, as they mix more smoothly into buttercream than liquid colours, providing consistent colour throughout.

3. Colour Bleeding

Issue: When piping intricate buttercream designs with multiple colours, you may notice the colours bleeding into each other, which can blur the details of your flowers.

Solution: To prevent colour bleeding, use stiffer buttercream, as a softer consistency increases the chance of colours blending unintentionally. Another useful tip is to allow each coloured section of your buttercream design to set for a few minutes before adding another colour next to it. This helps to "lock in" the colours, minimizing the risk of bleeding. If necessary, you can refrigerate the cake or cupcakes between steps to speed up the setting process.

Advanced Techniques for Creating Unique Effects in Buttercream Flowers

1. Ombre Buttercream

Technique: Ombre is a beautiful technique where one colour gradually transitions into another, creating a gradient effect. To achieve this look with buttercream flowers:

Prepare Multiple Shades: Start by dividing your buttercream into several portions. Begin with a base colour (usually the lightest shade) and gradually add small amounts of colouring to each subsequent portion to create darker or more intense shades of the same colour.

Layer the Shades: As you pipe the flowers, start with the lightest shade and gradually transition to the darker shades as you move through the petals. For a seamless transition, ensure each shade blends slightly into the next, creating a smooth flow from one colour to the other.

Application: This technique works particularly well for flowers with layered petals, such as roses or dahlias, where the outer petals can be a deeper or contrasting shade compared to the inner ones.

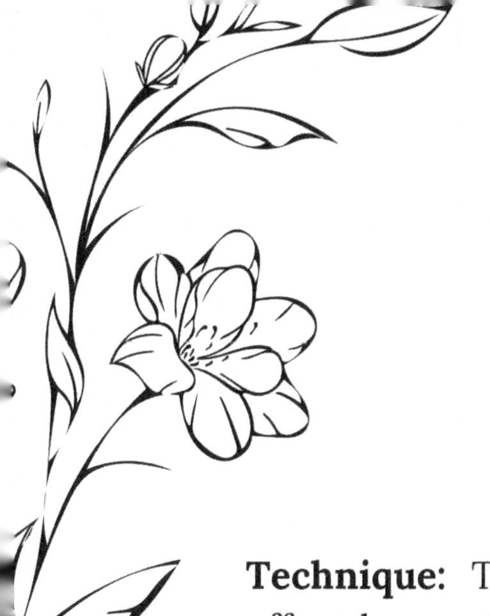

2. Two-Tone Piping

Technique: Two-tone piping adds a visually striking effect by combining two colours in one flower, creating a gradient or dual-tone look with each petal.

Prepare the Piping Bag: Start by loading two different coloured buttercreams into the same piping bag; placing each colour on opposite sides of the bag. You can achieve this by spooning each colour carefully into its side without mixing them in the centre.

Achieving the Effect: When you pipe the flowers, the colours will flow out together, creating petals with a gradient effect—one side of the petal will be one colour, and the other will be a different shade. This technique can create beautifully intricate petals with two distinct tones, ideal for flowers like roses, sunflowers or tulips.

Variation: You can experiment with contrasting colours for a bold look or use two similar shades for a more subtle, blended effect.

3. Dusting with Petal Dust

Technique: Petal dust can add an extra layer of depth and realism to your buttercream flowers, making them look more life-like.

Choose the Right Dust: Select a petal dust that complements or enhances the colours of your buttercream flowers. Use soft shades for a natural look and metallic or shimmer dusts for a more artistic effect.

Application: Once your buttercream flowers are piped and have set slightly, use a soft, fine brush to gently dust the edges or centres of the petals. Start with a light hand and build up the colour gradually. You can also focus the dust on areas where shadows would naturally fall, such as the bases of petals, to add dimension and depth.

Final Touch: This technique works well on flowers like roses, peonies, or orchids, adding a subtle realism and making the flowers appear more detailed and refined. By using these advanced techniques, you can elevate the artistry of your buttercream flowers, creating designs that are more sophisticated, intricate and visually stunning.

Cleaning Up After Piping Buttercream Flowers

After finishing your creative session, it is essential to clean up properly to ensure your tools stay in good condition and that your workspace remains tidy for future projects. Here are some tips for effective cleaning:

1. Clean Up Spills Immediately

Prevent Stains: Gel food colours in particular can stain countertops, clothing, and even your hands if left too long. As soon as you notice a spill, wipe it up with a damp cloth or paper towel. For stubborn stains, a mixture of baking soda and water or vinegar can help lift the colour without damaging surfaces.

2. Wash Tools with Warm, Soapy Water

Effective Cleaning: Use warm water and a mild dish soap to wash all your piping bags, nozzles, spatulas, and bowls. Buttercream is fat-based, so warm water helps to break down the grease effectively.

Focus on Piping Nozzles: Buttercream can easily get stuck in the small crevices of piping nozzles. Use a small brush, like a bottle brush or pipe cleaner, to ensure that every part of the nozzle is thoroughly cleaned.

Drying: Once washed, allow your tools to air dry completely before storing them. This prevents any residual moisture, which could encourage mold or bacteria growth.

3. Store Colouring Agents Properly

Cool, Dark Place: To preserve the potency and vibrancy of your gel or paste food colours, store them in a cool, dark place, such as a cupboard or drawer. Exposure to heat, light, and air can cause colours to degrade over time.

Tightly Seal Containers: Ensure the lids or caps on your colouring agents are tightly sealed after use to prevent them from drying out or becoming contaminated. Proper storage helps extend their shelf life and ensures you'll get the best results next time you use them. By following these steps, you will ensure that your workspace and tools are ready for your next creative buttercream project, and your colouring agents remain vibrant and effective for future use.

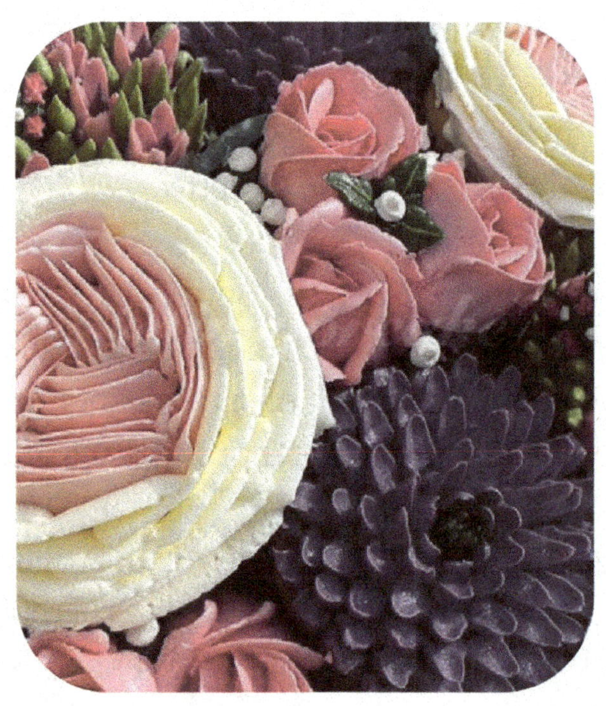

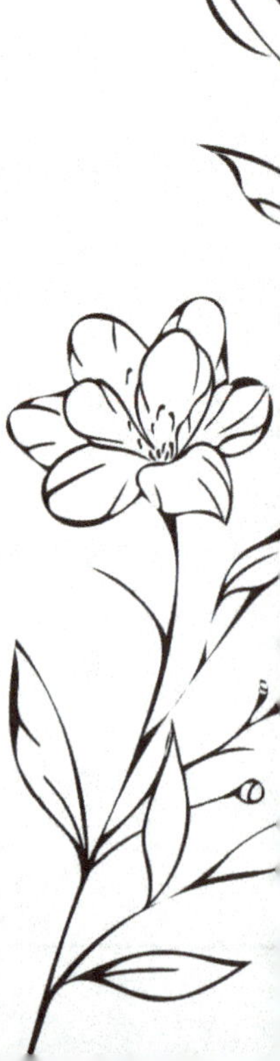

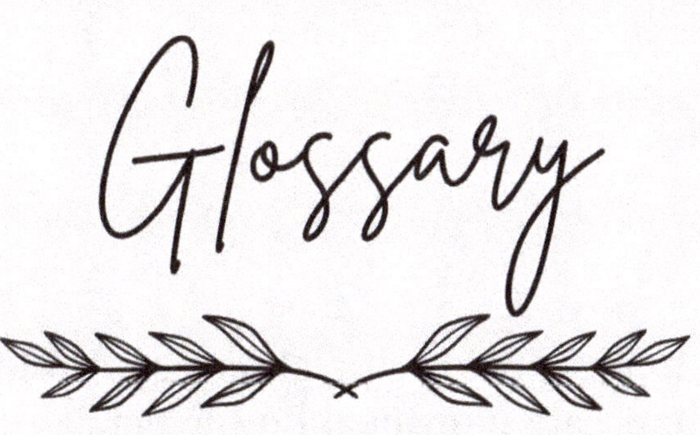

Glossary

- **Butter:** The primary fat used in most buttercreams, providing flavour and structure. It is important for achieving a smooth texture and consistency.
- **Buttercream:** A smooth, creamy icing made with butter, sugar, and flavouring. It is commonly used in cake decorating for piping flowers and other designs.
- **Colouring Gel:** Highly concentrated food colouring used to tint buttercream without affecting its consistency, especially important for vibrant flower designs.
- **Consistency:** Refers to the texture or thickness of buttercream. Different consistencies (stiff, medium, soft) are used for different techniques. Stiff consistency is typically used for piping flowers.
- **Coupler:** A two-part plastic device that fits into a piping bag and allows you to easily switch piping tips without changing the bag.
- **Flavouring:** Extracts such as vanilla, almond, lemon, or coffee are added to buttercream to give it a desired taste.
- **Flower Cupcake:** A small, flat, round metal tool with a pointed stem, used to pipe buttercream flowers. The flower is piped on the surface of the cupcake and then transferred to the cake.
- **Medium Consistency:** A slightly softer buttercream that can still hold its shape but is smoother, making it ideal for piping less detailed designs or writing.
- **Milk/Cream:** Small amounts of liquid are often added to adjust the buttercream's consistency, making it easier to spread or pipe.
- **Ombre Buttercream:** A gradient effect where buttercream colours gradually transition from light to dark across a cake or design.

- **Petal Technique:** Using a petal tip (e.g., No 104), buttercream is piped to create individual flower petals. This technique is used for flowers like roses, tulips, and peonies.
- **Piping:** The process of squeezing buttercream, royal icing, or other materials through a piping bag with a nozzle to create decorative shapes, lines, or designs.
- **Piping Bag:** A cone or triangular-shaped bag made of cloth, plastic, or disposable material, used to hold buttercream and fitted with piping tips/nozzles to create specific designs.
- **Piping Tip (Nozzle):** Metal or plastic attachments fitted to the piping bag to create different designs. Each tip is numbered to indicate the type of design it creates.
- **Powdered Sugar (Icing Sugar):** Finely ground sugar used to sweeten and thicken buttercream. It dissolves easily, creating a smooth texture.
- **Rosette:** A simple swirl created by piping in a circular motion, often used for borders or as the base for a flower.
- **Ruffle Piping:** A wavy, rippled effect achieved by using a petal tip or ruffle tip to create textured edges on flowers or as a decorative border.
- **Spatula:** A flat, flexible tool used for smoothing buttercream, mixing colours, or transferring piped flowers from a flower cupcake to the cake.
- **Stiff Consistency:** Buttercream that holds its shape well, used for detailed piping like flowers and borders. This is achieved by using less liquid or adding more powdered sugar.
- **Soft Consistency:** Buttercream that is spreadable and smooth, used for covering cakes or making swirls and simple decorations.
- **Two-Toned Piping:** A method where two colours of buttercream are placed side by side in a piping bag, resulting in a swirl with two distinct colours.

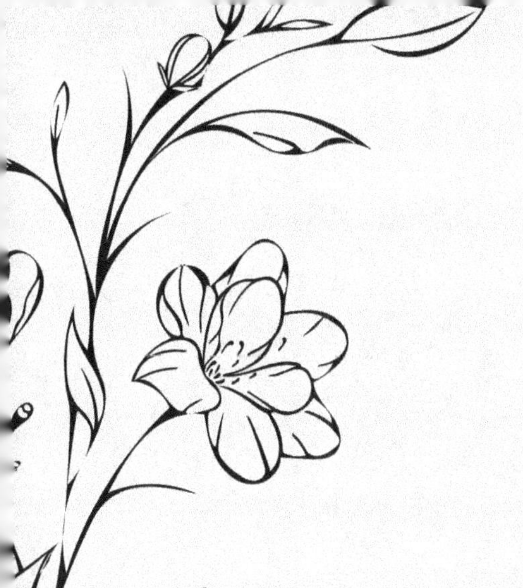

Acknowledgments

Creating this book has been a labor of love, and it would not have been possible without the encouragement, support, and talents of the people in my life.

To my dear family — thank you for your endless patience, love, and belief in me. Your support gave me the space to dream, create, and bring this vision to life, one buttercream petal at a time.

To my darling daughter for her photography skills – your patience and attention to detail made every flower bloom on the page.

To my closest friends — thank you for cheering me on, for being my taste-testers and for reminding me to keep going when I doubted myself. Your friendship over the years has been the sweetest gift.

To the baking and cake decorating community — I hope this book brings beauty, joy, and confidence to every reader who dares to pick up a piping bag.

To the designers and editors who helped shape this book — thank you for translating my vision into these pages with such care and creativity.

And finally, to every beginner who has ever felt nervous to start: this book was made for you. May it spark your creativity and remind you that practice really does bloom into something beautiful.

With heartfelt gratitude,
Farhana.

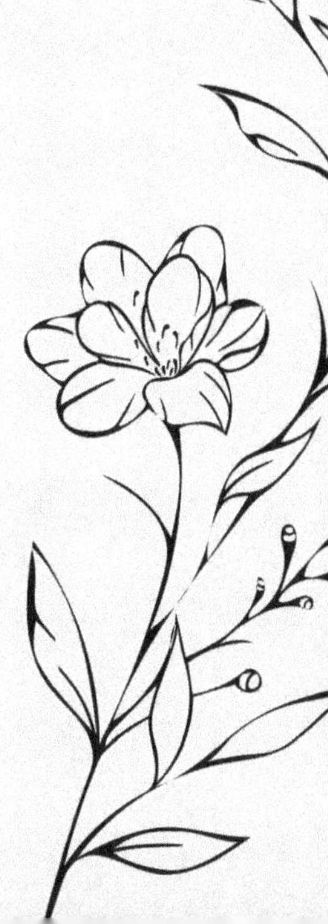